The Great Investors

Lessons on Investing from Master Traders

Glen Arnold

GW00371997

**Financial Times
Prentice Hall
is an imprint of**

Harlow, England • London • New York • Boston • San Francisco • Toronto
Sydney • Tokyo • Singapore • Hong Kong • Seoul • Taipei • New Delhi
Cape Town • Madrid • Mexico City • Amsterdam • Munich • Paris • Milan

To Flo and Trevor Badham, my in-laws, who welcomed me into their family. You are missed.

PEARSON EDUCATION LIMITED

Edinburgh Gate
Harlow CM20 2JE
Tel: +44 (0)1279 623623
Fax: +44 (0)1279 431059
Website: www.pearsoned.co.uk

First published in Great Britain in 2011

Pearson Education is not responsible for the content of third party internet sites.

ISBN: 978-0-273-74325-5

British Library Cataloguing-in-Publication Data
A catalogue record for this book is available from the British Library

Library of Congress Cataloging-in-Publication Data
Arnold, Glen.
   The great investors : lessons on investing from master traders / Glen Arnold.
      p. cm.
   Includes bibliographical references and index.
   ISBN 978-0-273-74325-5 (pbk.)
   1. Capitalists and financiers--Case studies. 2. Investments. 3. Investment analysis. I. Title.
   HG4521.A73 2011
   332.6--dc22
                          2010040718

10 9 8 7 6 5 4 3 2 1
14 13 12 11 10

Typeset in 10.5pt New Caledonia by 3
Printed by Ashford Colour Press Ltd., Gosport

Contents

Preface

There are some very special people who seem to possess an exceptional talent for acquiring wealth. It occurred to me that there are many other people, yet to make their big break-thorough, who would enjoy reading succinct analyses of the techniques used by the greatest investors to see if there are lessons they could absorb which would allow them to perform better than the average. I was thus motivated to investigate the investment approaches of nine great investors such as Warren Buffett, Benjamin Graham, Sir John Templeton and George Soros, asking questions such as: How did these people come to be so successful? What strategies have they used to make their fortunes? Can the 'ordinary' investor really draw on their techniques?

I needed to explore not just the past triumphs of the masters, but also the key factors they look for as well as the personality traits that allow them to control emotion and think rationally about where to place funds. How did masters of investment hone skills through bitter experience and triumph to develop their approaches to accumulating wealth?

What I discovered was that while there is plenty of material that provides hints and glimpses of the approaches used by the most successful investors it takes a long time (and much knowledge) to trawl through it all. The ideas are available; the problem is that this writing, speeches, etc. is scattered and often disorganised, thus the essential wisdom is not reachable in an easy to assimilate form. There is a need for a book that distils the essence that made such individuals millionaires and billionaires, one that systematically goes through key ideas and disciplines in a focused and easily accessible way.

Why Choose these Investors?

At first glance it would seem very difficult to choose just a handful of investors to be classified as 'great', but as I looked into it I found a high degree of consensus within the investment community about those who stand head and shoulders above the crowd. First, these people have a long track record of success, increasing the chance that their performances are based on underlying skill rather than luck. Second, when you examine their ideas and approaches you discover a great deal of shrewd understanding of the workings of markets and the minds of other market players. Third, they have an outstanding knowledge of businesses and how long-term returns are made. Fourth, they have put into the public domain enough infor-mation about their investment philosophy to allow us to gain insight into the key elements. In short, they are universally recognised as leading investors, i.e. there's no controversy about why they are included. As far as I'm aware other investors do not satisfy all four criteria for inclusion. These are the best.

What Do They Share in Common?

It was intriguing to discover that even though each great investor has developed a unique approach there are number of common factors. Indeed, the degree to which the investors draw on similar ideas is striking. Here are some of the common themes:

- **Be a business analyst rather than a security analyst**. Shares should not be seen as counters in a game of chance, but as claims on a business. Investors need to understand the underlying business, not focus on stock market price movements.

- **Do your homework**. Not only must you be prepared for hard work to analyse individual companies, but you must develop a broad social, economic and political awareness.

- **Controlling emotion**. They have developed the mental strength to withstand being carried away with the rest of the market when it becomes over-excited or overly depressed. Investors need resilience, self-discipline and courage. There will be long periods when patience is required, interspersed with the need to act decisively.

- **Consistency of approach**. Each investor differs from the others and yet they all maintain a consistency of their approach over decades – even when they have bad years they keep faith with their method.

- **Simplicity**. The key components of investment decisions are essentially simple – do not over-complicate. See the wood for the trees. For example, none of the great investors uses the complex modern portfolio theory constructs such as the Capital Asset Pricing Model with its beta analysis. True investment value should scream at you, so detailed and complex calculations are simply not necessary to give you the required margin of safety. All the maths you need you picked up before you were 16.

- **Constantly learning from mistakes**. Even those great investors now in their 80s learn new things every day, often from mistakes. These can be mistakes (a) of omission (e.g. Warren Buffett is forever publicly berating himself for missing a great opportunity – he finds plenty of compensating successes though!), (b) of commission (buying a share that turns out to be bad investment), and (c) of others – learn from the mistakes of others, you cannot live long enough to make them all yourself. You will find that the great investors are constantly reading and learning (biography, science, stock market history, newspapers as well as company reports) – they just never stop developing their minds.

- **Self-reliance**. They have the self-belief that comes from years of focused hard work and knowledge. They can then stand aside from the crowd and go with their own logic.

- **Reasonable risk taking**. They do not gamble. They make rational, careful analysis of the major risk factors and make moves when the odds are tilted in their favour. Mistakes and misfortunes are inherent in investing – even great investors are wrong more than 40 per cent of the time. They are careful to always be diversified so they are not risking a high proportion of their money on one outcome.

These are some of the commonalities that immediately come to my mind – you may notice a few more as you go through the book.

Is This Book for Me?

The typical reader will have some acquaintance with basic investing terms and concepts, but this is not a requirement to understanding – the book is written to be accessible to the relatively inexperienced investor. However, the absolute beginner might want to consult an introductory book on investing to gain familiarity with some of the investing terms. I've explain them in my book *The Financial Times Guide to Investing*.

Many professional investors and fund managers will buy this book; in fact, this may turn out to be the biggest market. This may seem odd – don't they already know this stuff?

No. Why not? It would seem that 95 per cent of them have a very superficial knowledge of investment philosophies because universities teach algebraic finance and the professional associations like numerical-based investment material. It is usually only later in their careers that they realise how limited these curricula are, and then they search out books on good investment approaches. Indeed, the ideas for each chapter were honed when I was asked to present a series of one-day courses at Schroders Asset Management focused on investment philosophies and stock market inefficiencies. While the attendees had been on the formal training courses that taught them about the technicalities of valuation and the workings of the markets, they recognised they needed to learn more about proven investment philosophies.

Do I Have to Read the Book in a Certain Order?

No. You can read the chapters in any order you like. They have been written so that they are self-standing.

I hope you enjoy reading this book as much as I enjoyed writing it.

Glen Arnold, October 2010

Acknowledgements

I would like to thank the following:

- Susan Henton and Rebecca Devlin, my personal assistants, who contributed greatly to the writing of this book.

- Christopher Cudmore, senior commissioning editor at FT Prentice Hall, who had such great faith in the project and helped improve the chapters, and everyone at FT Prentice Hall who contributed in many and various ways to create this book.

Publisher's Acknowledgements

We are grateful to the following for permission to reproduce copyright material:

Extract on p.210 from an interview with John Templeton in the *Financial Post*, 25th May 1987, p.25 (Toronto). From an interview by Professor Eric Kirzner, University of Waterloo. Reprinted by permission; Extracts on pp.286, 287, 289, 290, 300, 307, 312, 315, 317 from Lynch, P. with Rothchild, J. (1989) *One up on Wall Street: How to Use What You Already Know to Make Money in the Market*, © Copyright 1989 by Peter Lynch. Published by Simon & Schuster. Reprinted with permission.

In some instances we have been unable to trace the owners of copyright material, and we would appreciate any information that would enable us to do so. Every effort has been made to trace the copyright holders and we apologise for any unintentional omissions. We would be pleased to insert the appropriate acknowledgement in any subsequent edition of this publication.

CHAPTER 1

Benjamin Graham

Regarded by many as the greatest investment intellect of the twentieth century and the father of modern investing theory, Benjamin Graham became the mentor of many famous investors, including Warren Buffett, who worked for Graham for two years. Buffett was introduced to Graham's way of thinking by reading what he regarded as 'the best investment book ever written', *The Intelligent Investor*, when he was 19 years old, and later offered to work for him for nothing. Despite the low cost offer Graham kept turning him down. Buffett later joked that Graham had seen him as over-valued, 'he took this value stuff really seriously'. Graham did not accumulate a vast fortune for himself (merely millions) – he was often too preoccupied with numerous artistic and intellectual pursuits – but his ideas have influenced the creation of many multi-billion dollar fortunes.

Graham was the leading exponent of the value school of investing. His approach is far more sophisticated than the simplistic 'value rules' followed by some share punters today. He allowed for a multiplicity of factors when judging the value of a share rather than simply buying because the share fell into, say the low price-earnings ratio (PER[1]), category. He laid much more emphasis on understanding the business characteristics of the firm he was buying into, and on understanding the mind of the market. He combined this with powerful intellectual tools to control emotions when investing. If you can master these three areas then you are well on your way to joining the other Grahamites who have made investing fortunes.

---

1. **Price–earnings ratios, PER or P/E ratios** compare a company's current share price with its latest (or prospective) earnings per share (EPS), e.g.

$$PER = \frac{\text{current market price of a share}}{\text{last year's earnings per share}}$$

There is so much you can learn from Graham:

- Understand the difference between being an investor and being a speculator in shares.

- Determine the key factors to look for in analysing the value of a share.

- Be independently minded so that you can exploit the irrationality in market pricing rather than be a victim of it.

- Invest with a margin of safety – buy not only shares which are priced too low, but those that are priced very much too low.

The Early Years

Graham was born Benjamin Grossbaum in 1894 in London, and moved with his family to the US when he was one year old. His father was in the porcelain business, and the family lived a comfortable life. However in 1903 his father died, and the family drifted into poverty. To make ends meet, his mother turned the family home into a boarding house. Needing to boost the family income still further she speculated in shares, initially with some modest success, but lost everything in the 1907 stock market crash. The lesson of the perils of speculation, as opposed to the safety of investing, was to become a key driving force in the development of Graham's philosophy. If you have never really thought through the difference between speculation and investing then Graham's lifetime of thinking will help you.

Education

An exceptionally able student, Graham passed through grade and high schools with speed, simultaneously carrying out a variety of jobs that schoolboys routinely perform. He was awarded a full scholarship to the University of Columbia, excelling in all subjects despite working part-time throughout his studying and graduated only two and a half years later in 1914. Before graduating at the age of only 20, he was asked to join three different teaching departments at Columbia: English, Philosophy and Mathematics. He decided against this, and despite, or maybe because of, his mother's financial situation, he decided to work on Wall Street, first as a runner at a brokerage house, then as a clerk, an analyst and finally as a partner.

First Ventures into Investment

In 1923 he joined with former classmates to form the Graham Corporation, which traded for two and a half years, and returned a high percentage on capital. He was paid a salary and a percentage of the profit. However Graham felt that he was being used by his partners, and that he deserved a larger portion of the profits. Convinced that he knew everything about making money on Wall Street, he proposed that he forgo a salary, choosing instead to receive a percentage of the profits on a sliding scale, ranging from 20 to 50 per cent.

He proposed that he forgo a salary, choosing instead to receive a percentage of the profits on a sliding scale.

This led to the dissolution of the Graham Corporation and the forming of the Benjamin Graham Joint Account. The $400,000 capital for this came from Graham himself and a group of old friends, and Graham was paid according to the sliding scale he had proposed earlier. By 1929, the capital had grown to £2.5 million, and the number of investors increased, despite Graham refusing to accept funds from people he did not know.

Partnership with Newman

Jerome Newman was the younger brother of one of Graham's original group of friends from school and college and had graduated from Columbia Law School. He joined Graham in 1926, offering to work for nothing until he proved himself useful. Graham accepted this offer: obviously, he was considered better value than Buffett! He soon excelled, and this was the beginning of an association which would last until Graham's retirement. Although they were not good friends – in fact Graham made hundreds of acquaintances but no good friends – the pair of them worked well and harmoniously together. Newman had an excellent head for the practicalities of business and for negotiating, while Graham was the brains behind the new financial theories and strategies which were to revolutionise the way investing was done. Over time the Benjamin Graham Joint Account gave way to the Graham–Newman Corporation and Newman & Graham, and these companies were to employ some of the best investment analysts of the twentieth century.

Wall Street

Graham joined Wall Street at a time of great change. In his autobiography, *The Memoirs of the Dean of Wall Street*, he wrote, 'In the early days, the business of Wall Street was largely a gentlemen's game, played by an elaborate set of rules'.[2] Some gentlemen! The emphasis was on finding inside information with very little attention paid to financial analysis. Poring over dry statistics seemed a wasted effort when the real influences on shares were considered to be much more related to human emotions and 'contacts'. However, in the 1920s this system was starting to decline, and in its place were appearing the modern day tools of financial analysis. Graham was a pioneer of this new regime, using his considerable intellect to analyse securities.

He developed his philosophy of looking for shares that were selling significantly below true value. To do this he had to teach himself how to analyse the underlying value of a company. After much effort he figured out the key elements that we need to look for to allow us to confidently make good returns in a conservative fashion. Once you know how to value you can buy the underpriced and, just as importantly, avoid the overpriced. The great expansion in industries of all types and the accompanying bull market was the perfect time for Graham and his new theories, and he enjoyed a period of financial triumphs which saw his standard of living improve dramatically.

Academic Career

In 1927 Graham was thinking about putting his theories into book form; this would in time be *Security Analysis*, a book

---

2. Graham, B. (1996) *The Memoirs of the Dean of Wall Street*, p.205.

co-written with David Dodd, which gave the world the notion of value investing, and especially the 'Graham-and-Doddsville' school of thought. It has been in print continuously since its first publication in 1934. Prior to writing the book, to test his ideas, he set up a course at the University of Columbia; the course was successful and it was the start of 40 years of professorships and lecturing at various academic institutions as a sideline to his fund management role. Graham was a genuine polymath, knowledgeable in many fields and languages, and had a real curiosity for learning. In addition to his investment business and academic career, he found time to write a number of plays, one of which was produced; he acted for the US government as an expert valuation witness in a number of important hearings; he wrote poetry; and of course in 1949 he wrote *The Intelligent Investor*. As with his earlier work, this book has been a worldwide bestseller: even today it tops the rankings. I recommend it to you.

Early Setbacks

Graham was a *relatively* safety-first kind of investor in the late 1920s. Despite this he, too, admitted to getting carried away: 'I was convinced that I knew it all – or at least I knew all that I needed to know about making money in stocks and bonds – that I had Wall Street by the tail, that my future was as unlimited as my ambitions ... I was too young, also, to realise that I had caught a bad case of hubris.'[3]

During the Great Crash of 1929–32 Graham's previously profitable investing saw losses of nearly 70 per cent

---

3. Ibid., p.190.

of capital. This changed Graham's attitude towards material possessions and he resolved not to be driven by expenditure that he couldn't afford. He never again wanted to be manoeuvred or motivated by ostentation and unnecessary luxury. More than that, Graham reflected on the 1928–29 period to try and figure out what the fundamental errors were. He concluded that investors had converted themselves into speculators. In fact, the word investors should not be applied to them. They had distorted ideas of investment value and lost touch with key principles. They forgot that a great deal of circumspection is needed to evaluate stocks if a safety first approach is to be taken. Valuations based on projections of earnings can be very unreliable and the tangible asset base should be given more attention. We will explore these ideas later.

Graham felt honour-bound to perform well for the people who still trusted him with their money. He took no salary during the Depression and worked extremely hard to regain their money. Picking up the pieces after the crash and starting 1933 with client capital of only $375,000, the Graham–Newman Corp. made a profit of 50 per cent in 1933 and then went on to achieve one of the best long-term investment records over the next 20 years, until Graham's retirement in 1956. He stated to a US senate committee investigating market developments in 1955 that over a 'period of years' his clients had earned about 20 per cent gross per year and 17 per cent after deduction of Graham–Newman's management charges. This performance is about double the market return.

Developing a Theory of Investing

Graham rejected the long-held view that investors who could not afford to take risks should accept low returns on their investments. It was possible to achieve high returns combined with low risk, but only if the investors had sufficient knowledge of the key principles of investment (rather than speculation) and knowledge of industry and company analysis (have a genuine interest in how businesses work). It also required that the investor build up experience over time as the school of investing is one of hard knocks and you have to be open to continually learning from your errors. Finally, it required that investors control emotions. Analysis of value must be the central focus and the investor must learn to avoid getting carried away with the fleeting moods and fads of the generality of share punters. Avoid becoming too exuberant at just the wrong moment or too depressed and despondent at just the wrong moment.

How to be an Intelligent Investor

Having suffered considerable losses in the Great Depression, Graham subsequently did his utmost to avoid any kind of speculation, relying instead on his theory of financial analysis together with his 'searching, reflective and critical' attitude of mind. He emphasised the importance of comprehensive and detailed analysis which would lead to investments giving a satisfactory return with a margin of safety. Any operation not meeting these criteria he dismissed as speculative. Figure 1.1 overleaf shows you the key features of a Graham 'investment operation'.

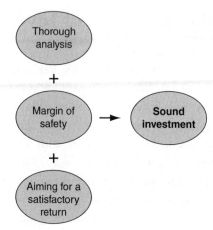

Figure 1.1   Graham's requirements for a sound investment operation

It is important to note that Graham spoke of an investment operation, not individual stocks. His reasoning is that a particular share may be considered as an investment at one price if there is a large enough margin of safety between the analysed value and what investors are currently selling the share for in the market, but would be speculative at a higher price where there was an insufficient margin of safety. Also, a share may be a sound investment if it is part of a portfolio but would not be sufficiently safe if bought on its own. Safety always comes first with Graham.

Graham was imprecise about the meaning of 'satisfactory return'. He warned us not to expect returns in excess of normal, unless you know as much about the security in question as you would about a private business that you owned outright. And he discourages investors from attempting short-term plays to beat the market because he strongly believed that there was no reliable way of making money easily and quickly, either in the financial markets or anywhere else. In a salutatory lesson Graham was trying to warn against the over-optimism and greed that could sweep individuals along, encouraging them to abandon sound investments, to speculate in stocks that appear to offer the prospect of rapid appreciation. The irony is that Graham, following his pessimistic, safety-first approach, outperformed the market. By not aiming for unreasonably high returns, but concentrating on sound investment principles in a disciplined framework, he achieved extraordinarily atypical results.

The irony is that Graham, following his pessimistic, safety-first approach, outperformed the market.

The following four sections discuss Graham's key ideas that can make those who understand them into value investors rather than speculators: thorough analysis, margin of safety, intrinsic value and controlling emotions in the face of market fluctuations.

Thorough Analysis

Intelligent investors should be able to analyse a business. This starts with the interpretation of a company's financial report and understanding its financial position. In theory, trying to estimate future earnings for a company simply means averaging past data and projecting it into the future. In practice this is no simple task. There are so many factors to take into account including the company's financial position, the quality of its management, its strategic position, its dividend record and dividend payout, interest rate changes and future prospects.

When looking at a company's accounts keep a sceptical mind and read the notes to the accounts because management (and pliant accountants) do have a tendency to paint a rosy view. Furthermore, Graham was distrustful of future projections. He said that while it is easy to extract any manner of statistics to analyse past figures, the difficulty of predicting future anything (especially the growth of a company's profits) means that there can be no effective confidence placed in any formula. He had witnessed so many rosy earnings projections in the late 1920s which turned to dust that, while he acknowledged that the investor should try to estimate future earnings, he would place a much greater weight on the proven past figures and very little on the hope value entailed in any forward projection.

When analysing a company, Graham identified two different elements in the analysis, quantitative and qualitative. Quantitative analysis is straightforward, being statistical and based on recorded facts classified by Graham as:

- the current market value of the company as determined by investors (shares in issue × price);

- past earnings and dividends;

- assets and liabilities; and

- operation statistics, such as efficiency of inventory control.

All of this information is generally available from published material and it is a fairly uncomplicated task for a competent analyst to undertake. The intensity of the analysis depends on the circumstances. For example the detail and scrutiny needed to consider the purchase a $1,000 bond is much less than that for a purchase of millions of shares.

The art of successful analysis is to be able to distinguish between important and irrelevant data. You need to develop a capability for concentrating on the essentials hidden in a mass of data. The elements that are 'essential' vary from industry to industry. For example, when judging a retail business in a stable environment the five-year history of turnover and profits may provide some indication of the attractiveness of the shares. But, when it comes to oil exploration companies the five-year history may as much deceive as enlighten, because the main factors for future profit are related to the world price of oil and the hit rate of wells drilled, which may be radically different in the future than in the past.

Qualitative analysis is much harder to get to grips with. Even though Graham recognised that qualitative factors were very important in valuation he was well aware that accurate appraisal was tough, and susceptible to being viewed through rose-tinted spectacles, as in 1929. The data is less tangible and includes variables such as the nature of the business, the ability of its management and its future prospects. While it's quite easy to understand what the qualitative factors are, it is not at all easy to observe them or to interpret them successfully. You won't find this is information in company reports, and you must look to other sources; too often this can simply be a matter of someone's opinion. Graham commented that the elements in this type of analysis 'are exceedingly important, but they are also exceedingly difficult to deal with intelligently . . . . Most people have fairly definite notions as to what is "a good business" and what is not. These views are based partly on the financial results, partly on knowledge of specific conditions in the industry, and partly also on surmise or bias.'[4]

---

4. Graham, B. and Dodd, D. (1934) *Security Analysis*, McGraw-Hill pp.34–5.

You've probably noticed that it's easy to spot a good business, but difficult to analyse the qualitative reasons for its success, and even harder to predict its future behaviour using qualitative analysis. Past performance may have a diminishing influence on future performance. Graham found numerous bargain investments in companies that were regarded as 'bad companies' situated in 'bad industries', which were thus avoided by the rest of the market. On the other hand, he also observed companies with superior records being bid up to absurd levels as investors flocked to the glamorous shares in anticipation of ever rising profits. The conclusion drawn by the generality of investors can be quite wrong because abnormally good or bad conditions do not last forever, for either the individual firm or for an industry. There are corrective forces that lead many poor performers to increase profits and lead to those companies with high expectations to disappoint. Academics call this mean-reversion. It is not that the poor companies swap places with the excellent performers, merely that the poor do not continue to decline and may even rise toward the average while the past 'growth' stocks fall off their pedestals as rivals enter the market, technological change lowers growth or something else slows growth from that expected. We look at the reasons Graham gave for expectation that many of the 'fallen' will rise later.

For Graham the most important factor in qualitative analysis was the inherent stability of the business. Again, he was looking for safety, and unstable business environments are unlikely to allow analysis that could, in any meaningful sense, be regarded as having a margin of safety. He cites the comparison between Studebaker, a car manufacturer, and First National Stores, a grocery chain. The grocery chain made steady and increasing but not spectacular profits, whereas the car manufacturer's profits, though greater, showed a greater degree of fluctuation, which would be expected in this cyclical industry. Graham therefore thought that the grocery chain was a far sounder investment because of its inherent stability, which would enable it to perform successfully for years to come, barring any reckless expansion policy. What we can take away from this is that some industries possess such a degree of inherent uncertainty as to their outlook that it is impossible, with any notion of safety, to analyse them. So, unless you have exceptional knowledge of say computer software or developments on the web don't even try to guess. The imponderables are legion. Will cloud computing take over the PC market? Will one social website triumph over another? Will Apple be able to maintain a stream of outstanding products that its competitors can't emulate? On the other hand the market place changes in the supply of soft drinks or chocolate are likely to be very small and so future demand and the competitive position of the current leaders can be assessed with some degree of confidence.

To try and get the right frame of mind to thoroughly analyse a stock market traded share Graham advised that we should imagine that we are buying an interest in a private business. Better still, you should estimate its value as though you owned all of the enterprise. Ask: how much is the business selling for? If you were buying a 10 per cent stake in a private business for $250,000 the first mental process you would go through is to multiply the amount by ten to see if the valuation for the entire business is reasonable – is it a good buy at $2.5 million? When looking at a private business you will be very keen to consider the assets being offered, the strength of its financial resources and its earnings potential. The same considerations should apply when you are considering a stock market investment. Unfortunately, a large proportion of investors focus their minds elsewhere: are telecommunication stocks due for a rise in the market? What do the latest GDP figures say about where the stock market is heading in the next six months? Focusing on the underlying business enables you to avoid the error of considering only short-term prospects for the movement of the shares. Often short-term unfavourable factors weigh heavily on the market price of a share. These temporary events have little bearing on the fundamental value of the business and yet the traders in the market hammer the price. It's rather like dumping a retail business with excellent long-term potential and with a fantastic position on main street and superb managers simply because the next quarter's result will be down because the road outside the store is being dug up. The stock market can get hung up on temporary negative news and unreasonably depress the share price.

In Graham's view the market was not a rational machine making precise calculations, but set prices after processing through the minds of human beings, who have a tendency to distort facts and use flawed reasoning due to cognitive failure, memory failure or emotional failure. As a result, he insisted that investors make their own calculation of value and not be guided by a market that sets prices not as a result of weighing the evidence but as a result of the votes (buying and selling) of thousands of flawed individuals: 'The stock market is a voting machine rather than a weighing machine'.[5] You must take an independent line based on sound reasoning. Critically evaluate the facts about the business. For this you need knowledge of how businesses work. You also need courage to act when the majority think you are wrong. Buffett said of Graham that his investing wasn't about various fads or fashions, 'He was about sound investing, and I think sound investing can make you very

---

5. Ibid., p.452.

wealthy if you're not in too big of a hurry, and it never makes you poor, which is better.'[6]

Notwithstanding Graham's call for independence of mind, be careful about always taking a contrary line to the market, because the market is not always mistaken – it is frequently correct. The independent and critically minded analyst must pay respectful attention to the judgement of the market but remain detached when the need arises.

Margin of Safety

Graham's emphasis on safety is one of the key factors that Warren Buffett learned from Graham. Value must be well in excess of the price paid, so that even if the bought security is found to be less attractive than it appeared at the time of the analysis it is still possible to obtain a satisfactory return. Margin of safety is analogous to the additional strength built into bridges or ships, which is more than needed to cope with all normal, or even imaginable abnormal, events. Graham told us to buy securities that are not only priced lower than calculated value, but are priced very much too low.

There have been moments in stock market history, such as the bull market of 1972, when Graham publicly stated that there was an inadequate margin of safety. In 1972 his reasoning was that while the estimated earning power of shares was greater than the rate of return on governments bonds the difference was not sufficient (providing a large enough premium given the high share prices) to afford a margin of safety given the

---

6. Warren Buffett speech, New York Society of Security Analysts, 6 December 1994.

vulnerability of equity returns to downturns in the business environment. Taking on risk was not sufficiently rewarded. This was judged to be prophetic following in the 1973–74 shake-out. Investors in 1972, like those of 1929, neglected the need for well-established standards of value and to ensure that any prices paid are not near the cut-off line where good value tips into bad value, but are well below that line.

Speculators seem to make up new standards as they go along, usually based on the current price. So, if the market has been through a rising phase speculators recalibrate what they consider a reasonable price. Regardless of how high the reigning price goes it continues to be a measure of value to the unthinking speculator.

In general, speculators operate under the belief that the odds are in their favour, that they have a 'feeling' for the market, and that they are therefore operating with a margin of safety. But their self-belief is not underwritten by any kind of factual reasoning and there is no margin of safety. On the other hand, a good investor will base choices on thorough analysis and interpretation of actual statistical data, and their margin of safety is the product of their intelligent effort.

I cannot offer you a formula or simple rule for deciding whether a share offers you a sufficient margin of safety. You need to think in terms of probable protection against loss under all normal or reasonable likely conditions or variations. Remember: you do not have to take a shot at every share that comes your way. Investing is not like baseball where you have three pitches and then you're out. In investing you can stand on the plate for a long time letting most of the balls go past because they do not have enough of a margin of safety. It is only when you are really convinced that the market is offering something that is way below your estimate of its value that you take a swing. Only swing when the ball is in the sweet spot.

Intrinsic Value

Intrinsic value is a concept given a great deal of weight by Graham. He regarded it as an elusive idea, but despite its fuzziness it is essential for the investor to estimate it. The nearest he came to a definition was to say that it was the value of the company to the private owner. It is the price at which a share should sell if properly priced in a normal market. That is, a price justified by the facts. These facts include the assets, earnings, dividends and definite prospects.

The concept is difficult to apply in a way that will pin down a single number. Analysts have tried. At first it was thought to be the same as balance sheet book value (after assets had been adjusted to reflect fair prices). This had serious limitations – book values of corporations generally have little systematic relation to earnings and hence value. Some firms have negative book value, but produce large profits and have a high stock price; others have massive quantities of assets, little debt, but poor profitability.

An alternative view, one supported by Graham, was to regard intrinsic value as being determined by its earning power. Again, this is very difficult to establish with any precision. Examining past earnings (the average, trend growth or decline) is of some use, but there must be good grounds for believing that the trend is a good guide to the future if simple extrapolation is to be used. In many cases the plausibility of this assumption is weak. Despite the difficulties it is necessary to somehow derive expectations of future earnings in which you have confidence.

Value should scream at you.

Graham said that it is not necessary to have a precise number; we need only establish either that the value is inadequate or that it is considerably higher than the market price. Graham, not famed for political correctness, would say if you see an overweight man walking down the street you do not need to weigh him to conclude he is fat. Value should scream at you.

The analysts should work in terms of a range of intrinsic values for a company, rather than a single number. For example in 1922 Graham assigned an intrinsic value in the range $20 to $40 to Wright Aeronautical. For the more risky Case in 1933 the range was much wider at $30 to $130. These may seem remarkably wide ranges compared with the precise estimates of value pumped out by brokerage firms these days, but Graham's wide range more accurately reflects the reality of investing. Today, as in 1922, it is impossible to be precise about the value of a share because it depends on the future cash that will flow to the holders and this depends on many factors, from new products to the behaviour of rival firms, and these elements are often extraordinarily susceptible to change. This is why we should insist on a large margin of safety – only buy below the estimated lower boundary of intrinsic value.

Market Fluctuations

Intelligent investors in shares should try to take advantage of the fluctuations, and not be too concerned about them. Making market fluctuations your friend is one of the three most important lessons Warren Buffett learned from Graham (the other two are looking at shares as small pieces of business and margin of safety). The degree of fluctuation that we witness in stock markets is not logical and the stock market often gets things wrong. Investors should ignore the innumerable predictions in the press, and not be persuaded to act on them. Graham had no faith in any method of market forecasting and thought it absurd to think that market forecasts could somehow lead to making money over time – they may work out every now and then but will, on average, let you down. Do not waste time on reading what some prognosticator has to say on the way the market or a share will move over the next few months. When you see these people on the TV or press remember that they don't have a clue, but are paid to take a view.

Companies recognised as successful are often those with the most fluctuating share prices. For example, Microsoft has had decades of impressive earnings, and has seen its shares rise and fall by large percentages. This does not mean that Microsoft had an uncertain future, but that the stock market had overvalued the shares at various points in time.

You can use price fluctuations to your advantage because they open up the opportunity to buy wisely when prices fall sharply and to sell wisely when they advance a great deal. For the rest of the time, when the share price is in neither the zone where it makes sense to buy with a margin of safety nor in the sell zone, it is best if you simply forget about the stock market and pay attention to your dividend returns and to year-by-year operating results being produced by the company. Graham's disdainful view of market speculators and the opportunities they bring, with their manic-depressive behaviour, is beautifully expressed in the parable of Mr Market:

> Imagine that in some private business you own a small share that cost you $1,000. One of your partners, named Mr Market, is very obliging indeed. Every day he tells you what he thinks your interest is worth, and furthermore offers either to buy you out or to sell you an additional interest on that basis. Sometimes his idea of value appears plausible and justified by business developments and prospects as you know them. Often, on the other hand, Mr Market lets his enthusiasm or his fears run away with him, and the value he proposes seems to you a little short of silly. If you are a prudent investor or a sensible businessman, will you let Mr Market's daily communication determine your view of the value of a $1,000 interest in the enterprise? Only in case you agree with him, or in case you want to trade with him. You may be happy to sell out to him when he quotes you a ridiculously high price, and equally happy to buy from him when his price is low. But the rest of the time you will be wiser to form your own ideas of the value of your holdings, based on full reports from the company about its operations and financial position.[7]

7. Graham, B. (1973 and 2003 – new material by Jason Zweig), New York: Harper Business, pp.204–5.

Speculation

People often think that securities divide into those that are inherently speculative (e.g. derivatives) or those that possess inherent investment characteristics (e.g. bonds). A second assumption is that the divide is between those who hold for the long term ('investors') and those who buy and sell quickly ('speculators'). Graham challenged this kind of shallow thinking, saying that it was neither. What matters is the attitude of mind of the person buying. A speculator is primary concerned with anticipating and profiting from market fluctuations, whereas an investor is focused on the underlying business, valuing it and buying with a margin of safety and not taking absurd risks to achieve unreasonable return goals.

Graham's philosophy was all about intelligent effort, not guesswork. He complained that the financial services industry was responsible for promoting speculation, with its brokers and other commentators continually emphasising the short-term prospects of a firm in terms of stock market price movement rather than prospects expressed in terms of the strength of the underlying business. Have things changed much, I wonder? The combination of financial market 'professionals' and an over-excited uninformed investing public can even push strong and relatively stable shares into a speculative situation if they became unduly popular; this has happened to the shares of Microsoft, IBM, General Electric and Intel at various points in their histories.

Unintelligent Speculation and Intelligent Speculation

In his later work Graham moved away from the simple split of investing and speculation and acknowledged that there is a speculative aspect to any investing because we are dealing with future uncertainties and therefore open ourselves to error and loss, but he insisted that this should be intelligent speculation. The investor must keep the speculative factor within minor limits. Unintelligent speculation he characterised in the following ways:

- buying and selling when you lack the proper knowledge and skill for it;

- risking more money in than you can afford to lose;

- ignoring quantitative material;

- placing the emphasis on the expectation of the rewards from a successful speculation rather than a considered assessment of your capacity to act intelligently.

Intelligent speculation requires a focus on information that is quantifiable by the calculation of probabilities. By drawing on the analyst's experience, a careful weighing of the facts will lead to a measurement of the odds of success. If the odds are strongly in favour of the operation's success then to go ahead would be intelligent. The share would have to be purchased at a price that allowed a margin of safety below the range of value found through the appraisal to be a truly intelligent speculation.

Speculation can be fun, and occasionally profitable, but Graham's views on the average speculator leave little room for doubt as to his opinion of their acumen: 'The speculative public is incorrigible. In financial terms it cannot count beyond 3.

It will buy anything, at any price, if there seems to some "action" in progress. It will fall for any company identified with "franchising," computers, electronics, science, technology, or what have you, when the particular fashion is raging.'[8]

You need to be able to look at yourself critically to be sure that you have the capability to intelligently speculate. Do you have a genuine interest in businesses and how they operate? Do you have the time needed to really understand the firm and its rivals? Can you keep your emotions in check when the market is irrational, exuberant or pessimistic? It is all too easy to fall into the trap of persuading yourself that you are intelligently speculating, when in fact, you are unintelligently speculating, with little knowledge or analysis of the securities bought.

Failure is to be expected even for the best investors (intelligent speculators). But when a position does not go the way you hoped always remember that even if your failure rate is as high as four out of ten you will still be in the super-league. Do not berate yourself if an investment goes wrong. If you are truly intelligently speculating then you can put failures down to the high degree of error inherent in this sort of activity. A failed share purchase does not put you into the unintelligent speculator category if you genuinely undertook sufficient study and used sound judgement.

Management

Graham had a very robust view of how the relationship between shareholder and management should be effected. Shareholders should be 'energetic' in their attitude toward

---

8   Ibid., pp.436–7.

their managements. They should be generous toward those who are demonstrably doing a good job, but demand clear and satisfying explanations when the results appear to be worse than they should be. They should be willing to support movements to improve or remove clearly unproductive managements.

Shareholders should be 'energetic' in their attitude toward their managements.

In present times it is in general harder to get away with fudging figures in the ways that Graham cites in his books, but there remain many reasons why shareholders need to be vigilant because bad management can be very inventive in deception and at covering up incompetence. There are three problems with management. Firstly there is plain dishonesty which is often difficult to detect but given that you cannot make a quantitative deduction when calculating value to allow for an unscrupulous management the only solution is to avoid all situations where you suspect deceit. Secondly is honesty combined with incompetence – shareholders should be on their guard and not simply presume that management is competent. Thirdly is the situation where managers are generally honest in the ordinary sense and competent in running the business, but they are only human and subject to pressure caused by conflicts of interest. This is a form of managementism at its most subtle. On many key decisions the managers are interested parties and care needs to be taken not to give them *carte blanche*. Watch out for non-shareholder prioritisation over the following:

- management withholding information from shareholders, using the excuse that it could be beneficial to competitors

– in this way they can maintain a tactical edge over the questioning shareholder;

- management benefiting from the expansion of the business by way of increased salaries or status;

- management being rewarded by share options or bonuses that do not align incentives with shareholders' best interests;

- management continuing to run a company even though it might be in the interests of shareholders for the company to be trimmed down or even liquidated, with capital being returned to shareholders;

- management having control of dividend payments – see the next section.

When private employers hire staff they naturally look for people they trust. However, this does not mean that they permit them to fix their own salaries or decide how much capital they should put into or remove from the business.

Dividend Payments

Graham was particularly troubled by companies whose management withheld dividends unnecessarily for inadequate reasons. Profits should be retained and reinvested in the business only where there is good reason to expect that they will produce a satisfactory rate of return. It is often the case that profits retained by companies for expansion are of less benefit to the shareholder in the future than that same profit distributed as dividends. This is a hugely complex problem, with no simple formula, as the management of each company must act as best suits that particular company, but we, as shareholders, must observe their actions and weigh up their explanations, and

always remember that we are looking for managers that understand that a corporation is merely a creature and property of the
owning shareholders. The senior officers need to show humility
by accepting that they are merely the paid employees of the
shareholders with the directors being trustees, whose legal duty
it is to act solely on behalf of the owners of the business.

Shareholders

Shareholders should have a significant voice in the running
of the companies in which they had invested, but far too
many of them do not: 'It is a notorious fact, however, that the
typical American stockholder is the most docile and apathetic
animal in captivity. He does what the board of directors tell
him to do, and never thinks of asserting his individual rights
as owner of the business and employer of its paid officers. The
result is that the effective control of many, perhaps most, large
American corporations is exercised not by those who together
own a majority of the stock but by a small group known as "the
management".'[9] It would be nice to report that matters have
improved. Alas, they have not improved nearly as much as they
need to – there are still a lot of docile animals out there.

As a shareholder himself, Graham was keen to use his
position to benefit all shareholders. In the late 1920s he had
his first taste of using his position as a shareholder to change
company policy. His fund owned shares in Northern Pipeline,
a company that was selling at only $65 a share, but paying a
$6 dividend. On top of that it had cash equal to $95 per share,
nearly all of which it could distribute to its shareholders without

---

9. Graham, B. and Dodd, D. (1934), pp.508–9.

harming its operations. Talk about a bargain security! By judicious buying of Northern Pipeline shares, and later winning over a majority of stockholders to his viewpoint, Graham was able to force the unwilling president and board to distribute the funds to shareholders against the expectations of Wall Street, most of whom thought that shareholders simply could not exert this amount of influence on a company.

Growth Shares

To Graham a growth share is one that *has* performed well in the past (in growth of earnings per share) and is expected to do so in the future. The term growth share should not be applied to companies which have an ordinary (or no) profit record where the investor merely expects it to do better than average in the future – these should be termed 'promising companies'.

Graham understood that, despite the risk involved, growth shares can hold a real attraction for the investor, offering as they do the chance to profit from their growth. However their very attraction tends to increase the share price, which can grow disproportionately high compared to average earnings and profits, only to fall considerably in a market downturn. He cites the example of IBM, once a wonder stock, making huge profits for its shareholders, which in the early sixties lost 50 per cent of its value, and almost the same percentage at the end of the decade. To emphasise the point, Graham also gives the example of Texas Instruments which in six years rose from a price of $5 to $256, without paying a dividend, while its earnings increased from 40 cents to $3.91 per share. Note that the price advanced five times as fast as the profits; this is characteristic of popular shares. However in the following two years earnings dropped off by nearly 50 per cent and the price by a massive *four-fifths* to $49. So following Graham's warning advice, the safety conscious investor should steer well clear of recognised growth shares. While he does admit that there can be spectacular gains to be made by buying the right share at the right time and selling at the right time, he thinks that the average investor is as likely to accomplish this as to find money growing on trees.

The safety conscious investor should steer well clear of recognised growth shares.

It is extremely difficult to know how much to pay for a share that offers rapidly rising earnings, and so obtaining any degree of dependability in returns is unlikely. The projection of future earnings based on a past trend is full of uncertainty; modifying the trend leaves you open to the self-critical charge of arbitrariness. Too often analysts have been persuaded to extrapolate a trend forgetting to allow for the impact of increasing competition to decrease the growth trajectory – or even eliminate it. Most growth shares are technologically based and any growth projections riding on the coat-tails of science are fundamentally a qualitative exercise.

Graham concluded that growth investing was at a pre-scientific stage because of the inability to find *conservative* (erring on the side of understatement) projections of future earnings and therefore rational analysis and margin of safety could not be applied. In contrast, the value of the neglected or bargain share could generally be established to see if it is selling at a price that affords some protection against the effect of miscalculation or worse than average luck. Those that buy based on predictions of growth are not seeking value for money in concrete, demonstrable terms whereas those that buy on the basis of protection against adverse developments are. Prospects and promises of the future do not compensate for a lack of sufficient value in hand.

Graham did not exclude the possibility that some individual analysts could be smart and shrewd enough to pick winning growth shares where the current price did not already reflect the prospects. But he regarded these qualities as rare, and advised investors to avoid trying to compete with these highly gifted and focused people. Instead of smart and shrewd the investor should aim for wise. This means that instead of brilliant insight into the future trading environment and managerial qualities of a corporation, the analyst should be merely technically competent, experienced and prudent.

Graham's Three Approaches to Investing

Graham developed three related approaches to investment – current asset value investing, defensive value investing and enterprising value investing – each with certain essential factors, see Figure 1.2 overleaf. Always the most important factor was sound business-like analysis and appraisal of the shares to be purchased.

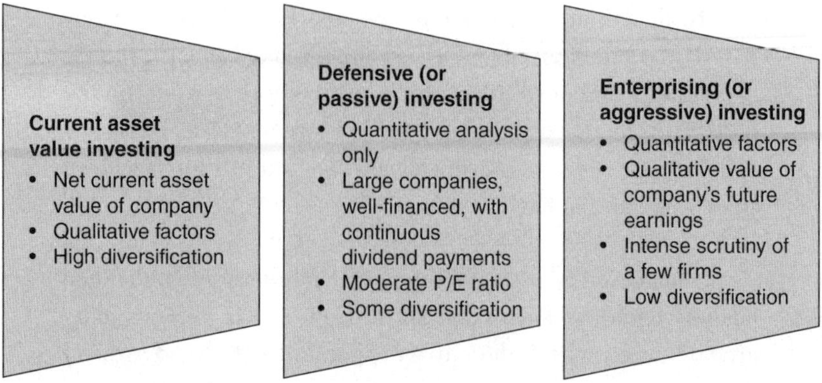

Current asset value investing
- Net current asset value of company
- Qualitative factors
- High diversification

Defensive (or passive) investing
- Quantitative analysis only
- Large companies, well-financed, with continuous dividend payments
- Moderate P/E ratio
- Some diversification

Enterprising (or aggressive) investing
- Quantitative factors
- Qualitative value of company's future earnings
- Intense scrutiny of a few firms
- Low diversification

Figure 1.2   Graham's approaches to investing

Current Asset Value Investing

This type of investing formed the foundation of Graham's success in the 1930s and 1940s. On analysing financial reports he found that there were numerous companies whose shares were undervalued in relation to the liquid assets held on the balance sheet. He looked for shares that sold for less than the company's net working capital alone, that is, the value of the current assets after deducting all liabilities, both current and long-term. Graham did take note of the possible market rationalisations justifying why companies sell for less than the value of their net working capital but frequently found them inadequate. In reality the negative factors were not of sufficient detriment to the financial strength of the company to justify pushing the share price so low – at least this was the case for the majority of shares within a portfolio of shares of this kind.

He took current assets without placing any value on fixed assets, intangibles or goodwill, deducted all liabilities, and divided this by the number of shares, thereby giving a net current asset value (NCAV) per share. If this was more than the actual share price, then the company's share was under-valued and therefore was a serious contender for investment. However, there is another stage of analysis: once a company passes muster on its quantitative elements, its qualitative elements are addressed, and an investor will then feel ready to invest. When a share selling for less than its NCAV is found the analyst should then check that its earnings are stable, its prospects are good given its strategic position and it has a good team of managers – see Figure 1.3.

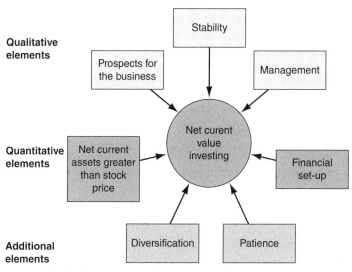

Figure 1.3   Net current asset value investing

Why do these bargain issues occur? Can it really be true that you can find companies so undervalued that their shares sell for less than their liquidating value? It would seem to defy logic that this could happen, but it did and it does today. In his book *Security Analysis* Graham gives numerous examples of companies which fell into this situation. In the 1930s and 1940s, and again in the 1970s, Graham was astonished by the amount of liquid resources in some of the companies whose shares were selling at a low price; he found that there were established companies whose long-term assets, such as valuable land and buildings, or patents and brand names, were valued at nothing. In an article in *The Journal of Investing* (Winter 2008) Ying Xiao and I demonstrated that this approach worked when applied to UK stocks in the period 1981–2005, and research carried out in other countries confirms that bargain issues are there to be found, even in modern times.

There are three main areas where mistakes are made which can lead to shares being seriously undervalued:

1. The stock market is fundamentally mistaken in its judgement of companies' profitability and prospects for survival.

2. Management has mistakenly gone in pursuit of value-destroying activities which will gradually waste away the company's assets.

3. Shareholders are mistaken in their attitude towards their property. They are not pushing the management to set the company on the right course.

It would seem that many equity market participants lose the habit of looking at the balance sheet and focus all their tests of value on the income statement. Those that have low (no) profits in the near term are dumped until the shares are changing hands at a fraction of the value that can be realised by selling off the assets. They seem to assume that the net assets are simply locked away, out of their reach, and so the value of them is irrelevant. They think assets are of little practical import since the company had no intention of liquidating. There is the anticipation of the continued dissipation of firm assets as management continues to make poor capital investment decisions. In many cases they are right, as we have experienced with many internet stocks over the past decade or so.

Why Should Prices Rise?

It is therefore possible for you to profit from errors made and pick up a bargain stock, but why would you have reason to think that the shares would rise in value?

At times of market downturns share buyers become fearful that there is worse to come; that a high proportion of quoted companies will fail to survive, waste resources in their struggle and then die, leaving the shareholders with nothing. This is exactly what happens to dozens of corporations. Graham accepted this but believed that a sufficient proportion of the shunned companies would regain value, so that buying a portfolio would be worthwhile. He believed that market pessimism can be indiscriminate. In the rush for the exit people dump shares for which there are good grounds for believing that recovery will eventually occur, as well as the real dogs.

He believed that market pessimism can be indiscriminate.

In 1932 he asked rhetorically: 'Is it true that one out of three American businesses is destined to continue losing money until the stockholders have no equity remaining? ... In all probability it [the stock market] is wrong, as it always has been wrong in its major judgements of the future.'[10]

---

10. Graham, B. (1932) 'Is American Business Worth More Dead than Alive? Inflated Treasuries and Deflated Stocks: Are Corporations Milking Their Owners?', *Forbes*, 1 June.

His reasons for expecting a revival of most of these companies are as follows:

- Industries recover from downturns; in an overcrowded, over-supplied industry with low prices some companies do go under, leaving the survivors with a greater share of an improved market and higher profits.

- Management can change their policies or be replaced, enabling their company to pursue a more profitable route. Managers in many of these poorly performing companies wake up and realise that they have to do better – after all their livelihoods are under threat. They switch to more efficient methods of production, introduce new products, abandon unprofitable lines. Sometimes shareholders need to apply pressure and force them to take a more commercial strategy focused on shareholder returns. The shareholders may replace the current team to do this.

- Companies may be sold or taken over and their assets better used. The bid premium will give a satisfying lift to the share price.

- The management of a company selling below liquidation value must provide a frank justification to the shareholders for continuing. If a company is not worth more as a going concern then it is in the shareholders' interest to liquidate it. If it is worth more than its liquidating value then this should be communicated to the market.

Asset Value

Graham was not prepared to accept accounting entries at face value when estimating net current asset value. He used to remind analysts that when calculating liquidating value you should regard the liabilities as real but the assets of questionable value. Liabilities should be deducted at face value, while assets should be adjusted according to the schedule in Table 1.1.

Type of asset	% of liquidation to book value	
	Normal range	Rough average
Current assets:		
Cash assets (including securities at market price)	100	100
Receivables (less usual reserves)	75–90	80
Inventories (at lower cost or market)	50–75	$66\frac{2}{3}$
Fixed and miscellaneous assets:		
(Real estate, buildings, machinery, non-marketable investments, intangibles, etc.)	1–50	15 (approx)

Table 1.1   Adjustment factors for asset values

Financial Set-up

Of great importance is the analyst's study of the financial reports. Satisfactory current earnings and dividends, or a history of good earnings, are essential, but are not necessarily an indicator of future performance. While maintaining that a past trend is a fact, a future trend is only an assumption, Graham did acknowledge that past performance can give clues to the future. If a hundred enterprises which had average profits of $10 per share over the past ten years are grouped together, and another group of hundred is formed with average profits of only $1 per share, there are good reasons to expect the first group to report larger aggregate profits than the second over the *next* ten years. Future profits are not determined entirely by luck or by competitive managerial skill. The major influences are likely to be the same as those that reigned in the past, including factors such as the amount of capital the firm has at its disposal, the experience of the managerial (or technological) team, and the reputation it has established with customers and suppliers.

Earnings power is an important concept, but must be treated with caution. Earnings power is most definitely *not* the current earnings. Graham said that it is derived from a combination of actual earnings shown over a period of years (5–10 years), and estimated future earnings. The latter are the 'average expectable earnings' over some period in the future. In examining the past and considering the future we should have in mind the average of earnings over a period of years because abnormal conditions may appertain to particular years, leading to a distorted view of earnings power due to factors like the business cycle. Underlying earnings might also be obscured by inclusion or exclusion of interests in affiliated or controlled companies, or by changes in policy regarding depreciation or reserves for contingencies. It is up to the analyst to differentiate between normal average earnings, and average earnings featuring a non-recurrent element which affects the figures.

Other factors to be considered in the financial set-up which may assist in assessing a company's position include production and cost statistics, capacity of the firm to fulfil orders, unfilled orders, asset make-up and liability structure (When do various debts have to be repaid? What type of debt? etc.). Rapid loss of quick assets (e.g. cash, receivables) is a danger sign, especially if there is no suggestion that the run-down is ceasing.

The Qualitative Factors

Graham insisted that the quantitative factors cannot be regarded as conclusive. They must be supported by a qualitative survey of the business. By analysing the nature of the enterprise, the analyst can get some indication of the extent to which the firm's profits will bounce back if they are in a temporary trough.

This qualitative analysis focuses on the following:

- competitive position of the firm within its industry;
- the operating characteristics of the company;
- the character of management;
- the outlook for the firm;
- the outlook for the industry.

Although Graham said it was important to study these qualitative areas he did not provide many clues to help the reader examine the nature of the business and its future prospects. One is left a little sceptical whether Graham actually gave the qualitative elements any significant weight. He did not want to move too far away from the objective facts. So, to judge managerial quality he would often revert back to the earnings record rather than make a more qualitative assessment.

The scars inflicted by the 1930s meant that he was uneasy about relying on judgement. He looked to the factual base. Opinion is too vulnerable to persuasion in the passion of the moment. Thus we have some degree of contradiction in Graham's writing. Qualitative factors are very important, but because they are non-quantifiable they are subjective and so cannot be regarded as 'facts'. Therefore the analyst should not place much weight on them unless they have some link to the quantifiable evidence. In other words, the investor cannot trust his own judgement in the evaluation of a business's most important features: its competitive strengths and quality of management.

After all, Graham would argue, investors in 1928–29 believed they could accurately predict bright futures for many firms, and later found they had been deluding themselves. Graham's message seems to be that qualitative factors are vital, but you need to be very cautious in interpreting the results, so you probably need to revert to the quantitative facts.

Qualitative factors are vital, but you need to be very cautious in interpreting the results.

To guard against relying too much on qualitative assessment of future change in the competitive position of the firm/industry or the operating characteristics of the firm he recommended that we concentrate on inherently stable businesses; those that were relatively simple to understand and not in a rapidly changing arena. This dependability/stability will be evident in the past statistical record of the firm, but this is by no means sufficient because qualitative considerations may completely vitiate them – perhaps a distrust of management or a strategic positioning error will cause a rejection.

Diversification and Patience

NCAV investing needs the investor to be diversified because some of the companies will fail and many will not live up to expectations. In the 1930s and 1970s it was possible to construct a portfolio of 100 or more of these companies. Today, you might come across five to 20 at any one time in a large stock market and so wide diversification using this investment strategy alone is often not possible. I suggest that you combine this approach with others so that you have diversification of strategies as well as within strategies. In other words, don't devote all your money to the handful of shares that look under-valued on their NCAV.

Once bought the investor has to control urges towards impatience if stocks do not advance soon after acquisition. It may take years for the market to recognise the fundamental worth of a NCAV stock. It would be most unfortunate to sell because nothing is happening – just as you do, the chances are that the stock will be re-rated. In our 2008 study we found that NCAV shares continued to out-perform the market by a large margin in the fourth and fifth year of holding.

So, if you can find a company that is

- selling below NCAV;
- run by honest and competent managers who will work hard to prevent dissipation of assets; and
- has shown high and stable earnings power in the past which is likely to continue in the future,

then you have found an investment bargain without the need for decimal point precision. Eventually the market will recognise its true value. In the meantime you can enjoy the high degree of safety that a stock with little chance of loss of principal possesses.

Defensive Investing

Following on from his theory of net current asset value investing, Graham developed his ideas further and formulated two other approaches based on the fundamental principles of intrinsic value and margin of safety: defensive (or passive) investing, and enterprising (or aggressive) investing. Those that opt for defensive investing can generally expect merely a normal or 'satisfactory' return. Rather than exceptionally high returns they focus on: (1) safety and (2) freedom from concern. There is a simple checklist resulting in little effort and the absence of the need to make frequent decisions. The enterprising investor, on the other hand will, if alert, intelligent and skilful, achieve above normal returns. The main difference in the two types of investing is the amount and quality of intelligent effort put in by the enterprising investor, for whom a high level of well-directed effort means reducing risk and increasing reward.

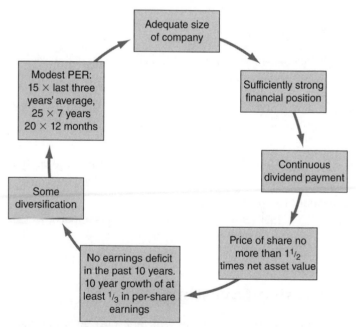

Figure 1.4 Requirements for companies in a defensive investor's portfolio

Defensive value investing is for investors who do not have the leisure or ability to spend a lot of time on their portfolio. All the criteria are quantitative and modern financial websites have made it incredibly easy to take all the shares in a market and filter out all those that do not fit the criteria. The requirements for the selection of stocks for the defensive investor are shown in Figure 1.4 on page 42.

- Each company should be large, prominent and important: small companies are, generally, subject to more than average vicissitudes. (He would use the first third in industry group as a cut-off.)

- The companies are in a strong financial position. Look for companies whose current assets are double the value of current liabilities; whose long-term debt is less than the net current assets.

- The company should have a continuous record of paying dividends over the past 20 years.

- The share price should not be significantly above the net asset value in the balance sheet: Graham used 1.5 times the last reported book value.

- Companies should have produced profits in each of the past ten years, and the earnings per share should have increased by at least a third in the past ten years.

- He thought that there should be some, but not too much, diversification, and recommended somewhere between ten and 30 issues.

- The price–earnings ratio should be moderate. In his writings he sometimes used 15 times the average of the past three years' earnings, at other times he used 25 times the average over seven years or 20 times those over one year.

These requirements are very restrictive, and Graham realised that companies that met all these criteria would be few and far between, but it was his intention to weed out companies which were (1) too small to be stable, (2) in a relatively weak financial condition, (3) showing unreliability in their earnings record deficit, and (4) not having a long history of continuous dividends. Graham knew that his rules excluded nearly all growth stocks, but thought that this was a reasonable stance to take given that growth stocks were more likely to be risky investments.

Even though I said earlier that it is possible to filter down from a list of all the shares on an exchange to a few that meet all the defensive value investing criteria, when this has been done by academics they end up with very few shares – too few to conduct statistical tests on performances. The rules are just too restrictive when taken together. The few papers to have looked at defensive value investing have dropped the number of requirements to only those three or four that the authors consider to be the 'most important'. Thus we do not have any proper tests of the efficacy of this approach. Despite the lack of evidence, it seems reasonable to propose that if you can find shares meeting all these requirements you will be able to purchase a bargain portfolio and should do well. You may not, however, be well diversified, so diversify in other ways, e.g. only devote one-third to one-half of your overall portfolio to this approach if you find only a handful of suitable shares.

Enterprising or Aggressive Investing

In the requirements for enterprising investing (see Figure 1.5) Graham proposes that similar criteria be used as for defensive investing as a starting point, but he relaxes their boundaries and changes emphasis. If, for example, a company failed to produce a profit three years ago, but performs satisfactorily in all other tests, then its shares could be considered for purchase. He dispenses with the large company criterion because if groups of small companies are bought this will afford enough safety.

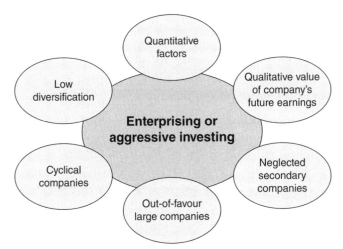

Figure 1.5 Graham's enterprising investing

As well as requiring informed judgement to weigh up the importance of key statistical data, the analyst needs to estimate the average earnings over a period of years into the *future*. Future earnings power estimation can be informed by knowledge of past physical volume, prices received and operating margin. Assumptions then need to be made concerning future growth prospects. This takes us much more into qualitative analysis, requiring a knowledge of strategic positions of firms and judging the quality and decency of the managers. Clearly enterprising investing requires much more work and thought than the defensive approach. Because it requires a high level of knowledge it makes sense to concentrate your efforts on those corporations or industries where you have a special knowledge or interest. This will help give a competitive edge over other analysts, an insight others lack.

The intensity of analysis required means that low diversification is sensible – confine your effort to a few shares in companies (under ten) whose future you think you know the best. It is better to concentrate on those that you *know* are going to prove highly profitable, rather than dilute your results to a mediocre figure, merely for diversification's sake. The reward for acquiring and using this specialised knowledge is better than average returns than are achieved by the defensive investor.

Graham insisted that the approach did not shift the share-picker too far along the continuum away from investment and toward speculation. Only shares which are clearly not over-valued using conservative measures and which meet objective and rational tests of underlying soundness are permitted to be considered for purchase.

However, he did have a warning for those who attempt enterprising investing without possessing the requisite skills or time. Do not attempt this approach if you bring *just a little* extra effort, knowledge and cleverness to the activity. If you make a half-hearted attempt at enterprising value investing then

---

Do not attempt this approach if you bring just
a little *extra effort, knowledge and cleverness to
the activity.*

---

instead of achieving slightly more than average results you may well find that you have done worse. People are often tempted to believe that since anyone can achieve a market average return simply by buying a broadly based portfolio representative of the market that if a little extra effort is applied then it is relatively easy to beat the market. Experienced hands, however, will tell you that there have been a lot of smart people who tried this and failed.

Contrary to what might be expected, Graham's enterprising investing does not involve taking any more risks than defensive investing, but this assertion rests on the assumption that the investor is skilled at qualitative analysis, and is able and willing to put in the quantity of work required. The more that intelligent effort is put into analysis the less the risk of loss and the more the return from the investment (see Figure 1.6 overleaf).

An investor should not try to be an enterprising investor simply for the possibility of greater rewards, when he is not fully equipped with the essential competence, dedication and wisdom. The effort required to be a successful enterprising investor is such that you need to view it as a business enterprise and not a hobby. Given that most people who invest in shares can only devote a small part of their time and mental effort to choosing companies whose shares prove worth purchasing, it would seem advisable that they engage in defensive or net current asset value investing and be prepared to accept the satisfactory returns offered by these approaches. Compromise is more likely to produce disappointment than achievement. The constant theme running through Graham's advice to a would-be enterprising investor is always application of time and effort; without this application, there is no possibility of sound investing with an adequate margin of safety.

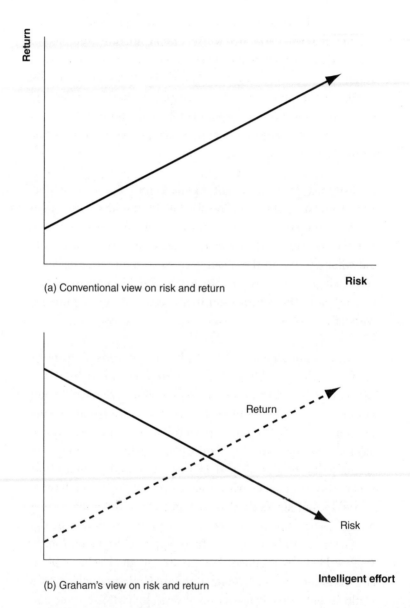

(a) Conventional view on risk and return

(b) Graham's view on risk and return

Figure 1.6   Return and risk

Enterprising value investing shares are found in a number of areas in the stock market. Unpopular but sizeable companies can prove a sound investment. They have the resources to come through a bad period and are able to respond quite quickly when improving circumstances allow. The fashion tide of the market pulls speculators' attention toward the current areas of glamour, leaving other shares stranded. The lack of interest may be due to recent unsettling news that is of a temporary nature – the market often sees molehills as mountains and ordinary dips as major setbacks. Secondary companies can also be good performers if bought at a time when they are suffering from neglect despite good past records and good prospects. Cyclical companies may also offer value, e.g. when the immediate outlook is unfavourable, near-term profits are dropping and the share price more than fully reflects the negative factors. The approaches of buying out-of-favour large company shares, neglected secondary company shares or cyclical shares are three distinct categories of investment strategies. They each require different types of knowledge and temperament. It is preferable to specialise and develop appropriate specific knowledge and attributes, rather than spread intellectual and emotional resources thinly.

When to Sell

Graham would hold shares for a considerable time, usually years rather than months, if there was a reasonable expectation of good income and enhancement of value. However, he would sell if (1) the quality of the company deteriorated, or (2) because the price has risen to a level not justified by demonstrable value.

He advised us not to be stampeded or unduly worried by market declines caused by speculators making judgement errors. The true investor focuses on intrinsic value and does not sell when the market mood changes. While he was generally against trying to predict up or down market moves he did say that there were extreme situations when the market is very high when it is better to keep a high proportion of the fund in cash or government bonds. These situations are rare and there is a real risk of being wrong.

Difficulties with Graham's Approach

Over-simplification

There are some serious difficulties for us in trying to implement a Grahamite investment approach. The first comes from not fully understanding what Graham was saying, or from over-simplifying the technique. For example, not allowing for qualitative factors in net current asset investing.

Torturing the Data

There are a number of derisory terms used in academic circles to describe the process of examining past data for patterns leading to a formula for success – 'torturing the data until they confess' is one. Here the 'researcher' tries out dozens of formulae on past data until he or she finds the one that gives the desired result. Along the same lines, we have 'mining the data-set' until something 'useful' is found. The point the academics are making is this: just because you have found some sort of statistical relationship in the numbers you have in front of you, does not mean that it is a reliable relationship upon which you can make decisions about the future; it could be a pure fluke. Alternatively, perhaps it was a reliable relationship in the past, but because so many people are aware of its past existence it no longer exists, because security buyers have acted on new information, and thus the price discounts it. Even Graham's purely quantitative approach – defensive value investing – has a long list of tests for a stock to pass before it is accepted. Graham goes further; he says this simple approach with its inattention to qualitative factors (e.g. management quality, competitive position of industry and firm, etc.) will produce merely satisfactory results and not the extraordinary returns that investors using simple criteria are looking for.

All those 'value funds' on Wall Street or elsewhere using absurdly simple criteria are as distant from Graham's ideas as are those which chase the latest fashion in hi-tech stocks.

Hard Graft

Even assuming away the temptation to over-simplify Graham's principles, there are some difficult obstacles blocking the path to market-beating investment performance. Firstly, it is hard work. It is vital to obtain high quality data and this is not handed to the investor on a plate. A good knowledge of accounting is needed to make the necessary adjustments for accounting artifices. The analyst needs experience and skill to try to uncover information which has been deliberately concealed. Awareness of crucial factors such as the business environment, corporate strategy and the behaviour of managers are also crucial to two of his methods. These are demanding fields of knowledge and must be properly cultivated.

Temperament

Certain personality traits are considered necessary. Strength of character is required to resist the temptation to go with the crowd when it is panicking, or when it is irrationally exuberant. Fortitude and courage are often needed to persist when all around you appear to be doing well and you have to wait for your harvest. Graham saw the investor as often his own worst enemy. Intelligence is not at the heart of the issue. There are many individuals who rank as ordinary on intelligence but who out-perform because they are temperamentally well-suited for the investment process. Extensive knowledge of finance, accounting and stock market lore come second to emotional control.

Idle Hands

For long periods of time two of Graham's methods – the net current asset value approach and defensive value approach – can be practised to only a limited extent because of the low number of shares that meet the criteria. Thus they cannot be the only approach used for a portfolio. They would tell you to buy few or no shares because the market is at a high level. 'My guess is the last big time to do it Ben's way was in 1973 or 1974, when you could have done it quite easily.'[11] This criticism by Warren Buffett seems a little harsh; it is rare when the market is so high that it is impossible to invest using one of Graham's three approaches, but you may need to combine some of Graham's ideas with those of other investment approaches to fully invest in a portfolio (unless you develop the skills and have the time for enterprising value investing).

---

11. Lenzner, R. (1993) 'Warren Buffett's Idea of Heaven: I Don't Have to Work With People I Don't Like', *Forbes 400*, 18 October.

Keeping an Eye on the Distant Horizon

Value investing can be dangerous for short-term traders. The strongest 'buy' signals occur at times of market (and usually economic) recession, e.g. 2002 and 2008. These tend to be periods of high volatility and the future is seen through a fog of depressing near-term news. Furthermore, the value investor's buying confidence rests on two assumptions:

- that the market price can be out of line with intrinsic value;

- that the disparity will correct itself.

Perhaps in the long run the second point is true, but to an investor with a short-term investing horizon the results may be unsatisfactory. Neglect and prejudice may result in the under-valuation persisting for an inconveniently long time. When the price does eventually reflect the previously calculated value, it may be found that the circumstances of the firm, and thus the key facts and reasoning on which the decision was reached, have changed, thereby altering the intrinsic value.

Used Cigar Butts

Used cigar butts may *or may not* give you one last puff. Warren Buffett abandoned Graham's net current asset approach because:

> … first, the original 'bargain' price probably will not turn out to be such a steal after all. In a difficult business, no sooner has one problem been solved than another surfaces – never is there just one cockroach in the kitchen. Second, any initial advantage you secure will be quickly eroded by the low return that the business earns.

> For example, if you buy a business for $8 million that can be sold or liquidated for $10 million and promptly take either course, you can realize a high return. But the investment will disappoint if the business is sold for $10 million in ten years and in the interim has annually earned and distributed only a few per cent on cost. Time is the friend of the wonderful business, the enemy of the mediocre.[12]

Buffett refers to buying a share which is so cheap that there is an expectation of some hiccup in its fortunes to allow you to offload the shares at a profit as the 'cigar butt' approach. Buffett followed Graham's value investing philosophy for a number of years. Berkshire Hathaway, his holding company, was itself a cigar butt. It engaged in the very unpromising textile manufacturing business in the United States. Its shares were cheap in relation to its assets, but the economics of the business were awful, and Buffett lost a lot of money on its operations. He also bought the Baltimore department store Hochschild Kohn at a substantial discount from book value, plenty of unrecorded real estate values and a significant inventory cushion. After three years he sold at about the price he paid. His comment was that:

> 'It's far better to buy a wonderful company at a fair price than a fair company at a wonderful price ... when a management with a reputation for brilliance tackles a business with a reputation for bad economics, it is the reputation of the business that remains intact.'[13]

---

12. Buffett, W.E. (1989) Letter to shareholders included with the 1989 Annual Report of Berkshire Hathaway Inc. www.berkshirehathaway.com.
13. Ibid.

In fairness to Graham it must be said that his net current asset approach *requires* a consideration of the key qualitative characteristics of the business, including an assessment of the industry economics, firm economics and strategic position. This is essential to be able to calculate earnings power. Perhaps the key to this controversy lies in the matter of emphasis: did Graham overwhelmingly emphasise the quantitative to the virtual exclusion of the qualitative as apparently suggested by Buffett, or did he give as much time to the intangible aspects of the company's position as he did to the historical facts and figures? It is difficult for us to judge this today. I have to acknowledge that Warren Buffett knew Graham and studied under his tutelage. He said, 'Ben tended to look at the statistics alone',[14] but my interpretation of Graham's writing is that qualitative factors were regarded as crucial in two of his methods; net current asset and enterprising value investing. What can be said with certainty is that with all three of Graham's methods, large numbers of companies would fall at the first hurdle, because they have inadequate net assets. This means that a long list of potentially good stocks, with few tangibles but with high levels of intangible assets, are not given any further consideration. Corporations such as Disney, Coca-Cola or Washington Post (all excellent investments for Buffett) would not have passed the first stage with Graham.

---

14. Bianco, A. (1985) 'Why Warren Buffett is Breaking His Own Rules', *Business Week*, 15 April.

In Conclusion

Unlike many of his successors who made billion-dollar fortunes, Graham himself did not make a huge amount from his investing. When he died in 1976 his estate was valued at $3 million, a small sum compared to other successful investors. For Graham, investing was not simply about accumulating wealth *per se*; he relished the intellectual side of investing, the cerebral challenge of picking companies whose shares would increase in value and prove to be a profitable investment over time because they met his exacting standards.

He bequeathed to posterity his theories of value investing and security analysis, which proved to be the most important tools in the armoury of investors, both the professional and the hard-working amateur. He showed us how to invest with a minimum effort and capability, but the quid pro quo is that we should only expect to achieve a 'creditable' performance. He reminded us that to out-perform requires much application and more than a trace of wisdom. We should not fool ourselves into believing that we fall into the out-performing category. A price has to paid if you want to be an enterprise investor.

As long as there are serious investors on this planet Benjamin Graham's key concepts will be influential:

- margin of safety;

- independence of mind – analysis based on sound reasoning;

- speculation versus investment;

- stocks to be treated as pieces of businesses and therefore business analysis rather than security analysis is required;

- intrinsic value;

- Mr Market – make market fluctuations your friend: the market is a voting machine, not a weighing machine;

- net current asset investing;

- defensive investing;

- enterprising investing.

CHAPTER 2

Philip Fisher

Philip Fisher is the leading light of growth investors. There is a common misconception that growth investors overlook whether the share is selling at a value price. While some growth investors are careless in this regard, Fisher was always insistent that the growth share was selling at a value price. Even high growth potential companies can be overlooked or fall out of favour and sell for less than their underlying worth from time to time. These companies are rare because the vast majority of companies with fast earnings growth are well recognised and selling at high prices – but they are well worth seeking out.

What you can learn from Fisher is that you *can* out-perform the market, but only by having a laser-like focus on a particular industry or a small group of industries. There's no point in trying to understand a wide range of industries because this will not allow you to develop the depth of insight needed to succeed in a focused area. Considerable dedication and experienced judgement needs to be brought to bear on the task of understanding all the firms in an industry; what drives their strategies and the calibre of the managers.

There is so much you can learn from Fisher:

- Use the business grapevine to gain knowledge about companies and their managers.

- Evaluate the competitive position of the company.

- Assess the research and development capability of a company.

- Judge the quality of management – especially marketing.

- Examine the most important financial data.

- Exploit the irrationality of other players in the stock market.

You will also have some appreciation of the need for patience when buying true growth companies.

Fisher was born in 1907 and enjoyed an incredibly long 74-year career in the investment world, before retiring at the age of 91. He came from a large family, and his mind was opened to the world of investment at an early age, when he heard a conversation between his grandmother and an uncle, discussing her investment stocks. He was intrigued and excited at the possibility of buying a share in the future profits of any one of hundreds of companies. His grandmother was concerned that he might have been bored by the subject of the conversation; on the contrary, this brief glimpse of the world of stocks and shares ignited a lifelong interest. In his teenage years he began investing, and made modest gains in the frenetic Bull Market of the 1920s, earning the disapproval and discouragement of his physician father, who was concerned that he was learning gambling habits. In reply, Fisher argued that he was not by nature inclined to take chances merely for the sake of taking chances. But he did admit that his initial foray into the stock market taught him almost nothing of any great value so far as sound investment practice was concerned.

Education and Beyond

Where Fisher did learn a lot was at Stanford University's newly-formed Graduate School of Business. As a first year student in the 1927–28 academic year, one day a week of the course was assigned to visiting large businesses in the San Francisco Bay area under the tutelage of Professor Boris Emmett. These visits provided invaluable insights into a number of companies. Not only did the students get to see the workings of the companies, they also had the opportunity to question the management, and under the shrewd guidance of Professor Emmett, they were able to gauge the strengths and weaknesses of each company. Realising how valuable this part of the course was, Fisher maximised his opportunity by offering to drive the Professor to and from the meetings, cleverly gaining crucial one-on-one time with him, and hearing his perceptive comments both before and, in particular, after the visits.

From these visits and comments, he formed two convictions that were to be the mainstay of his investment philosophy:

- He grasped the concept of a growth company, at a time when the term was relatively unknown.

- He became aware of the extreme importance of selling and marketing to the prosperity of a manufacturing company. Even at that young age he could see that great investments were often found in companies that are able not only to sell their products, but are also able to appraise the changing needs and desires of customers, i.e. marketing.

In the summer of 1928, despite not having graduated, he pushed for the position of security analyst (then called statistician) in a San Francisco bank which later became part of Crocker National. Stanford Business School, still in its infancy, did not have a suitable graduate for the job, but the bank was persuaded to give it to Fisher, on the understanding that he would return to Stanford if he could not fulfil the task. The job proved to be not to his liking. His role was to provide statistical data for the security salesmen who were selling high interest rate bonds, and the data was simply paraphrased from existing literature such as Moody's or Standard & Poor's. To Fisher the work was both boringly simple and intellectually dishonest.

Branching Out

In the autumn of 1928, he had an idea and his understanding boss at the bank gave him time to follow up it and undertake some real analysis of radio stocks. Introducing himself as a representative of the bank, he visited the radio departments of several retail stores and asked the buyers their opinions on the three major competitors in the industry. He was surprised by how similar their opinions were. The company which was the stock market favourite was not at all well-rated by buyers or customers. RCA, a popular company at the time, was just about holding its own; Philco however was the clear winner, with attractive new models and an efficient manufacturing process.

> *This investigative attitude is one of the central cornerstones of Fisher's investment philosophy.*

Nowhere on Wall Street was there a single negative comment about the first company, despite the trouble that was obviously in the offing given the opinion of its customers. Over the next 12 months, he watched with interest as this company's shares dropped in value in a rising market. Here then was a clear lesson which is important to learn: reading the printed financial records about a company is never enough to justify an investment. You need to get out and discuss the company and its prospects with those who have some direct familiarity with them. This investigative attitude is one of the central cornerstones of Fisher's investment philosophy.

The Great Crash

In 1929 Fisher became increasingly convinced that there was a wild unsustainable boom in share prices. He even wrote a report for the bank in August 1929 predicting that the next six months would see the start of the greatest bear market in 25 years. Sadly he was one of only a few voices opposing the accepted wisdom that share prices would continue to climb to ever higher prices on the amazing theory that economy and businesses were in a 'new era', where earnings per share were obviously going to rise and rise year after year. These optimists pointed to all the new technologies (e.g. radio, cars, electricity) that were going to propel the economy at a much faster pace than in the past.

I remember a similar sentiment in the late 1990s as people believed the internet, computers and telecommunication would push us to ever greater heights without interruption. We have had a lot of 'new eras' in the last century or 'this time it's different' assertions to explain away very high share prices. A knowledge of stock market history and the perspective it brings is a prerequisite for a good investor – the more we understand the past the further we can see into the future.

Despite Fisher's sound reasoning, he found himself caught by the market frenzy, and spent his carefully acquired savings on shares that were still cheap and had not yet risen, without making enquiries or obtaining information about them, totally ignoring what he had just learned in his analysis of radio stocks. After the crash he was left with only a tiny proportion of his original investment. It was a chastening experience and he learned a number of lessons, one of which is that a low price is no guarantor of value. What the investor needs is a share with a low price relative to its earnings a few years hence. He started to think in terms of predicting (within fairly broad limits) the earnings of firms a few years from now.

In 1930 he joined a regional brokerage firm with the task of finding stocks which were suitable for purchase because of their characteristics, and for eight months he enjoyed putting into practice what he had learned and thought about. Unfortunately it was to no avail, as the brokerage firm became yet another victim of the Great Crash, and Fisher found himself jobless.

Moving On

Fisher had already thought about branching out on his own, to manage investments for clients, and in 1931 he formed his own company, Fisher & Co., in a tiny rented office with no windows. It was a difficult time to strike out with a new business, and profits were abysmal; $2.99 per month was his net profit for 1932, followed by a 1,000 per cent improvement to $29 per month in 1933. Despite the lack of financial reward, Fisher remembers these years fondly and regarded them as two of the most profitable years of his life because they provided him with time to think through his philosophy. Furthermore he was able to bring in a group clients who were dissatisfied with the performances of their old investment managers and were looking for someone new. This group proved to be extremely loyal – which is not surprising given the high returns he achieved.

It was at this time that he hit upon an opportunity that perfectly matched his burgeoning investment philosophy; the Food Machinery Corporation. This company, which was a leader in its field, was formed by a company from Illinois merging with two California companies that Fisher had been interested in during his time with Professor Emmett. It had a very strong marketing position controlling its own sales, with a captive market in selling spares for the machinery it supplied; it had a superbly creative research and development department and its managers were efficient and well regarded by both customers and employees. It was selling at a price which was far lower than the intrinsic value of the company warranted, and Fisher seemed to be the only analyst to recognise the company's true value.

You can learn at lot by thinking about what Fisher was looking for in his search:

- Are the people running a firm outstanding?
- Does it hold a strong competitive position?
- Are operations and long-term planning handled well?
- Are there enough high potential new product lines for growth to continue for many years?

He had moderate success at 'in-and-out' investing (trading for short-term gains), but decided that it took too much time for too little profit. He had seen a lot of in and out trading conducted by extremely brilliant people, but observed that while they could be successful for a time it usually ended in disaster. He therefore determined to use all his considerable efforts to making major gains in the long-term.

The Second World War and Beyond

During the Second World War Fisher did a number of desk jobs in the Army Air Corps, and during this time he was able to reflect on his ideas and further hone his investment philosophy. After the war, he decided to concentrate on finding unusual companies which had the possibility of significant growth in earnings and to restrict his client group to a few large investors (12 was the maximum number of clients Fisher had during the 1950s and 60s). He also decided that the chemical industry would enjoy substantial expansion after the war, and set about finding the most attractive large chemical company. Researching the chemical industry to find out everything he could about the companies and their managements, he talked to anyone who had some knowledge of the industry. All the qualitative pieces of information (e.g. innovations, inventions and competitive conditions) that he had gathered were added to his analysis of financial data.

Dow Chemical

By spring 1947 Fisher had managed to single out one firm which met all his criteria – this was Dow Chemical Company. The reasons for his choice were:

- A culture of high achievement as a team. As he began to know people in the Dow organisation, he found there was a very real sense of excitement at many levels of management about the growth that had already occurred, about their accomplishments as a team. A belief permeated the organisation that even greater growth lay ahead.

- Senior managerial wisdom. One of his favourite questions in talking to any top business executive for the first time was what he considered to be the most important long-range problem facing his company. The president of Dow gave a tremendously impressive answer. This was to avoid becoming more 'military-like' as they grow very much larger, to resist becoming bureaucratic and to maintain the informal relationships whereby people at different levels and in various departments can continue to communicate with each other in an unstructured way.

- A focus on those areas where they had a special competence and refusal to step outside of that circle of competence. Dow only worked in those areas of the chemical sector where it either was already, or had a reasonable chance of becoming, the most efficient producer in the field. This might be as the result of greater volume, better engineering, a deeper understanding of the product or for some other reason.

- A strong research and development emphasis allowing it to get to the front, and also to stay in front for decades ahead.

- Nurturing of people throughout the firm. Senior managers were fully aware of the need to identify people of unusual ability early. These people were indoctrinated into the Dow way of doing things. Real efforts were made to discover the talents of a person and find a role that suited their characteristics.

Despite the pessimism of the post-war period, in which it was difficult to achieve good performance for clients, Dow Chemical Company and most of Fisher's other investment choices advanced significantly more than the market as a whole. There were exceptions where his choices did not prosper, but Fisher accepted that he was at fault and had either not done enough research, or chosen an industry that he did not know enough about.

These obscure little underdogs – Texas Instruments and Motorola – eventually gave spectacular performances.

Fisher subsequently specialised in technology shares, particularly those companies supplying other companies, and he made sure that he had a good understanding of the industry. To bag the bargains he was after he hunted for those that were relatively unknown. Two of these were small companies, and regarded as very speculative by the generality of investors. They were beneath the notice of conservative investors or the big institutions. A number of people criticised him for risking clients' money on two such small risky young companies which they felt were bound to suffer, be attacked and killed by the corporate giants. But Fisher kept right on with his usual approach of trying to understand the management and the industry better than anyone else. As you can guess, these obscure little underdogs eventually gave spectacular performances, earning great rewards for Fisher and his clients. You may have heard of them: Texas Instruments and Motorola.

Fisher's Investment Philosophy

Fisher's investment philosophy grew over decades, partly as a result of logical reasoning and partly from observing the successes and failures of others. However, the most powerful element was the painful method of learning from his own mistakes. Through experience, Fisher realised that for an investment to be a good choice, the most important criterion was to spend time finding out about a company; talking to managers and other knowledgeable people about an industry or company. This was what he termed 'Scuttlebutt', and we'll look at this in a little more detail below. Scuttlebutt surrounded all the other qualities Fisher looked for in a company, reinforcing the facts available from reports and normal sources. What he was looking for was a company that would be outstanding in its field, with all the qualities he had so admired in the Food Machinery Corporation; a company that had the probability of spectacular earnings growth with efficient management throughout.

When he found such a company, an 'investment bonanza', he held onto the shares for at least three years, believing investors should not be seeking quick returns or an easy way to fortune. Having conducted thorough research and made use of Scuttlebutt, Fisher's ideal company is one which performs exceptionally well in every single aspect of its business. These companies were generally in the technology industry, where failure is part and parcel of progress. Less well-informed investors tend to sell when things go wrong and earnings are less than expected, thus depressing the price, and this gave Fisher a chance to pick up a bargain. If the people who run the company are exceptionally able, and the mistakes that have occurred are only transient, then the company still provides an excellent investment vehicle, and is a better choice than a company which never takes any pioneering risk.

Scuttlebutt

As we've seen, Scuttlebutt is Fisher's name for research into a company, but not via the usual methods of reading reports. It is using the business grapevine, seeking the opinions of anybody and everybody associated with the company; employees, customers, suppliers, contractors, rivals, academics, trade association officers, industry observers, ex-employees etc. An amazingly accurate picture of the strengths and weaknesses of each company in an industry can be built up through soliciting the opinions of a representative cross-section of those who in one way or another are concerned with any particular company. If people feel sure there is no danger of their being quoted they will tell you freely about their competitors. If you ask people from five companies in an industry intelligent questions about the points of strength and weakness of the other four, then they will, generally, help you construct a very detailed and accurate picture of all five (see Figure 2.1).

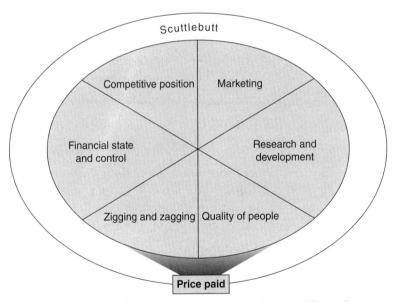

Figure 2.1   Crucial factors in Fisher's investment philosophy

Suppliers and customers are great sources of first-hand information; from them you can gather the strength of a company's sales and marketing ability and the strength of its finances. Other sources all contribute to the pool of information, until from all the different pieces a complete picture of the company and the character of its management can be formed. Care must be taken to cross-check facts where possible and to make allowances for feelings of resentment, especially when talking to former employees. Most importantly, people providing information must be reassured that their identity will never be revealed. If there is the slightest doubt about the analyst's ability to observe the rules of confidentiality, the sources of information will dry up or be noncommittal and therefore useless. Sometimes there will be conflicting pieces of data, but this need not be a problem because for really outstanding companies, the preponderant information is so crystal-clear that an investor who knows what to look for will be able to tell which companies are likely to be of enough interest to make the decision on whether to continue with the investigation. Following on from customer, supplier and competitor Scuttlebutt the analyst can then contact the senior managers of the company to fill out some of the gaps still existing in the picture.

The drawback with Scuttlebutt is that it needs considerable prior knowledge of finance and company strategy to be able to ask the intelligent questions necessary to gain worthwhile information, and is therefore predominantly accessible to those already in possession of, or willing to learn, these subjects.

Competitive Position

For Fisher a good investment was one where the underlying company has special characteristics that will allow above-average profitability for not just the next year or two, but for decades into the future. Using Scuttlebutt, he sought companies which had a consistent history of performing better than their competitors, and never forgot the words of Dr Herbert Dow, the founder of Dow Chemical Company: 'If you can't do a thing better than others are doing it, don't do it at all.'[1] There are a number of ways in which a company can maintain its competitive edge, and the best way is to promote efficiency in all aspects of the company's activities, whether it be selling, buying, manufacturing, management or any of the other elements that contribute to the running of a company.

Economies of scale can be a potential source of competitive advantage.

Companies which make high profits invariably attract the attention of other companies who would like a share of their market. The best way to deal with this type of competition is to be so efficient that competitors cannot compete without committing themselves to considerable expenditure, or getting involved in a damaging price war which is likely to cause indignation in their shareholders, and thereby a loss of confidence in the company with a resulting loss in value. Economies of scale can be a potential source of competitive advantage. Fisher appreciated this, but also felt that any operating cost benefit gained was too often lost in the extra cost of the additional layers of management needed. Companies that run perfectly well at a certain size can lose their efficiency as they grow larger, and their executives can be increasingly isolated from

---

1. Fisher, P. (1980) *Developing an Investment Philosophy*, Financial Analysts Society and Business Classics. References are for 1996 reprinted Wiley Investment Classics book, *Common Stocks and Uncommon Profits*, New York: John Wiley and Sons Inc., p.231.

the company's activities; Scuttlebutt is useful in this situation and can give clues to company performance.

The biggest advantage for the largest company is usually not on the manufacturing but on the marketing side. If the largest company develops a new product, the average customer is likely to buy it because the large company has already established 'an atmosphere' in which new customers are more likely to buy from the industry leader. This is because the leader has an established reputation for performance and/or sound value. Thus the manager responsible for buying is unlikely to be criticised for making this particular decision. A company which is the leading company in its field seldom loses its position as long as its management remains competent. As an example of a large company, Fisher liked to use Campbell, the soup producer. A household name and market leader, it had achieved cost reduction through scale and backward integration (buying up suppliers); it had the most prominent position in retail outlets with the largest display area; and the cost of its marketing was spread over billions of cans of soup.

Sometimes high returns are not caused by a company being excellent at the core business. Rather it is able to maintain its competitive edge by the efficiency with which it handles what appear to be subsidiary matter such as its leases, insurance policies or real estate.

For Fisher, three factors combine to give a company dominance in some industries:

- a reputation for quality and reliability;

- an awareness by customers that they need to keep their own reputation high by sourcing reliable and high quality products;

- a leading position in its industry with competitors only serving a small part of the market, so that the dominant company's brand becomes synonymous with the product.

To maximise profits, the cost of the product to the customer has to be only a small proportion of its input costs. This means that changing to another supplier will not save much money, but there is a risk to the customer of product inferiority. An efficient marketing team can use this to their advantage in persuading customers to reorder their products automatically, and this is something which is very difficult for a competitor to challenge.

Numerous small customers are preferable to a few large ones, and customers with specialised needs are ideal. This is because the company can build up a good working relationship with them, and a competitor would find it impossible to encroach on this territory. It would then take a major shift in technology or a decline in the company's efficiency to loosen its grip on the market.

Fisher did not think much of patent protection as a means of staying competitive because patents can only be used to block one of the paths taken by potential rivals to produce a product that customers will prefer. In other words, if the patented product is very profitable competitors will eventually develop similar or even improved products, by using a different route. We have seen this recently in pharmaceuticals and in smart phone technology. He thought it preferable for a company to maintain its edge in other ways, such as techno-logical prowess, manufacturing experience, an excellent sales and service department, and good relations with customers. He even went so far as to say that it is more a sign of investment weakness rather than strength when firms are dependent on patent protection for the maintenance of their profit margin. Even those patents that do effectively block market entry by rivals do not run on indefinitely. When the patent protection disappears, profits may suffer badly.

The company in a strong competitive position needs to guard against overexploitation of its position, and should not aim continuously to make profits way above those of its industry sector in general; this is likely to encourage other companies to compete for a share. It is quite sufficient for a good company to earn a profit margin of around 2 or 3 per cent more than competitors for the investor to gain a very large return. More than that and the company is just asking for the entry of destructive rivals to the industry.

Marketing

An essential component for a company to maintain its competitive position is through its marketing arm, which is capable of generating repeat sales to satisfied customers. If a company manufactures good quality products, and offers good after-sales service and spares, it is difficult for a competitor to move in. 'An efficient producer or operator with weak marketing and selling may be compared to a powerful engine that, because of a loose pulley belt or badly adjusted differential, is producing only a fraction of the results it otherwise would have attained.'[2] Among other things, the marketing team is in charge of making sure that the customer appreciates the quality and reliability of

---

2. Fisher, P. (1975) *Conservative Investors Sleep Well*. Previously published by Business Classics. References are for 1996 reprinted Wiley Investment Classics book, *Common Stocks and Uncommon Profits*, New York: John Wiley and Sons Inc., p.157.

the product, so that the customer is very wary about switching to a competitor whose product might be inferior and unreliable. Customers do not beat a path to the door of the man with the better mousetrap. It is up to the marketing team to extol the virtues of the mousetrap to the public.

Fisher was surprised by how little attention is paid to the issue of marketing by the majority of analysts who busied themselves with figures, but understood that it is a difficult factor to quantify compared to the relative simplicity of studying financial data. Again, Scuttlebutt can prove invaluable; competitors and customers will have definite opinions on the competence of the sales and marketing teams, and are more than likely to share them with an interested party. He said that those companies that have proven outstanding investments invariably have both aggressive distribution and a constantly improving sales organisation.

Research and Development

With Fisher's focus on technology companies he naturally regarded research and development as a key factor in the success of a company. If you choose to focus on an industry with less invention and innovation this factor may be downplayed.

It is not simply a matter of looking at the amount that is spent on R&D. It should be a straightforward task to divide the R&D figure by the total sales figure, and thereby work out how much R&D is spent on each dollar of sales. But there is a problem, in that there is not a set method for what is included in or excluded from the R&D figures published in company accounts, nor for how companies allocate their spending in this area. The quality of the R&D shows enormous variation, with well-run companies obtaining at least twice as much gain for each research dollar as less well-run companies.

A technological genius is all very well, but his or her skill has to be managed, and good teamwork is essential. The image of the isolated genius producing new products and processes no longer represents the reality. Today's innovations tend to come from teams of highly trained people, each with a different specialty. You may find a chemist working with a solid state physicist, a metallurgist and a mathematician. Their individual skills are only part of the equation. You also need leaders able to effectively coordinate the work of people of such diverse backgrounds and keep them driving toward a common goal. Indeed, so important is the coordination role that it often overshadows the importance of both the number of researchers or their intelligence. They must be helped to work as a team.

Furthermore coordination between R&D, production and sales is imperative, so that all departments are working together for the common good. If a new product is not designed in a way that makes it efficient to manufacture, or that makes it an attractive buy for customers, then sales efforts will be greatly hampered. In large companies it is important that top management understand the value of R&D, and create a stable environment with a long-term perspective. Crash programmes where researchers are taken off the current task and asked to start something new are both disruptive and demoralising, and abandonment of research which has not yet fulfilled its potential is wasteful. Fisher was not particularly interested in a company that had a current winning product, he looked for one which was likely to generate a steady stream of profitable new products. It must have the potential to be equally productive in the future, long after the current product has been superseded. Does it have systems and methods of management to produce a stream of new products and reinvigorate itself? Is it forward planning, and is it constantly inspiring R&D to come up with a regular supply of exciting new ideas?

---

*He looked for one which was likely to generate
a steady stream of profitable new products.*

A warning against investing in companies which spread their R&D efforts too thinly, across a range of technological areas: greatest success seems to come to companies that develop new products along the same lines as existing products, as this makes best use of existing resources. The researchers and managers play to their strengths *vis-à-vis* the opposition who tend to be focused on particular technologies. Look for companies that have a collection of research activities that can be viewed as a cluster of trees each growing additional branches from the trunk.

Financial State and Control

Fisher was aware of the importance of how a company's management handles its financial affairs; only when this is done well and accurately is management in a strong position. Those companies with above-average financial talent have several significant advantages. They know accurately how much profit they make on each product. They then have the ability to direct effort where this will produce maximum gains. Knowing each of the cost elements highlights where it might be worthwhile making a special effort to reduce costs, either through process changes or managing people more effectively. Most important

of all is to have skilful budgeting so that planning can be under-
taken and the company has an early-warning system to alert
managers to where things are not going according to plan and
where profits are threatened. In short, it is no good having an
excellent product, but not the financial skill to produce and sell
the product at the right price.

It is difficult for us to discover inefficiency in these areas.
As outsiders we cannot expect to obtain detailed figures, but by
talking to customers, suppliers, employees, etc. you can start to
build a picture of competence over time.

Fisher looked for companies with a consistent history of
high profit margins, as these are likely (but not certain) to give
an indication of future performance. Some companies have a
high degree of pricing power by which they are able to maintain
their profit margin. At the same time, it is just as necessary for
them to maintain constant downward pressure on costs, always
looking at ways of reducing expense and improving efficiency,
which can help offset the inevitable rise in wage costs. Look for
indications of a high level of ingenuity being directed at cutting
costs and improving profit margins.

You need to bear in mind that sometimes companies
may deliberately lower their profit margin in the short term
to accelerate their long-term growth rate; large outlays on
research or sales promotions are examples of this. Be careful
to draw a distinction between those companies showing a
rapid improvement in profit margin because of increasing
competitive strength in a conducive industry environment, and
those with an accelerating margin simply because of the stage
that their industry cycle has reached. Often, it is the marginal
(weak) companies which experience largest gains in margin
when the cycle is in an upswing. The lowest cost, quality firms'

profit margins do not change by such large percentages. The earnings of the weaker companies will decline more rapidly when the business tide turns.

This type of investing is concerned with very long-term holdings in companies promising steady growth and profit, not in companies which perform well in good times, but will inevitably decline when the business tide turns. By analysing profit margins over a number of years, it is possible to establish which companies fall into each of these two categories. Another issue to be considered is the possible demand for further equity finance. You do not want to be holding shares in companies that are continually needing to go to their shareholders to ask for more cash to sustain growth. The company may grow but the shareholders often get very low rates of return on the money they inject. A well-managed company should normally run using available cash and borrowing, without having to resort to its shareholders for extra funding. If such funding is required, it is important that it generates extra profit for the shareholders; if it does not then it would appear that the financial management is not up to scratch.

Quality of People

Fundamental to the success of any company, and therefore of great importance to investors, is the quality of its management and staff. The difference between the outstanding company and the average or mediocre company is the people running the organisation. Fisher identifies four different characteristics to define the quality of these people (see Figure 2.2 overleaf).

Figure 2.2   Quality of people

Business ability

Under business ability there are two different skills; first is the efficient day-to-day running of the company. Managers should be skilled at everyday tasks, and be constantly on the lookout for ways of improving efficiency in every part of the business. There is no time for them to sit back and relax when everything seems to be going well. They must also be prepared to accept that things do go wrong, and failures happen, especially if they are working at the leading edge of technology. The good manager will not overly criticise those who fail, but be more concerned with finding a solution to the failure and moving on efficiently, accepting that failure is part of the process of advancement. The company that is unwilling to take chances, and is satisfied with ticking along, will in the end become vulnerable to more daring competitors.

The rigid company that is not constantly challenging itself will sooner or later find itself in decline.

Secondly the management team must concern themselves with the long-range future; they need the talent to look ahead and ensure that the business is on track for significant future growth without taking undue risks. Fisher says that many companies have managers that are either good at day-to-day matters, or at long-range planning, but for real success, both are necessary. Managers must be encouraged to continually challenge what is now being done, pointing out that a way of doing things that worked well in the past is not sufficient justification for it to be maintained. The rigid company that is not constantly challenging itself will sooner or later find itself in decline.

Long-term prospects can be damaged by focusing on producing unduly high short-term profits because of the effect such a policy might have on customers and suppliers. It is important that companies keep good relations with their customers and suppliers. Companies can, for example, refrain from being overly aggressive in obtaining the keenest terms from suppliers and squeezing every ounce of profit from them. Paying a little extra will generate goodwill and cement a relationship which will stand firm when trouble strikes, ensuring reliable supplies of raw materials or components. Helping regular customers who find themselves struggling due to unexpected circumstances may cause some additional expense and reduce short-term profits, but will be rewarded by higher profitability in the future. The good manager will have long-term vision which will enable his or her company to build and maintain excellent working relationships with suppliers and customers, resulting in lasting prosperity all round.

Two types of fortune

Fisher thought that companies which have shown consistently high growth over a considerable number of years fell into two groups, 'fortunate and able' and 'fortunate because they are able'. In both groups management ability is a prerequisite. The Aluminum Company of America (Alcoa) is an example of a company which is fortunate and able. Its founders were extremely able people who took advantage of a developing market for their goods, at the same time managing to beat off competitors. They then had the fortune to be in a position to expand into totally new markets, opened up by the rise of air transport, and so their company grew even faster. Alcoa was fortunate in finding itself in a good position to exploit its advantages in an industry even better than the attractive one envisioned by its early management.

For Fisher, companies which are fortunate because they are able are Du Pont, Dow and Union Carbide. All these companies were able to build on existing skill and technology to develop new products. Founded in 1802, Du Pont started out making blasting powder. Its managers and technologists were later able to use the technical knowledge from this process to branch out into a plethora of chemical-based innovations such as Nylon, Cellophane, Neoprene, Teflon and Lycra, to name but a few. The brilliance of the management's business and financial expertise teamed with superb technical capability led to lasting success, with a steady stream of new products.

Integrity

Shareholders need to feel confident that their investment is in good hands; that the CEOs and management possess honesty and personal decency in their business dealings. It is only too easy for executives and management without integrity to benefit themselves at the expense of the owners of the company. If there are any doubts about the integrity of company management, then investors should take their cash elsewhere. This is where Scuttlebutt can prove essential; how else can you find out about the character of the CEO and his team without speaking to them directly or obtaining the views of those who know them?

Bad news happens, and management with integrity does not try to conceal it. They have to be able to stand up in front of their shareholders, and inform them of adverse events, as well as favourable developments. Warren Buffett gives a masterful example of honesty in the event of bad news in the Berkshire Hathaway Annual report for 1999:

> The numbers on the facing page show just how poor our 1999 result was. We had the worst absolute performance of my tenure and compared to the S&P, the worst relative performance as well ... Even Inspector Clouseau could find last year's guilty party: your Chairman. My performance reminds me of the quarterback whose report showed four Fs and a D but who nonetheless had an understanding coach. 'Son,' he drawled, 'I think you're spending too much time on that one subject.' My 'one subject' is capital allocation, and my grade for 1999 is most assuredly a D.

Even the best-run companies with excellent prospects are still prone to failures and setbacks. Unexpected difficulties, changes in demand and disappointing new products will occur sporadically, and should not deter the investor who is confident in the management team. Any suspicion that management has covered up a setback or problem should be taken as a warning sign; management may not have a plan to solve the problem; it may be in a panic, or it may have the arrogant attitude that it need not bother to report such things to shareholders.

Dividend policy is another area where managerial competence and integrity is crucial. Bad management can hoard cash, far beyond what the business needs and therefore not in the best interests of shareholders. Bad management may also divert cash into projects which offer poor returns for shareholders, but are good for their own position and salary. Conversely, bad management may increase dividends needlessly and sacrifice good opportunities for reinvesting earnings in the company. Here they act like the farm manager who goes to market to sell his young cattle the minute he can sell them rather than holding on until they have grown to the point where they can create the maximum value. While the cash produced from the quick sale is welcome he has (or rather the farm owners have) paid a frightful cost.

Because Fisher's main interest was in high-growth companies with a steady flow of new products, he looked for companies with a zero or low dividend, as by their very nature, such companies plough back their profits to create more profits.

Outstanding labour and personal relations

Management's behaviour towards the workforce is crucially important to the success of a company. If the senior management, through their actions, can persuade their employees that they are doing everything they can to create a good working environment and they are trying to take care of the employees' interests, then they could reap a rich reward in terms of greater productivity and lower costs. If employees feel that they are treated fairly and with respect, then it is usual for the company to benefit; production may rise, costs may fall, and employees will put the extra effort into their work. Time has to be allocated to mutual communication and to address grievances; wages will be higher than the average and pension schemes and profit sharing plans will be generous. However these additional costs pale into insignificance when compared to the cost of poor labour relations. A high turnover of labour is disruptive and causes additional recruitment and training costs. Strikes are an obvious cost, and there is the insidious cost of employing a workforce which does not give of its best; far, far better to treat employees well. Scuttlebutt will help here, enabling the investor to gauge the feelings of employees and ex-employees, and evaluate the firm's reputation as a good employer. The wise investor will also make use of labour turnover rates, and the length of the waiting list of job applicants wanting to work for the company.

Outstanding executive relations

The management of a company must have total confidence in the CEO and the team at the top. 'These are the men whose judgement, ingenuity, and teamwork will in time make or break any venture.'[3] Company policy derives from the attitude of

---

3. Fisher, P. (1960) *Common Stocks and Uncommon Profits*, PSR Publications (originally published by Harper & Brothers in 1958). References are for 1996 reprinted Wiley Investment Classics Book, *Common Stocks and Uncommon Profits*, New York: John Wiley and sons Inc., p.40.

those at the top, and they must create a working environment where cooperation, ingenuity and endeavour are both respected and rewarded. In any fast-growing company there may be occurrences of tension, friction or resentment. These must be dealt with quickly and sensitively. Promotions should be based on merit, not factionalism or nepotism. Salaries should be reviewed regularly without managers feeling the need to demand a pay rise. The best-run companies do not have to resort to going outside the company to recruit executives, but promote from within the company, having nurtured talent among their employees. This is an important factor, as existing employees know how the company functions, whereas an outsider has to learn all the hidden risks, all the idiosyncrasies, which can lead to problems. The investor should be wary of a company which relies on one person for its success; there must be depth in management.

A vital role for senior management is to identify and train motivated and talented juniors to succeed seniors when necessary: 'If from the very top on down, each level of executives is not given real authority to carry out assigned duties in as ingenious and efficient a manner as each individual's ability will permit, good executive material becomes much like the healthy young animals so caged in that they cannot exercise. They do not develop their faculties they just do not have enough opportunity to use them.'[4] Senior management must be able to let their juniors do their jobs without undue interference so that their talents can develop and new ideas can emerge. Once more Scuttlebutt is the foremost source of information in this matter, but good use can also be made of a commonly available statistic, the difference between the salary of the top person

---

4. Ibid., p.41.

and that of the two or three below him. If the gap is significant it is a warning sign.

Market Behaviour is to be Exploited

Zigging and Zagging

Zigging when others are zagging is something that Fisher is particularly fond of doing; using the knowledge gained from financial analysis and Scuttlebutt to invest in companies which analysts disregard. Most investors tend to follow the crowd and invest in what is deemed by the professional analysts to be a good investment. Fisher looked fondly back at the Food Machinery Corporation, whose true worth went unrecognised by the financial community, but which gave him spectacular returns. He sought out companies of this type; unpopular, inaccurately appraised but intrinsically sound. He zigged, putting faith in his research and sources of information, while the rest of the financial community zagged, following each other like sheep. This was where exceptional profits could be realised, and the risk of failure was relatively small if, and only if, all his test requirements were satisfied.

Share Prices and Price–earnings Ratios

The movement of share prices is governed by appraisals made by the financial community, and is sometimes disconnected from what is actually happening in the company. It should never be forgotten that an assessment of value by an analyst in one of the brokerages is a subjective matter. It comes from that person interpreting what is going on rather than necessarily reflecting what is really going on in the real world about us. Many analysts lack the skills or the time to accurately assess the facts and as a result their judgements are frequently faulty. Thus an individual share price does not rise or fall at any particular moment in response to what is actually happening or will happen to that company. Rises or falls are caused by the current consensus of the financial community as to what is happening and will happen regardless of how far off this consensus may be from what is really occurring or will occur. As a result of the difference between the financial community's appraisal of a company and the actual underlying facts, shares may be priced considerably lower than the facts warrant for a long period.

Trends and styles dominate the financial market just as they do in the fashion industry.

The markets tend to play 'follow the leader', where someone steers a whole herd of investors away from the track of rationality. Trends and styles dominate the financial market just as they do in the fashion industry. The trendy investment is paraded to possible investors with all its positive attributes accentuated and irrational optimism pushes prices up and up. Irrational pessimism then sets in, and all the worries, problems and doubts come to the fore. This was particularly apparent in many technology, media and telecommunication stocks in the 1990s. For investors, it can be an interminable wait for rational behaviour to return to the price of shares. The wide variation between the market's appraisal and the actual conditions may last for a long time. But remember the bubble always bursts – sometimes within months, sometimes only after years have passed, but it will burst.

When a share has been overpriced and its price is then corrected, the psychological pressure of the lowered price causes over-emphasis of all the negative factors, and the result could be severe underpricing. Serious investors must stand back from all the turmoil of the market and calmly analyse the facts. This is the way to find one of Fisher's bonanza shares, which the financial community has rejected, and then sit back and wait for the share to improve. Patience and self-discipline are needed, as the wait may be considerable. To be a good investor you need a good nervous system more than you need a good head. Investors must hold their nerve with fortitude, and they will reap the rewards, benefiting both from rising earnings and the simultaneous increase in the price-earnings ratio (PER).

Pay for Quality Earnings

It is not possible to rely on a simple comparison between PERs; consider two companies, A and B. Both companies' earnings have been the same in recent years, and they are expected to double over the next four years. The PER of both companies is 20. Similar companies in the same industry, but with no prospect of growth in earnings, are selling at ten times earnings. Move on four years, and assume that investors still value shares with no growth prospect at a PER of ten. Company A is expecting earnings to double over the subsequent four years as they did over the previous four years, so it will still be selling at a PER of 20 and its share price has doubled. Company B on the other hand does not have any future growth potential, so it is now valued at ten times earnings because it is a no-growth company. Despite its earnings doubling over the previous four years, its share price remains the same. Investors must invest in shares whose earnings they are confident will continue to grow over the coming years.

If a company has a proven policy of developing new sources of earning power, and if the industry it is in is one which is likely to continue to show substantial surges of growth, then its PER ratio in five or ten years' time is likely to be as high compared to the average stock as it is now. It is often the case that shares with truly fast growth potential are underpriced as the market does not discount the future as much as you might believe. If you have conducted a thorough analysis and estimated a very rapid growth in earnings for a company then, while at first glance the share price may appear very high, it may actually be the best bargain on the market among a host of shares on much lower PERs.

Investors must beware of trying to predict the future with numerical precision; this is a futile pursuit and not possible in any sphere, most definitely not in the financial world. What does matter for the future is that all the building blocks are in place – quality management, excellent marketing, strong competitive position, superb R&D, etc. If this is the case, then the surge in price and profits is bound to come sooner or later.

Diversification

The commonplace concern is that you have too many eggs in one basket; Fisher is more concerned with the other extreme. This is the disadvantage of having eggs in so many baskets that a lot of the eggs do not end up in really attractive baskets. Furthermore it becomes impossible to monitor all the eggs. Fisher was appalled that investors were persuaded to spread their funds between 25 or more shares, thinking that it is impossible for a person to keep track of so many companies in a satisfactory manner. In reality the real problem for investors is finding enough outstanding investments, rather than choosing among too many. He dismissed those who would fill their portfolios with a very long list of securities as share punters who were unsure of themselves rather than it being a sign of brilliance.

The investor has to keep in touch with their managements directly or indirectly. He cannot do this if he has to look after holdings in dozens of companies. Over-diversification will lead to a worse performance than if the investor had owned shares in too few companies. Having said this, an investor should always realise that some mistakes are going to be made and that he or she should have sufficient diversification so that an occasional mistake will not prove crippling. However, beyond this point he or she should take extreme care to own not the most, but the best. In the field of share investing it is better to hold a few of the outstanding rather than a little bit of a great many. Conventionally managed funds are being invested in companies about which far too little is known, leaving insufficient money to invest in companies that have been thoroughly researched. Buying shares without sufficient knowledge of the company's strategic, managerial and financial strengths and weaknesses is even more dangerous than having inadequate diversification.

To illustrate how much diversification he thinks is adequate, he draws an analogy with an infantryman stacking rifles. Two rifles would give an unstable stack; five or six placed correctly would be much firmer. But he can get just as secure a stack with five as he could with 50. In this matter of diversification, however, there is one big difference between stacking rifles and shares. With rifles, the number needed for a firm stack does not usually depend on the kind of rifles used. With shares, the nature of the shares itself has a tremendous amount to do with the amount of diversification actually needed. Risk can be lessened by choosing companies run by a management team rather than by one manager. Investment in cyclical companies should be balanced out by investment in shares less subject to fluctuation. It is not a good idea to invest wholly in one particular industry, but on the other hand investing in ten shares in ten different industries may be over-diversified. For investors focused on large, well-entrenched growth companies (such as Dow, Du Pont and IBM in the 1960s) Fisher's suggestion is that there should be a minimum of five such shares, with no more than 20 per cent in any one, and each separate company's products should not overlap. Well-entrenched but not yet leading companies which meet Fisher's criteria could each warrant an investment of 8–10 per cent of the fund. Finally, for small companies, which offer outstanding potential for gain for the successful, but complete loss of investment for the failures, you should only invest money that you could afford to lose, and never more than 5 per cent in any one share.

What Fisher Avoided

Rejecting Companies That Have Made Mistakes

Most of the companies Fisher invested in were technology pioneers. Failures of projects will happen in such firms if they are really striving as they should. Look for a good average success to average failure ratio. If the firm is run by good managers bad performance will be transient. Short-term focused investors have a habit of over-responding to earnings drops: 'time and again the investment community's immediate consensus is to downgrade the quality of the management. As a result, the immediate year's lower earnings produce a lower than the historic price earnings ratio to magnify the effect of reduced earnings. The shares often reach truly bargain prices.'[5]

Playing the In and Out Game

Fisher said he could not predict short-term price movements. Imagining that you can look at one of the shares in your portfolio and say that over the next six months I think it will go down and therefore I will sell it now and buy it back again in six months from now is foolish. Equally foolish is the policy of looking for shares not yet in your portfolio that you estimate will rise over the next six months. None of the great investors profiled in this book believe that they have sufficient knowledge to be able to say whether a particular share will be higher or lower six months hence. And yet so many less experienced people think they know! What does that tell you about over-confidence untempered by long experience or learning from the those with greater wisdom? The long-term holder will out-perform the short-term holder.

Macroeconomic Forecasts

Relying on these is 'silly'. Our current state of knowledge of economics is like the science of chemistry in the days of alchemy. Occasionally (perhaps one year in ten), however, things get extreme and a macro perspective can be of some

---

5. Fisher, P. (1980), p.231.

use. The financial community puts a great deal of mental effort into its this constant attempt to guess the economic future. It is a great pity that so much time and energy is wasted in this way. So much more can be accomplished if the investor ignores guesses on the coming trend of general business or the stock markets and instead focuses on looking for soundly positioned, soundly run companies that are underpriced.

Impatience

It sometimes takes what seems an age for the rest of the market to catch up and recognise the value of a company you have bought into. While it is easier to estimate that a share will rise it is not so easy to say how much time will elapse before it happens. Keep to rational investing principles while waiting for others to become more rational.

Trying to 'Come Out Even' on a Poor Investment

Many investors have compounded their losses by holding a share until they could 'at least come out even'. They may not like the company as an investment anymore but they are loath to give up and admit defeat and crystalise a loss. Not only is there a danger that the share will keep going down but there is often a large opportunity cost as the investor forgoes profits that might have been made through the reinvestment of the money that could be realised. To hold on so that you do not have to tell anyone (including yourself) that you made a mistake and have made a loss is mere self-indulgence. Accept your mistake and move on.

Judging a Share on the Basis of its Previous Price Range

To refer to the trading range of a share in the past when considering a purchase or a sale is to spend time on and be influenced by an irrelevance. The crucial facts needed as inputs to the appraisal are found in the current and future influences on the performance of the underlying business. Stupid statements are: 'well, the price has traded in a range for a few years, it is due for a rise'; 'because the price has risen a lot it will not go any further' (growth over future years may mean that it will rise a lot more). Understand the business not share charts.

Start-ups

At least two to three years of operating history are needed to evaluate the operations of the major functions of the business.

Saying No to High Price–earnings Ratios

Fisher was willing to pay PER of 35 or more if the potential growth in earnings was there.

Selling

Fisher's advice on when to sell stocks is succinct: almost never. That is, if the analysis was done correctly in the first place. Fisher however did occasionally sell stocks, for two main reasons; firstly when an error had been made in the original assessment of the company, and the company factors were less favourable than supposed. In this case it is vital that the error is recognised and corrected quickly, and that the investor has the honesty and self-control both to accept that he or she is fallible, and also to learn from the misjudgement.

Secondly there are companies whose development over time causes them no longer to qualify as a Fisher growth stock.

Secondly there are companies whose development over time causes them no longer to qualify as a Fisher growth stock. There are countless reasons for this deterioration, such as less able management, complacent executives or the loss of competitive advantage. The most important point is that the problem is recognised. Fisher suggested a test to see if a company still qualified as a growth stock: ask yourself if at the next peak of a business cycle the per-share earnings of the company will probably show at least as great an increase from present levels as the present levels show from the last peak of general business activity. If you cannot answer yes then you should probably sell.

A third reason for selling is when there is a better prospect on offer. Here one growth share is sold to purchase another. You need to be very sure of your ground for doing this because it can be easy to persuade yourself that the grass is greener on the other side. You know the problems of your current holding while you are not so familiar with those of the prospective purchase and thus there is always the risk that you have missed some major element in the picture

Difficulties and Drawbacks with His Approach

Demanding Time, Knowledge and Personality

Fisher's rules of investing and the habits they require are very demanding. Scuttlebutt is time consuming, as is gaining and maintaining sufficient knowledge about finance, economics and corporate strategy to be able ask the right questions. Most people do not have the time to conduct Fisher-type analysis. Of those who do have the time only a fraction will have the personality traits or inclination to go out and talk intelligently to people associated with a company. They need to be genuinely interested in business problems to be able to persuade other people to tell them what they know about a company.

Will They Talk to the Little Guy?

While business leaders are willing to talk to investors and potential investors they obviously cannot keep on giving up time to answer questions from all of them. Thus, they tend to be far more willing to talk to the large investment fund managers who might invest millions in their company, and less willing to engage with the small investor.

Do it Properly or Not At All

Do not base decisions on superficial knowledge; you must be fully committed or leave the whole investment process up to someone who is fully committed. Just as you would not be your own doctor, or lawyer or accountant, when it comes to investment you should hire a specialist in the field.

Concluding Thoughts

Fisher's main advice is to gain knowledge, in whatever way possible, invest only in industries into which sufficient research has been carried out and use Scuttlebutt. He insisted that share analysis should be conducted correctly, and regarded the investor's task as being so specialised and intricate that amateurs are unlikely to be able to handle their own investments. The advice he gives is aimed at professional investors, unlike some of the other great investors, who do not exclude the possibility that a diligent amateur might be able to make a success out of their portfolio by concentrating on particular industries they know well. Investors should consider adding shares to their portfolio only if they are in command of information for each company about its events, strategic conditions, management quality and all the other factors involved in its make-up.

Fisher has had a great deal of influence on many investors over the past 50 years, whether they regard themselves as growth or value investors. The points that they value are:

- Realise the importance of Scuttlebutt.

- Invest in a small number of companies that you really understand.

- Look for good managers and a strong competitive position.

- Do not go with the investing crowd's evaluation – do your own.

- Focus on returns for the very long term.

- Always buy growth companies at a low price.

- Do not waste time on macroeconomic forecasts or forecasting short-term market movements.

CHAPTER 3

Warren Buffett and Charles Munger

Warren Buffett is Chairman and largest shareholder of Berkshire Hathaway, a company through which he has pursued his extraordinarily successful investment career, investing in everything from chocolate to furniture to jewellery to newspapers. In 2008 he was listed by Forbes as the world's richest man with a fortune of $62 billion, an outstanding success story, achieved by shrewd investments during a career that has spanned over 60 years and earned him the nicknames 'Oracle of Omaha' and 'Sage of Omaha'.

Charles Munger is Buffett's colleague in Berkshire Hathaway, coming from the same town of Omaha, Nebraska. He developed his own very successful investment business before joining Buffett as Vice-Chairman of Berkshire Hathaway in the 1970s, forming the partnership that would dominate the world of finance for more than 40 years.

There is so much you can learn from Buffett and Munger:

- Focus on the characteristics of a business that will lead to high increases in earnings over the long term.

- Make sure the companies you invest in are operated by honest as well as competent executives.

- Returns on equity capital used within a business are key.

- You may have to wait decades before an excellent company become cheap enough to be bought at bargain price, if it ever does.

- Avoid over-diversification.

- The investment crowd is not to be followed, but errors made by it may be exploited.

- It often pays to stay loyal to a business and its executives over many decades.

- There are some excellent equity investments outside stock markets

The two men came from similar backgrounds but their early investment careers followed substantially different intellectual paths; Buffett based his investments on quantitative factors following the philosophy of his mentor Benjamin Graham, whereas Munger, who favoured Philip Fisher's ideas, looked for the factors which gave a business its competitive edge. However once they were working together, their views on shares began to merge to such an extent that they can virtually read each other's thoughts: Buffett says that he and Charlie can handle a four-page memo over the phone with three grunts. They both took Graham's view that holding shares should be seen as being an owner of a business. Their emphasis is on business analysis rather than share analysis. They jointly run their successful investment company, Berkshire Hathaway, complementing each other to a remarkable extent. Buffett readily admits the intellectual debt he owes to Munger; he says that he would have been a lot poorer if he had only listened to Benjamin Graham.

It is important to appreciate the effect of Buffett's childhood and early work on his investment philosophy so I will cover this first. We then look at the remarkable performance of the investment partnerships he ran in the 1950s and 1960s. Berkshire Hathaway became his and Munger's main vehicle for using their talents as capital allocators starting in the late 1960s: the story of its progress from a declining textile firm to one of the largest corporations in the world is inspiring. Along the way we examine some of their greatest investment decisions.

This is followed by a closer look at their investment philosophy and criteria for investment. Then we have a run-down of their advice on what you should not do as investor – investing is time consuming so you do not want to be distracted by irrelevances such as equations with Greek letters in them (beloved of academics), forecasting short-term market movements (beloved of thousands of market traders) or using the wrong measure of risk (e.g. beta, which is beloved of both academics and traders!). Finally I outline some of the difficulties and drawbacks with their approach.

Early Times

Buffett was born in 1930 in Omaha, Nebraska, where he still lives. His father Howard ran a brokerage business and later served four terms as a US congressman. From a very early age Buffett showed a strong aptitude for money and business, demonstrating both enterprise and initiative, first working in his grandfather's grocery store, and at the age of 11 marked up the board at Harris Upham, a NYSE firm in the same building as his father's brokerage. He filed his first tax return when he was 13, claiming his bicycle and watch as tax deductible expenses for his job as newspaper delivery boy.

His first venture into investing came early. At the age of 11 he, along with his sister Doris, bought three shares of Cities Service preferred stock at $38.25 per share. From this first investment, he learned three valuable lessons, which were to prove influential throughout his investment career. Lesson one: don't panic if prices fall. The investor needs patience and strong will to stand firm in the event of adversity. The stock of Cities Services fell to $27. Lesson two: don't sell for a short-term gain. If the investor has the conviction that his investment is a good one, then it should not be sold for a quick profit. Cities Services rose to $40, at which point Buffett sold, but they were later to reach $202 per share, which would have yielded a profit to Buffett and his sister of over $490. These two lessons taught Buffett about the importance of investing in a good company over the long-term. Lesson three: Buffett learned about personal responsibility. He felt guilty when the share price fell, because his sister had entrusted her money to him. He was determined that he had to be sure of success if he was going to invest other people's money for them; this ethical stance was to be the mainstay of his professional life.

Education

Buffett graduated from Woodrow Wilson High School in 1947, having moved with his family to Washington DC when his father took up his post as congressman. While at school, his enterprising nature enabled him to accumulate a considerable sum of money, which was to be the basis of his first investment fund; he worked part-time as a newspaper delivery boy, building up five simultaneous paper routes, beginning his connection with the *Washington Post*; he bought multi-packs of Coca-Cola, and sold them individually at a profit; he collected and recycled golf balls; he published a sheet giving tips on horse racing; he bought a reconditioned pinball machine for $25, added six more machines and sited them in barbershops, taking $50 per week; he bought a 1934 Rolls Royce and rented it out for $35 per day; he also bought 40 acres of farmland in Nebraska and rented it out to a farmer. All these money-generating schemes he devised by the time he was just 14 years old.

Charles Munger describes much of what is
taught in finance classes as 'twaddle'.

From High School, at 17 he enrolled at the Wharton School of
Finance at the University of Pennsylvania, but after two years
found, as have many other successful investors, that the teaching
of financial theories is of little practical use in the cut and
thrust of the business world. Charles Munger describes much
of what is taught in finance classes as 'twaddle', and Buffett
was of the same opinion, resulting in him leaving Wharton
and completing his undergraduate degree at the University of
Nebraska. It was while he was at Nebraska that he read a book
which was to change his life; this was *The Intelligent Investor*
by Benjamin Graham. Prior to reading it he had been buying
shares, but ended up making the same mistakes as millions of
other investors. He had tried chart reading and other technical
analysis and he had listened to tips but reading this one book
was 'like seeing the light' – he now had sound principles on
which to build.

Leaving Nebraska in 1950 with a Bachelor of Science
degree in economics, he initially applied to Harvard, but was
turned down. This was a shock to his ego, but it was more
fortunate than he understood when he received the rejection
letter because he subsequently applied to Columbia Graduate
Business School, where he met and studied under Benjamin
Graham, who became not only his teacher but his friend.
He did well at Columbia and was the only student to whom
Graham ever gave an A+ in his security analysis class. He left
Columbia in 1951 with a Master's degree in economics and an
invaluable understanding of Graham's key principles: intrinsic
value and margin of safety.

Both his father and Graham advised him not to try to make a living on the stock market, but Buffett was determined that this was what he wanted to do, maintaining the interest in investment which had stimulated him as a child. He offered to work for his mentor at Graham-Newman for no reward, but was initially turned down, Graham favouring young Jews who suffered discrimination in many financial establishments. Temporarily rejected by Graham, Buffett settled in Omaha, working as a salesman for his father's brokerage, Buffett-Falk & Co.

GEICO

Whilst studying at Columbia, Buffett had learned that Graham was a director of a small automobile insurance company called GEICO (Government Employees Insurance Company) and was keen to know why. One Saturday morning early in 1951 he took the train to Washington DC in the hope of finding someone to talk to who could tell him about the company. After knocking up the caretaker, he was told that there was only one person working in the building; this was Mr Lorimer Davidson, assistant to the President, who would later become CEO. Unfazed by the interruption, and impressed by Buffett's intelligent attitude and questioning, Davidson gave up four hours of his time to explain how the insurance industry functions, and what were GEICO's advantages. GEICO clientele were low-risk and therefore generated handsome profit margins. The company had a good niche market and excellent growth prospects, an efficient sales team and most importantly a substantial cash float, i.e. insurance premiums paid but not claimed on, leaving the cash temporarily available for investment purposes.

Buffett was inspired by what he learnt – not only how the insurance industry functions but also the factors that enable one company to excel over others. Davy explained that GEICO's method of selling (direct marketing) provided it with lower costs than its competitors.

On his return to Nebraska, while working at his father's brokerage, he began his association with GEICO, investing about 65 per cent of his net worth in GEICO shares for the sum of $10,282, and trying to interest brokerage clients in GEICO without much success. He was not surprised that he failed to get many takers, describing himself as a skinny, unpolished 20-year-old who looked about 17. One client he did persuade was his Aunt Alice, who was a staunch supporter of Buffett and reaped handsome rewards from this and many future investments suggested by him. In 1952 he sold his GEICO shares for $15,259, a sizeable return, but if he had kept his shares for the next 20 years, they would have been worth $1.3 million. This taught him a lesson: if you have identified a wonderful company then as long as it stays wonderful do not sell your stake.

Buffett found time to attend a Dale Carnegie course which gave him the confidence to speak in public, something which had hitherto terrified him. His new-found confidence enabled him to begin teaching night classes at the University of Omaha, and also gave him the courage to propose to his wife Susie, whom he married in 1952.

Over the three years he spent at the brokerage, he contacted Graham with various ideas for investment, and in 1954 Graham finally offered him a position as a securities analyst. For the next two years, Buffett absorbed Graham's values and beliefs, which reinforced the ethical standards which he had taken on board from early childhood. When Graham retired two years later, the 25-year-old Buffett returned to Omaha, with a sound grounding in Graham's investment principles, full of confidence in his own ability, and with a fund of $174,000, the result of shrewd investments. His intention was to put all he had learned into practice, and start his own investment business, run with high standards of integrity and discipline. He regarded Omaha as a much better place to think about investments than New York where there was just too many stimuli hitting him all the time. If you keep on being hit by an avalanche of news, short-term shocks and tips there is a danger that you start responding to them. It may lead to crazy behaviour while you respond to the immediate and lose sight of the really important factors for an investor.

Buffett Partnerships

Between 1956 and 1969 he ran a range of partnerships, inviting investors to let him invest their funds, with the aim of outperforming the Dow Jones Industrial Average over any three-year period, three years being the minimum period of time over which he thought a fund manager should be judged. The first of these, Buffett Associates Ltd., had seven partners and an investment fund of $105,000 ($35,000 of which was invested by Aunt Alice); the final one, Buffett Partnership Ltd., had over 90 partners and the year before it was wound up, was worth $104 million, an astounding achievement, with returns exceeding the Dow by considerable amounts (see Table 3.1 overleaf).

How did Buffett realise such huge gains? By using all his ability, experience and knowledge, and holding fast to his guiding principles, which to begin with were largely influenced by Graham, investing in stocks which were underpriced compared to their balance sheet net asset value, and which had a good margin of safety. While earning large sums for his partners, he agreed to receive no fee if the funds did not do well. He said that he did not deserve to receive anything if he could not at least achieve a return for his partners that they could obtain from a savings account. Buffett received no fee until a 6 per cent annual return threshold was reached, whereafter he received one-quarter of any return. If in any year the 6 per cent was not attained, Buffett received no fee until the deficit had been made up. Needless to say, there was no occasion where the 6 per cent threshold was not exceeded,

Year	Overall results from Dow %	Partnership results %	Limited Partners' results (after fees to Buffett) %
1957	− 8.4	+ 10.4	+ 9.3
1958	+ 38.5	+ 40.9	+ 32.2
1959	+ 20.0	+ 25.9	+ 20.9
1960	− 6.2	+ 22.8	+ 18.6
1961	+ 22.4	+ 45.9	+ 35.9
1962	− 7.6	+ 13.9	+ 11.9
1963	+ 20.6	+ 38.7	+ 30.5
1964	+ 18.7	+ 27.8	+ 22.3
1965	+ 14.2	+ 47.2	+ 36.9
1966	− 15.6	+ 20.4	+ 16.8
1967	+ 19.0	+ 35.9	+ 28.4
1968	+ 7.7	+ 58.8	+ 45.6
Compound '57–'68	+ 185.7	+ 2,610.6	+ 1,403.5

Table 3.1 Annual return performance of the Buffett Partnership Ltd.
Source: Letter to limited partners by Warren Buffett, 22 January 1969.

keeping the partners happy, and making Buffett a millionaire many times over.

An important meeting took place in 1959, which would hold great significance to both parties: Warren Buffett met Charlie Munger at a lunch arranged by a friend. The two of them hit it off immediately, and thus began their legendary partnership, although for the first decade or so this was largely a partnership of ideas and discussion, as Munger ran his own business in California and they largely invested independently – although on some occasions they would invest in the same company.

Partnership Investments

The investments Buffett made covered a wide range of industries; in 1961 a farm equipment manufacturer, Dempster Mill Manufacturing Company, was bought, and in 1962 Buffett began to acquire stocks of Berkshire Hathaway, a large textile manufacturing company in an industry on the decline. He also bought stakes in some leading companies, notably American Express and Disney.

Amex

At the beginning of the 1960s American Express dominated the emergent charge card market; it had very strong brand recognition and millions of customers, but few tangible assets. In 1963 it fell victim to a fraud of enormous proportions, engineered by an unscrupulous businessman, who realised that he could raise loans on the amount of salad oil he was holding in tanks. Amex were duped into issuing receipts for the amount of salad oil in store, but the tanks in fact contained only a small amount of salad oil floating on top of sea water. When the fraud came to light, Amex was the biggest loser, and their shares lost nearly half their value. Buffett took advantage of Amex's sorry situation, using 40 per cent of his partnership's capital to purchase 5 per of Amex for $13 million. He was confident in having a sufficient margin of safety, based on Amex's future earnings resulting from its virtual monopoly of its business. It was not a margin of safety of which Graham would have approved, relying as he did on balance sheet assets, but Buffett was convinced (rightly) in the accuracy of his evaluation of Amex's future.

It is interesting to note that Buffett was not averse to 'putting his eggs in one basket'.

It is interesting to note that Buffett was not averse to 'putting his eggs in one basket'; earlier he had put 65 per cent of his worth in GEICO, and now he was happy to put 40 per cent into Amex.

Disney

Buffett's attention was caught by Disney in 1966, when the stock market valued it at $90 million. Buffett thought it a good investment; it had a brilliant franchise, had made $21 million gross profit in 1965, was the owner of an invaluable film library and possessed more in cash than the amount of its debts. He noted that the Pirates of the Caribbean ride at Disneyland cost

$17 million. He was excited at being able to buy the whole company for only five times one of its rides – it just seemed so obviously underpriced. Buffett invested a significant stake in Disney, selling in 1967 for a 55 per cent profit. In 1995 he re-invested in Disney, exchanging Capital Cities/ABC Inc. shares for Disney shares, and in the 1995 Berkshire Hathaway shareholders report he berated himself publicly for selling too soon in 1967, as Disney's shares rose 138 fold between 1967 and 1995. Despite his self-deprecation (something he is very skilled at) we need to bear in mind that he did use the proceeds of the sale to produce fantastic returns elsewhere. But this does provide another example of the mistake of selling too soon, which encouraged the development of a very long-term holding approach.

Unease at the Bull Market

During the 60s, despite amazing success which brought smiles to the faces of his partners, Buffett himself became increasingly uneasy at the behaviour of the stock market. The Bull Market, boosted by the demand triggered by the Vietnam War, was in full swing, with price–earnings ratios (PERs) commonly between 50 and 100 for the most popular stocks, e.g. Xerox, Avon and Polaroid. Buffett's attitude of focusing on long-term profitability and his dislike of paying high multiples made him out of step with the general philosophy of the times, and he seemed to be an old-fashioned reactionary.

By 1967 his unease had increased to the extent that he wrote to his partners: 'Essentially I am out of step with present conditions … I will not abandon a previous approach whose logic I understand … even though it may mean forgoing large, and apparently easy, profits to embrace an approach which

I don't fully understand, have not practised successfully, and which, possibly could lead to substantial permanent loss of capital.'[1]

Partnership Dissolved

Twenty months after writing the letter, during which time the fund had increased even more, gaining 59 per cent in 1968 to be worth $104 million, the partnership was wound up in May 1969. Each partner was given three options (see Figure 3.1). Buffett stuck with Berkshire Hathaway (and Diversified Retailing for a time), along with some of the other partners. His share of the partnership, worth $25 million, funded a 29 per cent stake in Berkshire Hathaway, and Buffett was appointed chairman. By the age of 40 Buffett was a multi-millionaire, and could have retired in comfort, but he enjoys the buzz of the investment world so much that it makes him feel 'like tap dancing all the time' – according to his long-time associate Charlie Munger, when he walks through the office door his spirits are lifted, when he talks about tap dancing when investing he really means it.

Buffett continued investing, and in the 1973–74 crash bought more shares in Berkshire Hathaway at a steep discount to book value, eventually holding 43 per cent.

1. Buffett, W.E. (1967) Letter to Buffett Partnership partners.

Figure 3.1 Partners' options on dissolution of Buffett Partnership

Berkshire Hathaway

In its first incarnation, Berkshire Hathaway was a textile manufacturing company. Buffett and his managers did all they could to bring the company into profit to justify the amount of capital it used, but they were defeated by the economics of the textile industry; the commodity they produced was run-of-the-mill and they were unable to compete against foreign imports using cheap labour. To compete, vast amounts of capital would be needed, with no guarantee of a good return. Buffett decided that the capital would be much better used investing in businesses which had better future prospects, and with the example of GEICO in his memory turned his eye towards the insurance industry.

Investments in Insurance

In 1967 Buffett's previous experience with GEICO encouraged him to use $8.6 million of Berkshire Hathaway funds to buy two insurance companies, National Indemnity Capital, and National Fire and Marine Insurance Company. As Buffett had already realised, the big attraction of insurance companies is their float. When policyholders buy insurance, the policy money is put into a float. When a claim is made, money is taken out of the float to pay for the claim. Needless to say, if underwriters do their job properly, and no undue risks are taken, the float increases, and can be used to generate profits by making investments. In 1967 Berkshire Hathaway's float was $17.3 million. Forty-one years later, at the end of 2009, this float had grown to $62 billion.

Buffett sees float as a useful source of capital for investment if the insurance underwriting business breaks even. This means that the premiums received from policyholders equal the losses (claims made) and expenses incurred running the firm. While he accepts that the underwriting business is volatile – sometimes profitable and sometimes making heavy losses – he has cleverly put in place people and a culture that encourage profitable underwriting; they will turn down huge volumes of underwriting business if they feel that the premiums they can charge, given the rates over-excited rivals are offering, are too low to make a profit.

Berkshire Hathaway's insurance underwriters have obviously done an excellent job over the years, giving Buffett and his investment managers 'free' money with which to make their investments (see Table 3.2 opposite and page 118). 'Free' money occurs when insurance premiums exceed claim payouts and running costs by more than the amount it would cost to obtain funding from other sources (say, by borrowing at an interest rate slightly above the ten-year US government bond rate), and Buffett has had free money available for most of his 40 plus years at Berkshire Hathaway. He says that in the analysis of his operations the growth of the float has 'probably never been appreciated fully ... nor has the interplay of our having zero cost money in terms of effecting our gain in value over time. People always looked at our asset side, but they haven't paid as much attention to the liabilities side. Charlie

	(1) Underwriting loss	(2) Average float	Approximate cost of funds ratio of (1) to (2)	Year-end yield on government bonds
		(in $ millions)		
1967	Profit	17.3	Less than zero	5.50%
1968	Profit	19.9	Less than zero	5.90%
1969	Profit	23.4	Less than zero	6.79%
1970	0.37	32.4	1.14%	6.25%
1971	Profit	52.5	Less than zero	5.81%
1972	Profit	69.5	Less than zero	5.82%
1973	Profit	73.3	Less than zero	7.27%
1974	7.36	79.1	9.30%	8.13%
1975	11.35	87.6	12.96%	8.03%
1976	Profit	102.6	Less than zero	7.30%
1977	Profit	139.0	Less than zero	7.97%
1978	Profit	190.4	Less than zero	8.93%
1979	Profit	227.3	Less than zero	10.08%
1980	Profit	237.0	Less than zero	11.94%
1981	Profit	228.4	Less than zero	13.61%
1982	21.56	220.6	9.77%	10.64%
1983	33.87	231.3	14.64%	11.84%
1984	48.06	253.2	18.98%	11.58%
1985	44.23	390.2	11.34%	9.34%
1986	55.84	797.5	7.00%	7.60%
1987	55.43	1,266.7	4.38%	8.95%
1988	11.08	1,497.7	0.74%	9.00%
1989	24.40	1,541.3	1.58%	7.97%
1990	26.65	1,637.3	1.63%	8.24%
1991	119.59	1,895.0	6.31%	7.40%
1992	108.96	2,290.4	4.76%	7.39%
1993	Profit	2,624.7	Less than zero	6.35%
1994	Profit	3,056.6	Less than zero	7.88%
1995	Profit	3,607.2	Less than zero	5.95%
1996	Profit	6,702.0	Less than zero	6.64%
1997	Profit	7,093.1	Less than zero	5.92%

▶

	(1) Underwriting loss	(2) Average float	Approximate cost of funds ratio of (1) to (2)	Year-end yield on government bonds
		(in $ millions)		
1998	Profit	22,762.0	Less than zero	4.57%
1999	1,400.00	25,298.0	5.80%	6.20%
2000	1,715.00	27,871.0	6.00%	5.19%
2001	4,067.00	35,508.0	12.80%	5.7%
2002	411.00	41,224.0	1.00%	4.8%
2003	Profit	44,220.0	Less than zero	5.0%
2004	Profit	46,094.0	Less than zero	4.8%
2005	Profit	49,287.0	Less than zero	4.6%
2006	Profit	50,887.0	Less than zero	4.8%
2007	Profit	58,698.0	Less than zero	4.5%
2008	Profit	58,488.0	Less than zero	3.1%
2009	Profit	61,911.0	Less than zero	3.8%

[†] The yields on government bonds for 2001–08 are taken from Barclays Capital Equity Gilt Study 2009, and the 2009 figure is from *The Economist*.

Table 3.2   The cost of the insurance float
Source: Figures taken from various Chairman's Letters to Berkshire Hathaway shareholders.

and I pay a lot of attention to that. It's not entirely an accident that the business developed in this manner.'[2]

The float from the insurance business together with cash generated from other business enterprises was used to purchase three different types of investment:

- significant minority stakes in publicly quoted large companies;

- controlling interests in insurance companies;

---

2. *Financial Times*, 11 May 1996, p.1.

- stakes in non-quoted businesses with sound franchises and outstanding management.

Washington Post

The purchase in 1973 of 10 per cent (the holding later became 18.2 per cent due to numerous buy-backs) of the *Washington Post* for $10.6 million is an early example of Berkshire Hathaway's acquisition of a minority stake in a publicly quoted company. Buffett understood the intrinsic value of the company at a time when the market ignored it. Here was a company with successful franchises – the *Washington Post* itself, *Newsweek* magazine and five television and radio stations. As a strong brand with a significantly loyal customer base, it could raise its prices with no likelihood of losing significant sales. Following his mentor Graham's philosophy Buffett realised that he had found a good business selling at a discount, but moving away from Graham, Buffett focused on future possibilities and management strength rather than the present assets. He realised that the market was seriously undervaluing WPC shares which had great future potential:

> Most security analysts, media brokers, and media executives would have estimated WPC's intrinsic business value at $400 to $500 million just as we did. And its $100 million stock market valuation was published daily for all to see. Our advantage, rather, was attitude: we had learned from Ben Graham that the key to successful investing was the purchase of shares in good businesses when market prices were at a large discount from underlying business values. Most institutional investors in the early 1970s, on the other hand, regarded business value as of only minor relevance when they were deciding the prices at which they would

buy or sell. This now seems hard to believe. However, these institutions were then under the spell of academics at prestigious business schools who were preaching a newly-fashioned theory: the stock market was totally efficient, and therefore calculations of business value – and even thought, itself – were of no importance in investment activities. (We are enormously indebted to those academics: what could be more advantageous in an intellectual contest – whether it be bridge, chess, or stock selection – than to have opponents who have been taught that thinking is a waste of energy?) Through 1973 and 1974, WPC continued to do fine as a business, and intrinsic value grew. Nevertheless, by year end 1974 our WPC holding showed a loss of about 25 per cent, with market value at $8 million against our cost of $10.6 million. What we had thought ridiculously cheap a year earlier had become a good bit cheaper as the market, in its infinite wisdom, marked WPC stock down to well below 20 cents on the dollar of intrinsic value. You know the happy outcome. Kay Graham, CEO of WPC, had the brains and courage to repurchase large quantities of stock for the company at those bargain prices, as well as the managerial skills necessary to dramatically increase business values. Meanwhile, investors began to recognize the exceptional economics of the business and the stock price moved closer to underlying value. Thus, we experienced a triple dip: the company's business value soared upward, per-share business value increased considerably faster because of stock repurchases and, with a narrowing of the discount, the stock price outpaced the gain in per-share business value.[3]

---

3. Buffett, W.E. (1985) Letter to shareholders included with the 1985 Annual Report of Berkshire Hathaway Inc. www.berkshirehathaway.com.

In 2010 Berkshire Hathaway's WPC holding was valued at $600 million, a spectacular 57-fold rise from the $10.6 million the shares cost. Despite this great return Washington Post is not one of those listed separately in Table 3.3 because it is one of the smaller holdings in what is now an enormous portfolio. Many

No. of shares	Company	% of Company Owned	Cost	Market
			$ (in millions) $	
151,610,700	American Express Company	12.7	1,287	6,143
225,000,000	BYD Company, Ltd	9.9	232	1,986
200,000,000	The Coca-Cola Company	8.6	1,299	11,400
37,711,330	ConocoPhillips	2.5	2,741	1,926
28,530,467	Johnson & Johnson	1.0	1,724	1,838
130,272,500	Kraft Foods Inc.	8.8	4,330	3,541
3,947,554	POSCO	5.2	768	2,092
83,128,411	The Procter & Gamble Company	2.9	533	5,040
25,108,967	Sanofi-Aventis	1.9	2,027	1,979
11,262,000	Swiss Re	3.2	773	530
234,247,373	Tesco plc	3.0	1,367	1,620
76,633,426	U.S. Bancorp	4.0	2,371	1,725
39,037,142	Wal-Mart Stores, Inc.	1.0	1,893	2,087
334,235,585	Wells Fargo & Company	6.5	7,394	9,021
Others			6,680	8,636
Total common stocks carried at market			**34,646**	**59,034**

Table 3.3   Berkshire Hathaway's large share holdings of common stocks at 31 December 2009
Source: The 2009 Chairman's Letter to Berkshire Hathaway shareholders.

other household names whose shares Buffett has invested in for some considerable time have also shown outstanding results, such as Coca-Cola, up eight-fold, and Procter & Gamble (originally a stake in Gillette), up nine-fold. American Express, POSCO and BYD (a Chinese electric battery and car maker) have shown substantial increases. Buffett has always admitted that he makes mistakes sometimes, just like everyone else, but the overall picture remains impressive.

GEICO Revisited

Since Buffett had sold his GEICO shares in 1952, Lorimer Davidson, the man who opened his eyes to the insurance world in 1951, had become CEO and managed the company splendidly until his retirement in 1970. The new team of managers decided on an aggressive expansion programme. Unfortunately this meant a fall in underwriting standards as they took on both inexperienced and higher-risk drivers. Needless to say this, coupled with a more expensive way of attracting new customers, led to such large losses that in 1975 GEICO nearly went under. It survived, just, but its share price fell from $61 to $2 in 1976.

It was the appointment of 43-year-old John Byrne that stopped the rot. Buffett went to meet him and talked to him for hours, just as he had talked to Lorimer Davidson years before. Byrne says that Buffett quizzed him about all sorts of things but mostly about the changes he would make and his assessment of the chances that the firm would survive. As the conversation went on, Buffett was impressed by Byrne and his ideas for the future of GEICO. He felt that with Byrne's strategies and leadership qualities, GEICO could be rescued, and once restructured would be able to compete successfully in the insurance market; GEICO's problems were temporary, not fatal. He likened Byrne to a chicken farmer, who rolls an ostrich egg into the henhouse and says, 'Ladies, this is what the opposition is doing.' He was intent on cutting costs, raising new capital and returning to GEICO's old standards of underwriting and customer care.

Buffett began to buy GEICO shares while they were still just over $2. He invested $4.1 million in shares and $19.4 million in convertible preferred stocks which were converted two years later. By the end of 1980, Berkshire Hathaway had spent $47 million buying 7.2 million shares in GEICO, a holding of 33 per cent of the equity. It soon became clear that Buffett's confidence in Byrne was not misplaced; at the end of 1980 the market value of the holding was $105.3 million. In his 1980 report to the Berkshire Hathaway shareholders, Buffett said that GEICO had the two key qualities that a long-term investor is looking for: (1) a very important and very hard to duplicate business advantage – low costs and contact with millions of government employees; and (2) an extraordinary management whose skills in operations are matched by skills in capital appreciation. He likened GEICO's position in 1976 to that of Amex at the time of the salad oil crisis. Both were unique businesses, suffering a temporary blow that did not destroy their exceptional underlying economics. They had a 'localised excisable cancer' rather than being in the category of the true turn-around situation in which the managers need to pull off a complete transformation (a corporate Pygmalion, as he put it). Buffett recognised that 'skilled surgeons' are needed to deal with a temporary cancer of the kind faced by these two companies but was confident that he had found such people.

Berkshire Hathaway's stake in GEICO had a market value of $1,678 million 14 years later at the end of 1994 and Buffett was keen to increase his stake to 100 per cent. He saw the logic behind investing in familiar, and successful, businesses rather than seeking out new investments. He says that if a business is attractive enough to buy once, it may well pay to repeat the process. With this in mind, in 1995 Buffett went ahead with the purchase of 100 per cent of GEICO, valuing it at $4.6 billion. Three years later in 1998 he paid nearly $22 billion for the insurance company General Re, and continues to buy insurance companies today. The acquisition of more insurance companies means an even larger float to be used for investments, which in turn generate their own returns.

Stakes in Non-quoted Businesses

Buffett had also begun to take an interest in companies not quoted on the stock markets; he allocated some Berkshire Hathaway capital into great businesses that were selling below intrinsic value; businesses with strong franchises and outstanding management. These companies cover a whole range of industries such as *Buffalo News* (newspapers), See's Candy Shops (chocolate and confectionery), Nebraska Furniture Mart (home furnishing retailers), Scott Fetzer (diversified manufacturing and distribution), footwear manufacturers and retailers, jewellery shops, Dairy Queen shops, Flight Safety International and Net Jets.

Buffett is happy be the provider of Berkshire Hathaway's capital to businesses, and let the managers get on with the business of managing, having already satisfied himself with the quality of the management. He is very much 'hands-off' in the running of the businesses, concerning himself and his partner Charlie Munger mainly with the task of capital and investment decisions. There are two further roles they see for themselves. Firstly, appointing the key person to run a business. They usually do not have to look too far as the founder of the business is often willing to carry on. Indeed, Buffett and Munger state that they are only interested in businesses that come with a good team of managers – they are not up to the task of providing management. Secondly, encouraging the managers who control the enterprises. Buffett is accessible by telephone to any of his managers if they want advice. Some call, some don't – he does not mind if they do not speak with him regularly. He also lavishes praise on them in his annual letter to shareholders of Berkshire.

See's Candy Shops

See's Candy Shops is a good example of the type of company Buffett favours – a company with excellent management, good market position and growth potential with no need for massive amounts of capital injection. It makes and sells boxed chocolates on the West Coast – and excellent they are too! In 1972 it was offered for sale at $40 million, with a cash excess of $10 million, meaning the price asked was in fact $30 million. The purchase was being made by Blue Chip Stamps, a company affiliated to Berkshire Hathaway[4] and one in which Charlie Munger also had invested. Buffett and Munger at this stage had not consolidated their partnership but were keen to do the deal. They had not fully developed their investment philosophy based on economic franchise and, still under Graham's influence, were reluctant to pay the asking price, as See's had only $7

---

4. Buffett, through Berkshire Hathaway and other holdings, had a controlling interest in Blue Chip Stamps.

million in tangible net assets. They offered $25 million, which, fortunately, the sellers accepted.

Pre-tax profits for See's rose from $4.2 million to $42.4 million over the next 20 years. This sounds good, but it is necessary for you to know how much capital was needed to generate the growth in profits. See's started off with $7 million capital, and over the next 20 years this rose to just $25 million, so while profits increased ten-fold, the capital required rose only four-fold. These low capital needs made it possible to distribute more dividends to shareholders, and See's distributed an amazing $410 million to shareholders during these 20 years. This made it an excellent investment compared to many industrial manufacturing companies, which by their very nature need regular and large injections of capital, and so are far less able to reward their stockholders. See's continued on its profitable way, and by 2007 its accumulated pre-tax profits since acquisition had risen to $1.35 billion, a substantial portion of which was used to purchase further investment prospects.

Buffett and Munger are always focused on returns on capital and See's Candy provides an excellent example of its importance. Take a hypothetical steel producer to compare with See's Candy. It too is producing $4.2m profit but it is making use of $40m of capital. Conventional investors may value this company more highly than See's because of the extra value of its asset backing – it has a much larger balance sheet (assuming the same profit projections). However, Buffett and Munger would value the steel producer at much less because of its great need for additional capital as it grows. Let's imagine that both firms increase output and profit by ten-fold. The steel producer is now producing $42 million while making use of $400 million of capital. See's produces the same profit, but its capital has risen from $7 million to $70 million. The steel producer has to come up with an additional $360 million to invest in plant and machinery, etc., while See's needed only $63 million. Compared with the steel company See's can distribute an extra $297 million to shareholders to invest elsewhere. Buffett commented in his 2007 letter to Berkshire Hathaway shareholders that it is far better to have an ever-increasing stream of earnings with virtually no major capital requirements – he pointed at Microsoft and Google as further examples.

As soon as the purchase of See's Candy had been finalised Chuck Higgins was put in charge, a man in whom Buffett was supremely confident. This confidence was not misplaced; Higgins steered See's through the next 30 plus years producing a constant stream of growth and profits, see Table 3.4.

Year ended	Revenues $ million	Profit after taxes $ million	Amount of candy sold (£)	Number of stores
31 Dec 2007	383.0	53.3	31.0m	About 200
31 Dec 1982	123.7	12.7	24.2m	202
31 Dec 1973	35.1	2.1	17.8m	169

Table 3.4   Data for See's Candy Shops[5]

It is interesting to note that the profits Higgins engineered were made by good management. The number of shops and the amount of candy sold did not increase dramatically, but Higgins cut down on costs, and was able to increase the selling price of his products, thus generating the outstanding profits mentioned above. He stuck to what the business was good at, ending up with a niche product with very strong brand recognition. Buffett summed up:

---

5. Munger, C.T. and Koeppel, D.A. (1982) 1982 Annual Report of Blue Chip Stamps, p.34.

See's strengths are many and important. In our primary marketing area, the West, our candy is preferred by an enormous margin to that of any competitor. In fact, we believe most lovers of chocolate prefer it to candy costing two or three times as much. (In candy, as in stocks, price and value can differ; price is what you give, value is what you get.) The quality of customer service in our shops – operated throughout the country by us and not by franchisees – is every bit as good as the product. Cheerful, helpful, personnel are as much a trademark of See's as is the logo on the box. That's no small achievement in a business that requires us to hire about 2,000 seasonal workers. We know of no comparably-sized organization that betters the quality of customer service delivered by Chuck Higgins and his associates.'[6]

Unlike See's a good many retail businesses struggle to retain their position in the market place; they do not operate an economic franchise and have little pricing power; it is relatively easy for competitors to enter the market and subsequently win over customers; suppliers often have too strong a position.

They have something special that allows them some freedom to make mistakes and still thrive.

Buffett has always been cautious about investing in retail businesses, unless they meet his exacting requirements. The retail sector is susceptible to the 'shooting-star phenomenon'

---

6. Buffett, W.E. (1983) Letter to shareholders included with the 1983 Annual Report of Berkshire Hathaway Inc. www.berkshirehathaway.com.

in which managers have a great idea or a special formula which serves them well for a while; until competitors react that is. The problem for retailers is that they must be smart every day because competitors can easily copy and then top whatever they do. There is always a constant a stream of new merchants pulling customers away. You cannot coast as a retailer. The comparison with some other industries is remarkable. They are not have-to-be-smart-every-day businesses. They have something special that allows them some freedom to make mistakes and still thrive. For example, if you own the franchise to Mickey Mouse, Snow White, Coca-Cola or Gillette you can have bad managers running things for a while and still the franchise is there. This is an example of what Buffett and Munger call a 'have-to-be-smart-*once* business'.

Despite their caution, Buffett and Munger have found the 'right' retailing businesses, See's Candy, shoe outlets, jewellery stores and one of his favourites, Nebraska Furniture Mart (NFM). What attracted him to NFM in the first place?

Nebraska Furniture Mart

NFM is a furniture and home furnishings store in Omaha, Nebraska, started and still run by the Blumkin family. In 1983, it generated $100 million in sales from its single 200,000 square foot store. The management is totally focused on giving outstanding value to their customers, and expanding the business as much as possible on the single site. When evaluating a business for possible purchase, Buffett asks himself if he would like to be in competition with it, given ample capital and good staff. About NFM, his opinion is that he'd rather wrestle grizzlies than compete with Mrs Blumkin and her family. He regards NFM as one of the best businesses in the country.

NFM is managed with amazing efficiency and astute volume purchasing and is deliberately run on a gross margin which is about half the industry norm; this makes for a good return on invested capital.

Under the watchful eye of the its founder, the formidable Mrs Rose Blumkin, affectionately known as Mrs B, the company built up its reputation for value for money and good products, attracting customers from hundreds of miles away. The quality of the management is what attracted Buffett to NFM; he insists on a high standard of integrity in anyone with whom he has a long-term business relationship, and Mrs B and her family excelled in this sphere. When purchasing 90 per cent of NFM for $55 million in 1983, Buffett trusted the Blumkins implicitly, to such an extent that no audit, inventory or property searches were ever done; 'We gave Mrs B a check for $55 million and she gave us her word. That made for an even exchange.'[7]

Buffett buys not just the physical assets of a company; far more important and valuable to him are the people themselves, who have shown themselves to be both honest and competent. If he can trust them at the outset, then he can trust them to run the business well in the future. The success of a business is moulded by the quality of its management; if there are any niggling doubts as to their integrity, don't deal with them – trust is paramount. There were absolutely no doubts with Mrs B and her family – her reputation for strategy and morality was second to none. Her motto was: 'Sell cheap and tell the truth.'

---

7. Buffett, W.E. (1984) Letter to shareholders included with the 1984 Annual Report of Berkshire Hathaway Inc. www.berkshirehathaway.com.

Mrs B's story

Mrs B's story was legendary, an American dream come true. At the age of 23, about the time of the end of the First World War, she talked her way out of Russia and into America, speaking no English and with no formal education. She sold used clothing, and when she had accumulated $500 she opened a furniture store in 1937. This was NFM, the company bought by Berkshire Hathaway for $55 million in 1983. Aged 90 in 1983, she refused to retire, and still worked seven days a week, despite the fact that Louie, her son and President of NFM, and his three sons were more than capable of running the business. Buffett admires the fact that all the family are really nice people and: 'they all (1) apply themselves with an enthusiasm and energy that would make Ben Franklin and Horatio Alger look like dropouts; (2) define with extraordinary realism their area of special competence and act decisively on all matters within it; (3) ignore even the most enticing propositions falling outside of that area of special competence; and, (4) unfailingly behave in a high-grade manner with everyone they deal with.'[8] Defining your area of special competence and behaving decently are factors Buffett and Munger look for and we come across them again and again.

Mrs B continued to 'outsell and out-hustle' at NFM until she left at the age of 96. Even then she was not content to retire, and started up a new business selling carpets and furniture, working seven days a week. Three years later, when she was 99, she agreed to sell the new business and land to NFM, but insisted that she continue to run the carpet side of the business in her own way. When she reached the age of 100, she still worked her usual seven days per week.

---

8. Ibid.

Finding and keeping managers such as Mrs B is the absolute aim of Buffett, and his partner Charlie Munger. The quality of the management they acquired and appointed made it possible for them to be 'hands-off' in the running of any business, while having total confidence in the ability of the management.

Charles Munger

Munger was born in Omaha in 1924, a few years before Buffett. He shared Buffett's mid-Western roots and ethics, which kept their feet on the floor, even when they were making billions of dollars. Munger worked for Buffett's grandfather in the family grocery store. Munger says tongue-in-cheek that the store was a great introduction to business, because as a lad you had to work so hard you were encouraged to look for an easier career, to count your blessings when you found one and be cheerful upon finding disadvantages therein. His father was a lawyer, but the young Munger studied mathematics and physics at the University of Michigan. His studies were interrupted by the Second World War, and he joined the Army Air Corps as a meteorologist in Alaska. After the end of the war, although he did not have an undergraduate degree, he was accepted at his father's alma mater Harvard Law School, graduating from there in 1948.

He worked as a real estate attorney until 1965, after which he decided to concentrate on investing. By this time he had met Warren Buffett. The two of them got on well from the start, and began discussing investment projects. Buffett tried to persuade Munger that investing would be a more lucrative career than the law: 'I told him that law was fine as a hobby but he could do better.'[9] Although his fame is very much tied to his association with Warren Buffett, Munger himself ran a very successful investment partnership of his own in California. He concentrated his portfolio on the very few securities which he knew well, which meant that his performance could be quite volatile. He chose to invest in shares whose price was at a significant discount to value. Munger's investment partnership generated compound annual returns of 19.8 per cent during the 1962–75 period, nearly four times as much as the market as a whole.

During the 60s and 70s, Munger and Buffett met up fairly regularly to discuss investments, and sometimes they bought shares in the same companies. However it was not until 1978 that Munger officially joined Buffett, and became Vice Chairman of Berkshire Hathaway.

Munger, now a billionaire, joins with Buffett in not flaunting his wealth, and could be said to be thrifty. He is diligent, patient, has a very dry wit, can be blunt even to the point of rudeness on occasion. He takes pride in his own talent and intelligence, fully aware of how special those talents are. He says that nobody has ever accused him of being humble and while he admires humility, he thinks he did not get his full share. He has no truck with academics who advocate modern portfolio theory, calling it a type of dementia, and is of very much the same opinion regarding the quality of most investment bank analysts.

---

9. Buffett, W.E. (1984) 'The Superinvestors of Graham-and-Doddsille', transcript in *Hermes*, Magazine of Columbia Business School, Autumn. Reproduced in the reprinted version of Benjamin Graham's *The Intelligent Investor* (1973).

Munger and Buffett are mutually
complimentary about each other's
abilities

Munger and Buffett are mutually complimentary about each other's abilities; they are both strong supporters of ethical business practices and abhor any kind of shady dealing; they understand that their achievements have been accomplished by sharp wits, good strategy and firm discipline, and they both take the view of their mentor Benjamin Graham that investing in shares in a business is to take part ownership of it, and to be interested in its staying quality rather than the chance to make a quick buck from buying and selling shares.

Graham's philosophy dwelt mainly on tangibles; he was wary about investing in companies unless they were backed up by inherent stability and net assets. He did consider future earnings prospects, but only if backed up by quantitative assets and when there was an acceptable margin of safety. Buffett and Munger gradually moved away from these tight restrictions, and took an interest in companies whose future earnings prospects looked good.

Some of the companies which would have met with Graham's approval, those with high net assets, inherent stability, and a consistent history of earning power, found themselves struggling in the new era of worldwide competition. Manufacturing companies in particular were at a disadvantage as they could not compete with overseas labour and manufacturing costs. Earlier Buffett had found this out with Berkshire Hathaway, once a thriving textile company, which even he could not put back into profit without massive capital injections, which could potentially to be used far more profitably elsewhere. Buffett found that many shares which qualified as Graham's bargain stocks were in fact mediocre companies in declining industries and as such had unpredictable future earnings.

Under the influence of Munger, Buffett's investment approach moved away from a strict adherence to Graham's principles, and he turned towards the qualitative elements; future prospects and in particular, the quality of the management. Few if any of the companies mentioned in Table 3.3 would meet with Graham's strict requirements; companies such as Coca-Cola, Procter & Gamble and the *Washington Post* simply do not have sufficient assets to meet with Graham's approval and therefore would not have been suitable as investments.

Buffett spoke about his change of thinking, and credited John Maynard Keynes, the famous twentieth century British economist, with finding the key to his dilemma:

> My own thinking has changed drastically from 35 years ago when I was taught to favour tangible assets and to shun businesses whose values depended largely upon economic Goodwill. This bias caused me to make many important business mistakes of omission, although relatively few of commission. Keynes identified my problem: 'The difficulty lies not in the new ideas but in escaping from the old ones.' My escape was long delayed, in part because most of what I had been taught by the same teacher had been (and continues to be) so extraordinarily valuable. Ultimately, business experience, direct and vicarious, produced my present strong preference

for businesses that possess large amounts of enduring Goodwill and that utilize a minimum of tangible assets.[10]

Munger, under the influence of Fisher, and Buffett began to focus on high-quality businesses with enduring competitive advantages, businesses with superior economics, growing earning power, a margin of safety in the price, and of course the mandatory exceptional management. Their goal is not to find mediocre companies at bargain prices. Rather, they want outstanding businesses at sensible prices.

Business Philosophy

With their years of education (mostly self-education) and varied experience Buffett and Munger together developed an investment philosophy that has been extraordinarily successful. They came to realise that to be a successful investor you must be able to evaluate a business well. Many so-called investors spend their time analysing the stock market, trying to work out where and when the next trend will occur, or trying to foresee future trends by studying numbers, figures and charts. Buffett and Munger think that the term 'professional investor' to describe many fund managers is an oxymoron because they do not focus on what businesses will do in the years ahead but on what they expect other fund managers to do in the days ahead. They treat shares as merely tokens in a game, like the thimble and flatiron in Monopoly.

Buffett and Munger try to understand any business in which they take an interest, as if it were their own business.

---

10. Buffett, W.E. (1983) Letter to shareholders included with the 1983 Annual Report of Berkshire Hathaway Inc. www.berkshirehathaway.com.

They find out how the business and its management function, its day-to-day activities and the underlying economics of the industry and make sure everything works satisfactorily. Buffett has said that the most important nine words ever written about investing were in Graham's book *The Intelligent Investor*: 'Investing is most intelligent when it is most businesslike.'

Thinking Like an Owner

If they are thinking of buying some shares in a company, Buffett and Munger treat the investment as if it was the only company owned by their families; as if they were buying the whole company, thinking like a business analyst, rather than a market or security analyst. They put themselves in the frame of mind that they had just inherited the company, and it was the only asset the family was ever going to own. After that the questions are automatic: Which firms compete against us? What am I worried about? Who are my customers? How do we grow the business? The way to answer these sorts of questions is to go out and talk to people who understand the company – customers, competitors, managers, suppliers, etc. Discover its strengths and weaknesses relative to others.

Investing successfully entails a fair amount of hard work; it is not down to luck. The investor needs to be bright and disciplined, prepared to spend time reading not only company and industry reports on the company in question, but also other companies in its industry, and also willing to personally undertake research into the industry. When Buffett was interested in GEICO, he spent a lot of time in libraries investigating insurance company data, reading books on insurance and talking to insurance industry experts and managers. With

American Express he would sit in his favourite steakhouse noting the number of customers who used Amex cards, and with Disney he went to a cinema to see reactions to Mary Poppins. If you put this effort in up front you can purchase good shares at the right price. Then you just stick with them as long as they remain good companies.

Criteria for Investment

What then constitutes a good company? A good choice would be a company you know well and have thoroughly researched to ensure it has a durable competitive advantage; one with good-quality management who are both competent and honest, and a company whose shares are at a sensible but not too high price. The most important fact for the prospective investor is that he understands the company in which he is thinking of investing, and this requires not a high IQ but considerable concentration of effort. Buffett says that he and Munger are not smart enough to achieve good returns by dealing in companies that are less than great businesses. Nor does he think they can achieve long-term investment success by flitting from share to share. They are contemptuous of those who call themselves 'investors' but who nevertheless turnover their portfolios rapidly – it is rather like calling someone who repeatedly engages in one-night stands a romantic.

Figure 3.2 illustrates Buffett and Munger's vigorous criteria for investments. Their objective in establishing the criteria in Figure 3.2 is to calculate the intrinsic value of a company, which can be compared to the current price of the stock, and then the margin of safety can be determined – is the gap between value and price sufficiently great?

Available at a very attractive price

It is frequently possible to identify companies which fulfil the first three criteria. But such wonderful businesses usually sell for high prices. The price must be 'sensible' in terms of its relationship to calculated intrinsic value, leaving a large margin of safety. Fortunately, from time to time, excellent companies find themselves in unusual circumstances and the share is misappraised by the market.

A business you understand

In investing your scorecard is not computed using Olympic-diving methods: 'degree of difficulty doesn't count. If you are right about a business whose value is largely dependent on a single key factor that is both easy to understand and enduring the pay-off is the same as if you had correctly analysed an investment alternative characterised by many constantly shifting and complex variables.'[†]

Operated by honest and competent people

The management has to be both able and shareholder-oriented. They should be of the highest integrity and you should be able to like, trust and admire them. Their extraordinary skills in operations should be matched by their skills in capital allocation.

Favourable long-term prospects

The company must have a very hard-to-duplicate business advantage that has resulted in, and will continue to produce, consistent earnings power. The competitive advantage must be 'mouth-watering' and enduring. There must be an economic franchise castle surrounded by a very deep moat.

† Buffett, W. E. (1994) Letter to shareholders included with the 1994 Annual Report of Berkshire Hathaway Inc. www.berkshirehathaway.com.

Figure 3.2   Buffett and Munger's criteria for investments

Inevitables

Buffett's favourite type of business is what he calls an 'inevitable'; these are strong efficient companies who are dominant in their industry, and will continue to be so for the foreseeable future; companies in industries that do not experience major changes, and so it is possible to predict future earnings. Companies in volatile industries are far less likely to remain dominant. What sort of company is an inevitable?

One such company is Coca-Cola; conceived in 1886 and patented in 1893, it rapidly grew to dominate the market, and has retained its leadership ever since. The company went public in 1919, with a share price of $40. Anyone who bought one of these shares in 1919, and held onto it, would be a millionaire many times over by now, despite the report in *Fortune* in 1938 that suggested that it was too late to buy the share, as market saturation and competition had reduced its future potential. How wrong can you be! Coca-Cola has gone from strength to strength year after year; its strategic and operational dominance persist to this day.

Coca-Cola, and other inevitables such as Gillette, may find that analysts predict future demand for their products differently, but there is no suggestion that their dominance will not continue, so long as they have that most necessary of assets, a good management team combined with a competitive advantage creating strong barriers preventing new entrants to the industry. The managers will be able to keep up with the times, bringing in innovations when necessary, and maintain the efficiency which has kept them at the top of the tree.

Market leadership does not make an inevitable. General Motors, IBM and Kodak went through periods when they seemed invincible, but their dominance did not endure. For every inevitable you find you will come across dozens of 'impostors'; firms that are going through a good patch, but which are vulnerable to competitive attacks. Buffett thinks that he and Munger could not come up with as many as 20 inevitables. And even an inevitable can go off track as the management of great companies can get sidetracked and neglect their wonderful base business. Gillette and Coca-Cola both went through a periods of rash diversification before wiser management brought them back to the straight and narrow. Coca-Cola bought into the shrimp growing industry and Gillette went exploring for oil! One of things that most concerns Buffett and Munger is that the management lose their focus. They have seen too often management destroy value because they become hubristic, thinking they can run anything, or because they become bored and strike out in new directions that they are ill-suited for.

Punch Cards and Perfect Pitches

Needing to be absolutely certain of a share's suitability, an investor should realise that such companies are not common, and do not come up often; one or two good opportunities a year would be plenty, and the investor should take his time. Buffett says his style is lethargy bordering on sloth. He suggests that an investor should be given a punch card with 20 punches on it. Every time an investment is made, the card is punched, and the card has to last a lifetime. Using the card only for great opportunities means that it would never be used up. Even with a whole lifetime Buffett and Munger figure that it is just too hard to make hundreds of smart decisions. So they ask of themselves only that they are smart just a few times.

Buffett made a study when he was running investment partnerships into the success of small investments compared with larger ones – the larger ones consistently did better. There is a threshold of examination, criticism and knowledge that has to be overcome or reached in making a big decision that you can get sloppy about on small decisions. Thinking a share is 'OK' is not good enough, the investor has to be absolutely convinced of its suitability.

Buffett is fond of using baseball metaphors.

Private investors can have some advantage over the professional in that they do not have to keep on investing all the time, they can wait for the right time. Buffett is fond of using baseball metaphors; the private investor can stand at the plate and wait for the perfect pitch, and he won't get dismissed after three pitches. So you can let dozens, even hundreds, of companies go by and you do not have take up the option of buying. Wait for the fat pitch, do not swing indiscriminately.

Circle of Competence

The circle of competence is something that every investor should understand. It is impossible for anyone to research and understand a large number of varied industries and companies. What the investor must do is recognise this and draw a circle of competence round those companies/industries that the investor is capable of truly understanding. These companies must then be examined to see if they meet the criteria set out in Figure 3.2. On no account should any interest be taken in companies outside this circle of competence. At any one time the investor should not be focused on whether the area of their circle of competence is large or small. What matters is how well you've defined the perimeter. You must know where the edges are. By knowing your limitations you will perform better than somebody who has a much wider circle, but is fuzzy about where the edges lie. Of course, it is a good idea to learn more and widen the circle, but this takes a long time and much experience.

Understanding the degree of your competence allows you to resist the temptation to get out of your depth in uncharted waters. Charles Munger says that we should aim to profit from always remembering the obvious rather than from grasping at the esoteric. Be consistently not stupid, instead of trying to be very intelligent. He likes to point out that it is the strong swimmers who drown.

Anybody who tells you they can value all the companies on a stock market has a very unrealistic idea of their own ability. If Buffett and Munger cannot come even close to being able to do this, who are these people? Familiarity with a business means that it is understood, and within the circle of competence, and in this case familiarity does not breed contempt, but rather confidence and the ability to create profits.

Avoid Complexity

Buffett and Munger follow their own advice in sticking to businesses they understand. Despite all their accumulated knowledge they say that this means that the businesses must be relatively simple and stable in character. They say that they are not smart enough to value a business if it is complex or subject to constant change. They have avoided investing in technology shares purely because of the complexity. While this might mean that they have missed out on some notably good investments, such as Microsoft or Intel, they have nevertheless been able to concentrate on their circle of competence, and find good investments in areas they know well.

Margin of Safety and Intrinsic Value

Buffett and Munger believe Benjamin Graham's margin-of-safety principle to be the cornerstone of their investment success. They are not interested in a share selling at only slightly less than its value.

Intrinsic value is the discounted value of the cash that can be taken out of an asset during its remaining life. With bonds this is usually relatively easy to estimate as bonds have regular coupons and a date when they will be redeemed. There is a risk that the borrower might not be able to meet coupon payments, but in general bond valuation is straightforward.

With shares intrinsic value is much harder to estimate, depending as it does on qualitative factors such as the ability of the management or the firm's competitive position. It is the analyst's job to do the calculation and find out which shares give the greatest difference between current price and estimated value. No two analysts will come up with same figure for intrinsic value, as it is dependent on a personal judgement of elements such as estimates of future cash flows. Despite the concept being a little fuzzy, intrinsic value is all-important and Buffett and Munger regard it as the only logical way to consider the relative attractiveness of investments and businesses.

Cash Flow

Buffett and Munger agree with those financial analysts trained at the finest business schools and professional training organisations who believe that discounted future cash flow is what gives value to a share, but differ in how this is obtained. Although Buffett is interested in mathematics, he and Munger do not rely on endless complex cash flow estimates and mathematical analysis, whereas academics and many professionals like to see page after page of intricate calculations. At the 1996 meeting of Berkshire Hathaway shareholders, Munger said that they have a fingers and toes style about valuation. He said his partner talks about discounted cash flows, but he had never seen him do one. To which Buffett joked that there are some things you only do in private. From the research that they do on a company, a ball park figure is satisfactory, unencumbered by endless statistics, which can cloud the picture. If the value of a company does not scream at you, it's too close and you should drop the idea.

Because of his thorough understanding of companies, Buffett does not see the need to make any upward adjustment to allow for any additional risk in buying shares, and uses the current risk-free rate of return, the US government long-term bond rate, as the discount rate. Because he is certain of his facts he does not see the point in of adding a risk premium.

The 'cash flow' that Buffett discounts is the owner earnings, which he defines as $(a + b) - (c + d)$

where:

a = reported earnings
b = depreciation, depletion, amortisation, and certain other non-cash charges

c = the amount of capitalised expenditures for plant and equipment, etc. that the business requires to fully maintain its long-term competitive position and its unit volume

d = any additional working capital needed to maintain its long-term competitive position and unit volume

c and d can only be guesses, and therefore the owner earnings figure cannot be precise, but Buffett agrees with Keynes that he would rather be vaguely right than precisely wrong.

Poor owner earnings figures are produced by many businesses because they have to spend more than b just to maintain their long-term competitive position and unit volume; in other words, $(c + d)$ is greater than b.

Many analysts produce different cash flow figures to Buffett; they include a and b, but fail to take any account of c or d, with the hidden implication that the business is never in need of any fresh injections of capital and that nothing needs renewing, improving or refurbishing. This renders their figures meaningless, as c and d are vital in the future prosperity of the business; without them, the business will decay.

Scott Fetzer

Scott Fetzer provides an illustration of the use of owner earnings in calculating intrinsic value, see Table 3.5. The company, a conglomerate of 22 businesses including World Books and Kirby, was acquired by Berkshire Hathaway in 1986 at a cost of $315.2 million and with a book value of $172.4 million.

		$000s
a	1986 GAAP earnings	40,231
plus *b*	depreciation, depletion, amortisation, and other non-cash charges	8,301
		48,532
less		
c and *d*	Expenditure on plant, equipment, working capital etc. needed to maintain long-term competitive position and unit volume	8,301
		40,231

Table 3.5   Scott Fetzer's owner earnings 1986

Buffett and Munger judged that items under *b* were equal to *c* and *d* together. This calculation applies to most of Berkshire Hathaway's investment companies, but not in every case. During the late 1980s Buffett calculated that annual expenditure on *c* and *d* for See's Candy exceeded *b* up to $1 million, but this expenditure was necessary for the company to maintain its competitive position.

Table 3.6 overleaf shows Scott Fetzer's earnings for the nine years following its acquisition. If it is a sound assumption that owner earnings in these years are equal to reported earnings because *b* is equal to (*c* + *d*), then the figures in column 2 (plus an estimate of earnings after 1994) may be discounted when estimating the value of the company.

It is plain to see that the company was a bargain purchase at $315.2 million whether the earnings figures were discounted at 10, 15 or even 20 per cent.

Year	(1) Beginning book value	(2) Earnings ($ millions)	(3) Dividends ($ millions)	(4) Ending book value 1 + 2 − 3
1986	172.6	40.3	125.0	87.9
1987	87.9	48.6	41.0	95.5
1988	95.5	58.0	35.0	118.5
1989	118.5	58.5	71.5	105.5
1990	105.5	61.3	33.5	133.3
1991	133.3	61.4	74.0	120.7
1992	120.7	70.5	80.0	111.2
1993	111.2	77.5	98.0	90.7
1994	90.7	79.3	76.0	94.0

Table 3.6   Scott Fetzer's performance figures 1986–94[11]

The company also had the added bonus of surplus cash when it was purchased, and despite only earning $40.3 million was able to pay Berkshire Hathaway a dividend of $125 million in 1986, making the net investment by Berkshire Hathaway much less than what they paid. Scott Fetzer continued this earnings and dividends pattern, as well as reducing the amount of capital required and shrinking its modest debt to virtually nothing. It did this without resorting to any artificial cash boosting, such as sale and leaseback or selling receivables. By 1994 its return on capital employed reached such an extraordinary level that if it had been in the Fortune 500 list in 1993 it would have had the highest return on equity, with the exception of three companies emerging from bankruptcy.

Seeking, and finding, companies such as Scott Fetzer which produce high owner earnings while needing little additional capital has been a successful exercise for Buffett and Munger. Three of Berkshire Hathaway's companies, Nebraska Furniture Mart, See's Candy Shops and Buffalo Evening News, increased

---

11. Buffett, W. E. (1994) Letter to shareholders included with the 1994 Annual Report of Berkshire Hathaway Inc. www.berkshirehathaway.com.

their combined pre-tax earnings from $8 million in 1970 to $72 million in 1985, while using only about $40 million more in investment capital. This allowed Buffett and Munger to use the majority of the earnings they generate elsewhere. Compare this with US companies generally: for them to significantly increase their earnings they mostly needed large increases in capital. Buffett estimates that the average firm has required about $5 of additional capital to generate an additional $1 of annual pre-tax earnings. If that is translated to the three companies above then to generate the profit increase that they have they would have needed over $300 million in additional capital from their owners, not the mere $40m that they actually withheld from Berkshire.

Naturally, the low incremental capital businesses are very hard to find at a good price.

Thus, the best businesses to own are those that over the long run can employ large amounts of incremental capital at very high rates of return. The worst businesses are those that must, or *will*, use more and more capital at very low rates of return. Naturally, the low incremental capital businesses are very hard to find at a good price.

The Ideal Company

Buffett and Munger advise careful and thorough research into any possible investment. Not poring through endless financial reports and figures (although some financial research is necessary), but personal research, meeting and talking to anyone who might have some knowledge of the possible investment company.

Their ideal investment company is one which has a strong economic franchise, such as Coca-Cola, Gillette, Disney or See's Candy. The stronger the franchise, the more control the company has over pricing and increasing sales volume without large capital requirements. A trusted well-recognised brand name is a great asset, which can generate customer loyalty and can allow companies to price their products favourably. It also makes it overly difficult for competitors to enter the market.

Franchise

Coca-Cola is a wonderful example of this. Despite numerous attempts by competitors, its brand is unsurpassed. Customers ask for a Coke, not a fizzy soft drink, and their secret recipe has kept their customers happy for well over a hundred years. Disney has an unrivalled franchise, and the ability to produce film and products for the future using its film library, with no extra outlay. Chocolate companies benefit from brand recognition; 'If you own See's Candy, and you look in the mirror and say "mirror, mirror on the wall, how much do I charge for candy this fall", and it says "more", that's a good business.'[12] Cadbury is able to charge more than its rivals: if you went to buy chocolate and the store owner told you that he does not stock Cadbury but did have an unbranded chocolate bar that he recommends and your response is to leave the store and walk across the street to find a Cadbury bar or if you are willing to pay a few pence more for the Cadbury bar than the unmarked bar, then you know the company has franchise value. Gillette is another brand that is able to price its products favourably. Of

---

12. Rasmussen, J. (1994) 'Billionaire Talks Strategy With Students', *Omaha World-Herald*, 2 January, p.175.

the thousands of millions razor blades sold worldwide, 30 per cent in number are made by Gillette, but 60 per cent in value.

Moat

Another element of the ideal company is a 'moat', which puts up barriers to prevent rivals from being able to compete in the industry. The moat can take many different forms, but the most important is the ability of the management team to perform excellent day-to-day management, while at the same time creating features which are difficult for rivals to emulate or need significant capital outlay to reproduce or substitute, and maintaining a constant vigilance for ways to improve and innovate, and to attract and keep customers. Wells Fargo, for example, has developed a very close relationship with customers which would be difficult for a competitor to interrupt.

Tailwinds Prevail

The original Berkshire Hathaway textile company is an example of a company which could not afford any management errors. Despite their best efforts and good managers, its results were mediocre. When it comes to selecting shares it matters that the business is in an industry such as Coca-Cola or the *Washington Post*, where tailwinds rather than headwinds prevail.

Management Quality

The attitude and competence of the managers also matters a great deal. Managers need to love their work and should treat the business as if it were their own. They should have the long-term prosperity of the company and its shareholders at heart, not just a good performance for one year. Most of Berkshire's key managers are very wealthy and yet they continue to work in the business with great enthusiasm and interest. They work so hard because they love what they do. They relish the thrill of outstanding performance. They think less like managers working for a salary and bonuses on short-term performance and much more like owners looking to the long-term prosperity of the business.

Hands Off Attitude

Buffett and Munger are very strongly in favour of a 'hands-off' attitude towards their managers, thinking that this is the way to bring the best out of them. They get rid of all of the 'ritualistic and nonproductive activities' that senior executives normally have to waste time doing, e.g. meetings with share analysts, quarterly reports. Buffett and Munger do not tell managers how to spend their time; each manager has total charge over their personal schedules. What they are told is to stick to a very simple mission: to run their business as if: (1) they owned 100 per cent of it; (2) it is the only asset in the world that they and their family have or will ever have; and (3) it is impossible for them to sell or merge it for at least a century. These rules really help to get the required long-term focus.

Managers are also told not to let any of their decisions be affected even slightly by accounting considerations. Too many CEOs of other firms make poor long-term decisions because of the need to provide impressive short-term numbers to the markets – Buffett and Munger short circuit this sort of game playing in a very simple and effective way. They ask managers to think about what counts, not how it will be counted. Their ability to choose managers (choosing only people whom they 'like, trust and admire') and to trust them has paid off handsomely for Berkshire Hathaway.

Institutional Imperative

A point of concern is what Buffett calls the institutional imperative, which is the tendency for companies to stray from the path of rationality, decency and intelligence:

> I thought ... that decent, intelligent, and experienced managers would automatically make rational business decisions. But I learned over time that isn't so. Instead, rationality frequently wilts when the institutional imperative comes into play. For example:
>
> (1) As if governed by Newton's First Law of Motion, an institution will resist any change in its current direction;
> (2) Just as work expands to fill available time, corporate projects or acquisitions will materialize to soak up available funds;
> (3) Any business craving of the leader, however foolish, will be quickly supported by detailed rate-of-return and strategic studies prepared by his troops; and
> (4) The behavior of peer companies, whether they are expanding, acquiring, setting executive compensation or whatever, will be mindlessly imitated.[13]

---

13. Buffett, W.E. (1989) Letter to shareholders included with the 1989 Annual Report of Berkshire Hathaway Inc. www.berkshirehathaway.com.

Unfortunately, only too often CEOs of companies remain in their posts despite turning in a lacklustre performance. The CEO has to account for the company's performance to the board, but board members often lack business sense, and are in their position more because they know the right people or are good at playing the corporate system. They are not able to call the CEO to account. In too many companies it is considered socially unacceptable to criticise the CEO's performance. Interestingly, executives do not seem to be likewise inhibited when it comes to critically evaluating, say the substandard typist.

Decency and Integrity

Making the right choice of management is obviously a crucial part of running a business, and decency and integrity are what Buffett and Munger look for. They like to think of their managers as being the sort of person you would want your son or daughter to marry. The worst trait for a manager is any type of dishonesty. If you are looking for people to work for an organisation you want three qualities: integrity, intelligence and energy. It is important to note that if they lack the first then the other two will kill you. As Buffett says if you hire someone without integrity you really want them to be dumb and lazy. The person at the top sets the tone in any organisation; this is the person who must have integrity and by their behaviour set an example to everyone else involved in the company.

Manipulating Accounts

There needs to be honesty in the accounting area. It is quite commonplace for financial figures to be massaged and manipulated, and many accountants and auditors do what the managers expect and ask them to do, rather than provide unbiased figures for the company. There is too much of a ring of truth in the old joke about the CEO who asks how much does 2 and 2 equal and is answered by the accountant 'How much would you like it to be?'

Doing the Ordinary Extraordinarily Well

The whole idea behind running a company is for every employee from top to bottom simply to do the job well, and for managers to do ordinary jobs so well that they are able to perform extraordinarily well. They should not be focused on doing unusual, exotic or esoteric things, just the ordinary things with a sharp focus. Sometimes teamwork can make the ordinary extraordinary, as Buffett commented on Carl Reichardt and Paul Hazen at Wells Fargo and Tom Murphy and Dan Burke at Capital Cities/ABC:

> First, each pair is stronger than the sum of its parts because each partner understands, trusts and admires the other. Second, both managerial teams pay able people well, but abhor having a bigger head count than is needed. Third, both attack costs as vigorously when profits are at record levels as when they are under pressure. Finally, both stick with what they understand and let their abilities, not their egos, determine what they attempt.[14]

---

14. Buffett, W.E. (1990) Letter to shareholders included with the 1990 Annual Report of Berkshire Hathaway Inc. www.berkshirehathaway.com.

Operating Earnings to Shareholder Equity Ratio

A good way of measuring operating performance is the ratio of operating earnings to shareholders' equity. In 1989 Buffett reported that in Berkshire Hathaway's non-insurance operations, for every $1 of shareholders' money in the business, the managers had made a profit of 57 cents, an astonishingly good performance. Many companies report earnings per share figures, rather than earnings per dollar of equity. This can be extremely misleading, as any injections of equity capital from retained earnings may boost earnings per share simply because there is more money in the business. Earnings that could be distributed to shareholders but are retained in the business must produce at least their own amount in value (and preferably two or three times that).

Cost Control

Cost control is another area where managers must perform well. New ways of saving on costs should be continually sought. Managers of an already high-cost operation seem to be the ones whose overheads are always on the increase. On the other hand, the managers of a tightly-run business usually go on to find even more methods to reduce costs, even when operating costs are already well below those of his competitors. Buffett and Munger practise this frugality and tight cost control at Berkshire Hathaway; their corporate office staff totals only 19 people, running a $200 billion company with over a quarter of a million employees.

Buffett and Munger practise this frugality and tight cost control at Berkshire Hathaway.

They are very doubtful that high head office costs are beneficial to most companies seeing little correlation between central overhead and good corporate performance. In fact where head office costs are as much as 10 per cent this can act as a tithe on the productive parts of the business which only hurts earnings.

Value of Experience

Experience is invaluable, and Buffett and Munger are content for managers to carry on regardless of age so long as their competence in not in doubt:

> We do not remove superstars from our lineup merely because they have attained a specified age – whether the traditional 65, or the 95 reached by Mrs B on the eve of Hanukkah in 1988. Superb managers are too scarce a resource to be discarded simply because a cake gets crowded with candles. Moreover, our experience with newly-minted MBAs has not been that great. Their academic records always look terrific and the candidates always know just what to say; but too often they are short on personal commitment to the company and general business savvy. It's difficult to teach a new dog old tricks.[15]

New dogs must learn the ropes and prove that they have Buffett's essential qualities – integrity and decency.

---

15. Buffett, W.E. (1988) Letter to shareholders included with the 1988 Annual Report of Berkshire Hathaway Inc. www.berkshirehathaway.com.

Use of Capital

It is the owner's and management's job to make the best use of the capital available to the company, but it is no easy task to make the best use of the capital generated by a company. Unfortunately too many companies are run by managers who have neither the inclination nor the knowledge to make the best use of capital.

The airline industry is an example of a spectacularly bad use of capital. If you take all the profits of all the airlines in the world since the first flight of *Kitty Hawk* you will find a total that is less than zero. Investors every now and then are asked to put in more money via rights issues, but on average that money is wasted. The airline industry is in the unfortunate position of being an undifferentiated product in a market with over-capacity; customers tend to be price-driven rather than loyal to a particular airline. Any new demand is easily met by existing supply or new entrants to the industry:

> Businesses in industries with both substantial over-capacity and a 'commodity' product (undifferentiated in any customer-important way by factors such as performance, appearance, service support, etc.) are prime candidates for profit troubles ... If ... costs and prices are determined by full-bore competition, there is more than ample capacity, and the buyer cares little about whose product or distribution services he uses, industry economics are almost certain to be unexciting. They may well be disastrous. Hence the constant struggle of every vendor to establish and emphasize special qualities of product or service. This works with candy bars (customers buy by brand name, not by asking for a 'two-ounce candy bar') but doesn't work with sugar (how often do you hear,

'I'll have a cup of coffee with cream and C & H sugar, please'). In many industries, differentiation simply can't be made meaningful. A few producers in such industries may consistently do well if they have a cost advantage that is both wide and sustainable. By definition such exceptions are few, and, in many industries, are non-existent. For the great majority of companies selling 'commodity' products, a depressing equation of business economics prevails: persistent over-capacity without administered prices (or costs) equals poor profitability. Of course, over-capacity may eventually self-correct, either as capacity shrinks or demand expands. Unfortunately for the participants, such corrections often are long delayed. When they finally occur, the rebound to prosperity frequently produces a pervasive enthusiasm for expansion that, within a few years, again creates over-capacity and a new profitless environment. In other words, nothing fails like success. What finally determines levels of long-term profitability in such industries is the ratio of supply-tight to supply-ample years. Frequently that ratio is dismal. (It seems as if the most recent supply-tight period in our textile business – it occurred some years back – lasted the better part of a morning.)[16]

Bad Use of Capital – the Textile Industry

After determined but unsuccessful attempts to put the textile business of Berkshire Hathaway back into profit, Buffett decided in 1964 that this was not the best use of capital. Their biggest competitor at the time was Burlington Industries,

---

16. Buffett, W.E. (1982) Letter to shareholders included with the 1982 Annual Report of Berkshire Hathaway Inc. www.berkshirehathaway.com.

a much bigger and more profitable company with sales of $1.2 billion, compared to Berkshire Hathaway's $50 million. Burlington decided to invest heavily in the textile industry, and over the next 20 years injected an extra $3 billion of capital, the equivalent of $200 spending per share. Unfortunately over these same 20 years the decline of the textile industry and the increase in inflation meant that each share had only one-third of the purchasing power that it had in 1964.

> This devastating outcome for the shareholders indicates what can happen when much brain power and energy are applied to a faulty premise. The situation is suggestive of Samuel Johnson's horse: 'A horse that can count to ten is a remarkable horse – not a remarkable mathematician.' Likewise, a textile company that allocates capital brilliantly within its industry is a remarkable textile company – but not a remarkable business. My conclusion from my own experiences and from much observation of other businesses is that a good managerial record (measured by economic returns) is far more a function of what business boat you get into than it is of how effectively you row (though intelligence and effort help considerably, of course, in any business, good or bad). Some years ago I wrote: 'When a management with a reputation for brilliance tackles a business with a reputation for poor fundamental economics, it is the reputation of the business that remains intact.' Nothing has since changed my point of view on that matter. Should you find yourself in a chronically-leaking boat, energy devoted to changing vessels is likely to be more productive than energy devoted to patching leaks.[17]

17. Buffett, W.E. (1985) Letter to shareholders included with the 1985 Annual Report of Berkshire Hathaway Inc. www.berkshirehathaway.com.

Share Repurchase

Capital can also be used to repurchase shares. If shares are selling below intrinsic value, it may benefit shareholders for the company to repurchase some of them using existing capital and maybe sensible borrowings. If this happens, the shareholders benefit in two ways: firstly their shares have a higher intrinsic value due to the repurchase, and secondly the management is sending a confident message to shareholders and the world in general that the company is on the right track and not building a grand empire for the benefit of the managers at shareholders' expense.

Mergers

Managers should make rational decisions over mergers, including acquisitions and takeovers. Mergers should raise the intrinsic value of the shares of the acquiring company. Of crucial importance in what is being given in exchange, and good managers should have the interest of their owners (the stockholders) at heart and be sure that the merger will be beneficial to them. Some of the unsound reasons for mergers are:

- **Excitement** – managers revel in the extra activity, challenge and attention from the press.

- **Size of organisation** – managers judge their performance by the size of the company, and aim for irrational growth.

- **Overconfidence** – managers are so confident in their own ability they are positive that they have a magic touch and will transform the profits of the company being acquired.

- **Focus on short-term earnings** – managers concentrate on not diluting earnings per share, instead of making sure that intrinsic value per share remains undiluted.

Pitfalls to Avoid

Following Buffett and Munger's example, there are certain pitfalls for investors to avoid. It is not a good idea to place too much reliance on forecasting the way the stock market and shares will move over the coming few months. You may be lucky once, but a series of short-term bets on immediate-horizon forecasts will not be any benefit in the long term. It is also pointless to be constantly reading macro-economic projections. With a long-term holding strategy the current state of the economy is of limited impact because value is determined by owner earnings over many decades, when recessions come and go.

Don't do equations with Greek letters in them.

Investors should not try out any of the complex mathematic formulae which some academics and analysts recommend – don't do equations with Greek letters in them. Knowledge is the key, and the investors must do their homework so that they understand their chosen companies.

Impatience can be detrimental to investors. If investors cannot find a suitable company to invest in, they must keep their impatience in check, and wait. Buffett and Munger have had many years when no major investments were made, because there was nothing suitable that met their strict criteria. In the same way, impatience with shares owned must be curtailed. If the right investigations were made and the investment company is sound, there is every chance that it will perform well in the future, although there may well be ups and downs on the way. Losing patience and making a hasty decision can lead to heartache.

Independence of mind is a valuable asset. Investors should avoid following the crowd and being swayed by the horde of so-called experts, but they must also admit when they have made a mistake. It is far better to make your own mind up, having examined all the data within a rational framework. Mistakes should be examined and lessons learned from them.

Being too ambitious can cause investors to make bad decisions. Buffett and Munger aim for no more than 15 per cent per year on their investments. Trying to achieve more means taking more risks and too much trading can be disadvantageous as the various commissions on trades eat into any profit made.

Too much diversification can lead to investors not having sufficient knowledge of their investments; they should only invest in as many companies as they can thoroughly research and understand. At the end of 1999 and 2000 Berkshire Hathaway had 70 per cent of their investment fund in only four companies because Buffett and Munger felt unable to make purchases in businesses they truly understood at bargain prices.

Buffett and Munger on Risk

Buffett and Munger advocate not taking unnecessary risk, and their philosophy is defined in the following quotation:

In our opinion, the real risk that an investor must assess is whether his aggregate after-tax receipts from an investment (including those he receives on sale) will, over his prospective holding period, give him at least as much purchasing power as he had to begin with, plus a modest rate of interest on that initial stake. Though this risk cannot be calculated with engineering precision, it can in some cases be judged with a degree of accuracy that is useful. The primary factors bearing upon this evaluation are:

1) The certainty with which the long-term economic characteristics of the business can be evaluated;
2) The certainty with which management can be evaluated, both as to its ability to realize the full potential of the business and to wisely employ its cash flows;
3) The certainty with which management can be counted on to channel the rewards from the business to the shareholders rather than to itself;
4) The purchase price of the business;
5) The levels of taxation and inflation that will be experienced and that will determine the degree by which an investor's purchasing-power return is reduced from his gross return.

These factors will probably strike many analysts as unbearably fuzzy, since they cannot be extracted from a data base of any kind. But the difficulty of precisely quantifying these matters does not negate their importance nor is it insuperable. Just as Justice Stewart found it impossible to formulate a test for obscenity but nevertheless asserted, 'I know it when I see it,' so also can investors – in an inexact but useful way – 'see' the risks inherent in certain investments without reference to complex equations or price histories.

Is it really so difficult to conclude that Coca-Cola and Gillette possess far less business risk over the long term than, say, *any* computer company or retailer? Worldwide, Coke sells about 44% of all soft drinks, and Gillette has more than a 60% share (in value) of the blade market. Leaving aside chewing gum, in which Wrigley is dominant, I know of no other significant businesses in which the leading company has long enjoyed such global power.

Moreover, both Coke and Gillette have actually increased their worldwide shares of market in recent years. The might of their brand names, the attributes of their products, and the strength of their distribution systems give them an enormous competitive advantage, setting up a protective moat around their economic castles. The average company, in contrast, does battle daily without any such means of protection. As Peter Lynch says, stocks of companies selling commodity-like products should come with a warning label: 'Competition may prove hazardous to human wealth.'

The competitive strengths of a Coke or Gillette are obvious to even the casual observer of business. Yet the beta of their stocks is similar to that of a great many run-of-the-mill companies who possess little or no competitive advantage. Should we conclude from this similarity that the competitive strength of Coke and Gillette gains them nothing when business risk is being measured? Or should we conclude that the risk in owning a piece of a company – its stock – is somehow divorced from the long-term risk inherent in its business operations? We believe neither conclusion makes sense and that equating beta with investment risk also makes no sense.

The theoretician bred on beta has no mechanism for differentiating the risk inherent in, say, a single-product toy company selling pet rocks or hula hoops from that of another toy company whose sole product is Monopoly or Barbie. But it's quite possible for ordinary investors to make such distinctions if they have a reasonable understanding of consumer behavior and the factors that create long-term competitive strength or weakness. Obviously, every investor will make mistakes. But by confining himself to a relatively few, easy-to-understand cases, a reasonably intelligent, informed and diligent person can judge investment risks with a useful degree of accuracy.[18]

Difficulties and Drawbacks

While Buffett and Munger's investment philosophy is easy to state it is difficult to practise with skill. It requires a considerable amount of time and knowledge to understand a business and its competitive environment. You need a firm grasp of strategic analysis as well as accounting and finance. Also, getting to know the character of a manager is going to be difficult for the average investor. While Buffett or Munger can pick up the telephone and talk to chief executives we might have greater difficulty. At least we can attend the annual general meeting to

---

18. Buffett, W.E. (1993) Letter to shareholders included with the 1993 Annual Report of Berkshire Hathaway Inc. www.berkshirehathaway.com.

hear the senior officers speak – I find them particularly useful for the one-to-one chats after the formal meeting. Also, if you track a company and the management's pronouncements over a number of years then you can build up an impression of their consistency, openness and realism.

Clearly the followers of Buffett and Munger will have to narrow down the range of companies and industries that they try to understand so that they can develop the depth of knowledge required to create a circle of competence that has some real meaning.

To sum up

Warren Buffett and Charles Munger are now octogenarians, but their minds are as sharp as ever. If you would like to find out for yourself how they seem to be growing in wisdom and wit as the years go by you could buy a few shares in Berkshire Hathaway and attend the annual general meeting in Omaha where they respond with great erudition to questions from shareholders for six hours. I recently returned from the 2010 meeting and I think they were on the best form I can remember – yet again I learned a tremendous amount.

Warren Buffett and Charles Munger are now octogenarians, but their minds are as sharp as ever.

So what are the key elements you can take away from Buffett and Munger's lifetime of endeavour?

- Analyse businesses not shares, and do not buy shares in businesses you do not understand. Remember to draw your circle of competence sharply and not be fuzzy about its edges.

- Look for a company that scores well on both the quality of its long-term economic franchise and the quality of its management.

- Return on equity capital within the business is a vital element in any investment decision.

- Calculate intrinsic value from discounted cash flows and make sure the price paid has a large margin of safety below the intrinsic value. Owner earnings is the definition of cash flow that you need.

- Inevitables are great if you can find them at the right price.

- Hyper-activity is wealth destructive – remember the punch card and perfect pitch.

- Do not trade on: forecasts of short-term expectations of movements in the market; macro-economic forecasts; mathematical formulas with Greek letters in them; or because you are impatient.

- Do not be a crowd follower, or too ambitious in your investment returns or over-diversified.

- Do not sell so long as the company continues to increase intrinsic value at a satisfactory rate.

CHAPTER 4

John Templeton

John Templeton is widely regarded as the leading light of the global value investing approach. For seven decades he searched for bargains the world over. While the majority of his contemporaries refused to look at shares beyond their own back yard Templeton hunted down companies selling at, say, three times earnings in contemptuously neglected Japan in the late 1950s or in underrated South Korea in the 1990s. In the search for bargains you are going to come across more if you study a wide variety of countries and their companies rather than just your own; you also gain the additional safety that comes with greater diversification.

To take but one example of the advantages of a global value focus: in the six-year period 1968–74 US fund managers lost around 50 per cent of their clients' assets because they focused purely on US shares, while Templeton's international fund was bounding ahead. In fact, from the foundation of the Templeton Growth Fund in 1954 until he withdrew from active management of that particular fund in 1992 he turned a typical $10,000 placed in the fund at the start into $2 million, an average annual return of 14.5 per cent. If the same sum of money had been invested in US domestic shares over that period it would have grown to just over $550,000, an annual average of 10.85 per cent.

There is so much you can learn from Templeton:

- The importance of understanding securities markets beyond the confines of one nation. There may be years, even decades when your domestic market is over-valued and it makes sense to find undervalued shares amongst the other 90 per cent plus companies listed abroad.

- How to take the long view on your holdings.

- To be smarter than other analysts and go against the crowd.

- The importance of social, economic and political awareness.

- Guiding principles for work and life.

Sir John (he was knighted in 1987) was a man of quiet confidence, gentle cordiality and deep religious faith. He cared about much more than just money making. Despite becoming a billionaire he would always insist that the spiritual mattered much more to him (and to everyone else, if they could but recognise it). He devoted both his fortune and his time to worldwide study of the big questions connecting science, religion and human purpose. Despite being a man of fierce intellect he did not use it to intimidate; he remained reserved, polite and humble, true to his Christian beliefs.

He has supplied us with some of the best aphorisms to guide investors. Here are a couple of his most famous, which provide a flavour of his rational exploitation of the emotionalism of others:

> Bull markets are born on pessimism, grow on scepticism, mature on optimism and die on euphoria.[1]

> The time of maximum pessimism is the best time to buy and the time of maximum optimism is the best time to sell.[2]

I'll first explain the early influences that helped him shape his investment philosophy. Then I'll discuss his early triumphs

---

1. John Templeton foreword to Templeton, L.C. and S. Phillips (2008) *Investing the Templeton Way*, New York: McGraw Hill.

2. John Templeton quoted in the *Globe and Mail*, 19 July 1996.

as an investment counsellor and as a mutual fund manager. His Templeton Growth Fund had some amazing successes, including investing in Japan, Korea and China, long before the vast majority of western investment houses. Finally the key elements of his investment approach are explained.

The Shaping of the Man

Born, in 1912, into a community of 2,000 in Tennessee, Templeton was strongly influenced by the sense of decency and faith that can be found in small town America. Virtues of hard work, service to others, self-control, dependability, freedom of enterprise and thrift were taken to be the norm. As a boy, Templeton was free to do anything he thought best (apart from alcohol or tobacco); this gave him enormous self-confidence and the conviction that anything is possible. He cannot remember his parents giving him advice, nor spanking him. They did, however, provide impressive role models. His mother was a well-educated active member of the Presbyterian church. As well as keeping the church going through fund-raising she supported a Christian missionary in China. Templeton learned early how money could be used to help others.

His father, a self-taught lawyer, owned a small cotton gin to provide additional income. There was also a cotton storage business, a retail fertiliser business, and an agency for a number of insurance businesses. By 1925 he had bought six small farms, and, on some of the land, built 24 homes and rented them. Templeton watched his father's enterprising activities, some successful, others failures. There was ambition and drive, which resulted in the family becoming, if not rich, better off than most in Winchester.

His mother said he was 'born old'. A youngster possessing self-control, judgement, reliability and foresight. He achieved 'A' grades all the way through school, spurred on by the deal he had with his father whereby each time he got a report card with nothing but As on it he received a bale of cotton. But every time he had a card with anything less than all As – even one item – he had to give his father a bale of cotton. After 22 half-year school report cards the father owed the son 22 bales of cotton.

He went on to study Economics at Yale 1930–34, followed by a Rhodes scholarship to study law at Balliol College, Oxford.

The Doctrine of the 'Extra Ounce'

As a child Templeton observed that the people who were moderately successful worked *almost* as hard as those who were outstandingly successful. The additional effort required was only 'an extra ounce', but they accomplished so much more. There seemed to be an exponential pay-off.

When he was 13 he bought two old Fords. In six months, with the help of his friends, he combined the two to create one car, which he drove for four years. He loved to learn in-depth about new things, especially if they could make money. He had an inner drive and initiative to search for bargains.

In the summer of 1931, while in his first year at Yale, Templeton received what, at the time seemed like devastating news from his father. His father wrote that the business depression had affected him badly and that he simply didn't have any more money to put toward his college. Templeton prayed and talked to people about his predicament. His uncle lent him some money and he obtained a scholarship, but he still had to work to earn the majority. He would say that seeming tragedy can be God's way of educating His children. His financial problems further reinforced in him the value of hard work and thrift. He later regarded the bad news from his father as one of the best things that ever happened to him.

His financial problems further reinforced in him the value of hard work and thrift.

To hold onto the scholarship he had to get good grades. He developed techniques to avoid time wasting:

- He carried paper and books so that wherever he went he could study and write in any free moment. Those few moments added up.

- He worked 15 hours per day, six days a week (seven hours of sleep).

Nevertheless he had an active social life. Motto: 'Work first, play later'. This attitude continued throughout his life; even in his nineties he worked 60 hours a week.

The Mistakes of Others

Around the Winchester area, farms would occasionally fail, become subject to foreclosure and be auctioned off. They were auctioned on the town square where Templeton's father had a second floor office. From his window Harvey Templeton could follow the auctions, and if a farm did not attract a bid he would walk to the square, make an offer and buy farms for a few cents on the dollar.

Just as with farm auctions, when it comes to the pricing of shares we sometimes witness low prices and lack of buyer interest, generating even more disinterest, until there are few or no buyers. On the other hand, shares that have already been bid up attract increasing interest from buyers – making them even more expensive. Templeton's childhood lesson that farms could be bought cheap simply because of the absence of other buyers and not because of an absence of sound value can easily be transferred to the financial markets.

The converse lesson – that assets can become over-priced due to the over-excitement of the crowd – is illustrated by another anecdote from his childhood. One summer evening he raced down the street to join a crowd gathered outside the front porch of a house. Finally, the owner flicked a switch and the whole house was lit up. The crowd that had gathered yelled and clapped with joy. Electricity had arrived and there was much excitement about it. However, Templeton was smart enough to realise that exciting technology does not equal exciting shares. He figured the electricity companies were already over-hyped.

Valuable lessons were also learned about the behaviour of others when playing poker, which he played from the age of eight. People are occasionally foolish and frequently naïve, their actions leading to opportunities for those capable of taking calculated risks, keeping track of the cards, calculating the odds and evaluating the behaviour of the other players. About one-quarter of Templeton's funding for his education at Yale and Oxford came from poker. (He stopped playing at 24, and would never invest in gambling companies – he had seen too many people ruined through compulsive gambling.) One of Templeton's favourite poems is 'If' by Rudyard Kipling: 'If you can keep your head when all about you are losing theirs ...' Good advice if you are to be an investor who often goes against the prevailing consensus and buys when others are selling in a fit of panic.

Thrift

His father was so keen on get-rich-quick schemes that he entered the dangerous world of playing the cotton futures market in New York and New Orleans. One day he walked in and said 'Boys we've made it rich, we just made more money than you can imagine in the cotton futures market'. He told them that they would never have to work again, neither would their children or grandchildren. Days later he had to announce that he had lost it all and they were ruined. Henceforth, John and his brother, Harvey, Jr. scared by the ethereal nature of paper wealth created by financial markets adopted a policy of thrift, looking therein for comfort and security. In Winchester, a person who did not save lacked character, they were undisciplined or shiftless. Thriftiness indicated self-respect.

After graduating from Oxford he married Judith Falk in 1937[3] and took his first investment-counselling position in New York. His pay was $150 per month, as was Judith's (an advertising copywriter). They agreed that they would save one-half of their income, so they could build up a portfolio, with the goal of total financial security. They made this thriftiness into a fun game rather than a chore. Friends would join in, as they scoured New York to find a restaurant where they could get a good meal for 50c. They furnished a five-bedroom apartment for $25, buying at auction and second-hand, and refashioning wooden boxes as furniture. They took to heart what Rockefeller

---

3. Tragically Judith died following a motorcycle accident in 1951, John married Irene in 1958.

said about wealth. He said that you have to make your money work for you if you want to become really wealthy.

As a child he had been fascinated by the power of compound interest, his favourite example being the sale of Manhattan in the seventeenth century. The history books often say that the Indians were foolish to sell Manhattan for as little as a few beads worth $24. But Templeton would point out that if you assume that the $24 is invested at a compound interest of 8 per cent, they would now have trillions of dollars.

Being an investment-counsellor he was coming into regular contact with wealthy people and had a good income. He was regarded as eccentric in his extreme thriftiness, marching to a different drum, but personable, liked and respected.

No Personal Debt

As a teenager Templeton saw many farmers lose their land because of the debt they had taken on. He made a vow to be a lender if necessary, but never a borrower (at least, not for ordinary consumption – he borrowed for investment very occasionally). In his bargain hunting he followed the principle of paying for everything in cash, so that he would always be a receiver and not a payer of interest. He did not borrow to buy houses or cars. By following this policy he gained freedom from worry about being able to make monthly payments. He could also bargain a low price. For example, the house he and Judith purchased in 1944 had a replacement construction cost in that year of $25,000 (it was built 25 years earlier), but they paid a mere $5,000.

Worldwide Perspective

As a first year student at Yale he became interested in investment and began to read books on the subject in addition to his normal studies. He eventually bought his first shares with some money he had made from working his way through college. He bought seven dollar preferred stock of Standard Gas and Electric Company which was selling at only 12 per cent of par due to the Great Depression. Most of his classmates came from wealthy families who owned a range of stocks, but Templeton observed a strange common phenomenon: they did not own any shares outside of one nation. To this 20-year-old student it seemed that you could find better value if you looked elsewhere.

He made up his mind to become an investment counsellor based on three reasons. First, his earlier experiences had convinced him that his strongest talent was that of judgement. He felt he could weigh a variety of factors affecting a decision better than most people. He could assess the relative strengths and weaknesses of businesses and then show courage and self-confidence to act on the decision made. Second, he thought he could make more money in this field than in others. Third, he could help people acquire wealth and security – a noble calling, aligned with his Christian faith.

In training as an investment counsellor he could learn about many different businesses.

There was also a fall-back rationale: in training as an investment counsellor he could learn about many different businesses, so if his path was blocked in investment counselling he could apply that knowledge to another line of work.

On winning his Rhodes Scholarship he was keen on studying a business-related subject. When he explained this to the Oxford professors the expression on their faces was of disgust. Templeton said that it was as if he had told them he wanted to study garbage. They just could not understand why an Oxford '*gentleman*' would be interested in studying business. He opted for law instead, but kept hold of his investment career ambitions. The knowledge of law was of some use in the investment counselling business, but more importantly, the size of the Rhodes Scholarship meant he did not have to work. Instead he travelled and cultivated friendships that were to prove valuable in later life. He made a number of short trips to Europe on a shoestring budget, but his big exploration was made when, following graduation in 1936, he visited dozens of countries travelling through Europe and Asia in order to return to the USA. For the eight months this would take he had a mere £100 in cash. (He refused to take money from his brokerage account. He often told his friends that if you put aside money for capital, you should not start to spend it.)

The travelling had a higher purpose. He wanted to understand, from the ground up, the way societies work in a wide variety of countries. By examining the social, political and economic systems from the grass-roots he might gain some insights that would allow him to gain high returns for potential future clients and himself. He travelled through 35 countries and at each place he tried to learn as much as he could that would give him greater understanding of companies around the world so that he could value them. He was convinced that you can only figure the true value of a company by studying more than one nation because products from one company in a single country are in competition with other companies worldwide. So, to calculate earnings power in the future you need to know the competitive features of the whole industry across the globe.

A Fortune Made in 1939

When he eventually arrived in New York he had 12 interviews with financial institutions and two job offers. He took the lower paying one with Fenner and Beane, a stock brokerage firm that had established its investment counselling division only a few weeks before with two employees. However, within a year he was offered a much higher salary as the vice-president of a small Dallas company, National Geophysical, by his old Oxford buddy, George McGhee. It was during this time that Templeton made a highly profitable investment decision by going against the consensus. On 1 September 1939 Hitler invaded Poland. There was widespread fear that America would go back into Depression as the Nazis systematically destroyed civilisation. Investors hurried to sell shares as they anticipated bad times; the stock market index halved.

Templeton remained calm, and drew on his experience. He had some familiarity with Europe and world affairs – he had even attended the 1936 Olympics in Berlin. He figured that the US would be dragged into the war and concluded that US industry would be asked to step up output to supply war resources. Thus demand would rise just as it had in the Civil War and in the First World War. Goods and commodities needed to be transported, therefore railroad companies would benefit.

He had the ability to focus on the longer-term prospects and disregard the current gloomy views. He looked at *probable future events* rather than on *current events*. He reasoned that even the most inefficient business would revive in the forthcoming boom; profit margins would soar. He sought to purchase where sentiment was most negative, so that when the market reassessed the prospects for these companies they would produce the largest pay-offs. He had spent two years studying the performance of shares selling at under $1 and concluded that if they were bought, given the extent to which they were over-sold due to very low expectations, he was unlikely to lose money.

By this stage he and Judith had built up a personal portfolio worth about $30,000 through a combination of wise investments, a generous company purchase plan and thrift. He was so convinced that his contrarian stance was correct that he borrowed $10,000 (the only time he borrowed in the next 40 years). With this he went back to his old firm, Fenner and Beane, to place an order. He asked them to buy $100 worth of stock in every company trading at less than $1. His dutiful broker pointed out that 37 of the 104 companies were in bankruptcy. Templeton replied that it did not matter, believing that in a war economy even bankrupt companies come back.

Note that he was careful to diversify his risk: even though individual companies within this portfolio might lose money, by investing in around 100 there was a good chance that the overall performance would be good; high risk, therefore high diversification. Note also his focus is on the profitability of companies years from now: maybe five years, maybe ten. His average holding period was four years for this portfolio.

In one year Templeton had made enough to repay all the borrowed money. The shares were gradually sold over a number of years, yielding $40,000. Only four of the companies failed. Templeton's wider perspective and his intense study of wartime economics allowed him to see before others that US shares were cheap. His historical analysis convinced him that in a major war the most depressed companies come back to life and provide the largest percentage gains.

One of the shares bought in 1939 was Missouri Pacific preferred. These shares were originally issued at $100 offering a $7 annual dividend. The company was in bankruptcy and the shares were selling for $0.125. If the railroad traffic did increase with a wartime boom then, Templeton estimated, the preferred shares should rise to $2 or $3. As it became profitable its prior-year tax losses would help it to avoid the high war-time corporate taxes. This is why he selected a marginal company (a loss maker) rather than a strongly profitable company. He knew his history: in the First World War strong companies faced high tax bills – partly justified because those firms benefited from the war-time increased demand – whereas weaker companies were overlooked. The company returned to profit in 1940, and rose strongly in 1941 and 1942. Templeton sold the shares at $5, a 3,900 per cent increase. He admits that he sold too early. He always said that you cannot expect to buy at the bottom and sell at the top. The best you can hope for is to buy something that is cheap. When it goes up buy something else that is cheaper. Sell the first to buy the second.

His Own Firm

In 1940 Templeton bought for $5,000 an investment counselling firm with only eight clients owned by George Towne, an elderly man. With a name change to Towne, Templeton and Dobbrow and the purchase of second-hand typewriters and a second-hand library of research material and books (thrift at all times!), Templeton had arrived as an independent investment counsellor, aged 28. He could not afford to pay himself a salary for two years, and had to rely on savings to see him through.

He was a conscientious manager, seeing his role as that of someone who could, through sound investment, allow his clients to retire comfortably or send children to college. His clients received an investment programme individualised for their specific needs. He decided how to split a client's money between bonds, equities and property. He also helped with estate and financial planning, offering a service to reduce income and estate taxes. He always regarded serving people as a pleasure – a greater pleasure than spending thousands of dollars.

While cutting unnecessary cost he did not skimp on hiring the best talent.

While cutting unnecessary cost he did not skimp on hiring the best talent. He believed that you get a better bargain in the market place for executives and employees if you pay about 20 per cent more than the salaries available elsewhere. An excellent employee is worth more than two mediocre employees.

One of Templeton's personal mottoes is 'OPM is sacred'. OPM is other people's money. There is a major difficulty in scaling-up an investment-counselling business. Each account has a unique set of objectives and circumstances relating to risk tolerance, taxes and timing. Clients are on the telephone regularly and have a claim on the manager's time. It became increasingly apparent that a more rational, time-effective approach to managing money for other people was to set up mutual funds. He saw in this type of business a way of helping families of different income levels save money and accumulate wealth and security.

Templeton Growth Fund

Templeton, together with a few colleagues, set up the Templeton Growth Fund (TGF) in 1954, with the strategy of finding shares with the lowest prices in relation to their intrinsic value and long-term earning power, and to diversify into more and more nations. From the start the fund looked for value all over the globe for two reasons:

1. It widened and deepened the pool from which to draw bargains, allowing the investor to remain flexible. If you are looking for pockets of over-pessimism, fear and negativity then searching a number of markets increases the probability of finding it at any one point in time. On the other hand, sticking to one market may mean going long periods when the market is full of optimism and bargains are few and far between.

2. Diversification – one country's markets can fall unpredictably. It is not possible to time market rises and falls. To protect yourself, be in a number of markets.

The Templeton Growth Fund started with $7 million of assets. Over the first two decades it climbed slowly. The portfolio performance was outstanding, but the fund was not marketed effectively. In 1974 John Galbraith joined to market the fund to bring it to a wider public. Other funds were added to the Templeton stable (e.g. a small company focus fund) and by 1992 they were managing £22 billion. By 1997 there were 4 million investors owning $80 billion.

To gain some impression of the quality of the Templeton Growth Fund consider the case of Leroy Pasley. He was an old friend of Templeton's who had made money applying his genius to electronics. He put $100,000 into the fund at the outset, and did not take a penny out for the next few decades. By the mid 1990s this holding had grown to be worth over C$35 million (TGF was set up in Canada).

Japanese Adventure

In the 1950s and 1960s Japan was perceived by American and other investors as a loser of wars, an industrial backwater and a small market. Clearly its reputation was low, making trivial low-cost products; made in Japan meant low quality. People dismissed the Japanese as never having the potential to lead on research or quality.

Templeton had studied the Japanese character and business practices since the 1940s. He knew far more than most. His observations were that the Japanese people were tremendously hard working and they saved to invest in future prosperity. Out of every yen earned one-quarter was saved, compared with the typical US saving rate of around 5 per cent. Japanese thrift enabled them to invest in more plant and machinery. There was also a sense of solidarity between companies and their employees; they considered it a privilege to work for a fine company. And they admired business leaders.

In the decade following the devastation of the Second World War Japan had already become an industrial producer on a big scale, focusing particularly on heavy equipment and machinery. Starting in the early 1950s Templeton invested much of his personal savings in the country, but was unable to put client funds into Japanese shares because of the strict exchange controls restricting withdrawal of money from the country: you could put money in, but you could not take it out. Templeton thought that the government would continue to liberalise the economy and eventually allow foreign investment to flow. When he was proved right in 1968 he was ready, and immediately invested client funds.

Japanese shares were trading at an average of only four times Templeton's estimate of annual earnings, whereas US stocks were trading at 19.5 times. Other investors were put off by extreme price fluctuations and a lack of information on the underlying companies. They clung tenaciously to their generally downbeat view of Japan. But Templeton found so many bargains that the TGF never paid more than three times earnings, even for the best companies.

Soon 50 per cent of TGF was in Japanese shares. He was criticised for (a) buying in Japan, and (b) devoting such a high proportion of the fund to Japan. His reply to which was that was where the bargains were to be found.

Accounting and Legal Complexity Present an Opportunity

Other investors avoided Japanese shares because of the complexity of the accounting and legal rules. Japanese companies did not report consolidated income numbers. So if a subsidiary earns $1 million, but hands over only $150,000 to the parent company, the unaware investor may think that the company parent has an interest in only $150,000 of its subsidiary's earnings. In reality, if it owns 60 per cent of the subsidiary it has an interest of $600,000. Templeton looked for the companies with the widest gap between the parent company reported earnings and the consolidated earnings.

Hitachi owned a number of subsidiaries, for which the relevant share of earnings were not consolidated in Hitachi's financial statements; thus Hitachi's earnings figures were artificially depressed, resulting in a seemingly high price-earnings ratio (PER) of 16. Templeton added back the subsidiary earnings and found a PER of 6. The consolidated earnings figures were two and a half times the parent-company reported earnings. He reckoned that there was a strong likelihood that Japanese investors would eventually bid Hitachi up to two and half times the price they had previously. When the government finally got around to requiring companies to report consolidated earnings Japanese investors started looking at the consolidated earnings and share prices rose.

Lesson to take away: take time to understand the situation from the top to the bottom, especially if it difficult for others to understand.

The Japanese economic miracle produced economic growth rates of around 10 per cent per year in the 1960s. Companies that TGF bought showed terrific earning figures, and the investment crowd around the world paid attention, but they were already ten steps behind.

The extraordinary performance of the Japanese stock market brought Templeton to the notice of the investing public.

The extraordinary performance of the Japanese stock market brought Templeton to the notice of the investing public. In 1969 the *New York Times* carried an article showing the top 25

mutual fund managers ranked by performance for the year to
September 1969. The Templeton Growth Fund was number
one, showing a gain of 19.38 per cent in net asset value, up from
19th position in 1968. Considering that Lipper surveyed 376
funds this was a great performance.

The next few years were not so good, but Templeton was
less concerned with the short-term performance than he was
with superior long-term returns. The Templeton Growth Fund
underperformed the Dow Jones Industrial Average in 1970,
1971 and 1975, and yet returned a compound 22 per cent in
the 1970s overall, compared with 4.6 per cent for the Dow.

Japanese shares became so 'hot' in the late 1970s that
typical PERs were 30, with the most sought-after companies at
over 70. The growth rate in earnings had slowed dramatically
compared with the 1960s, so investors were paying more and
more for less and less. There was just too much 'unreasonable
optimism'. Templeton identified bargains elsewhere in the
world and in order to buy them he took profits from Japanese
stocks.

He had unwound his positions in Japanese shares in the
early and mid 1980s, just at the point when their popularity and
market prices rose through the last frenzy of one of the biggest
stock market bubbles ever – the stock market increased 36-fold
between 1960 and 1989. Despite making huge profits he later
regretted not being around to benefit from the insane scramble
for everything Japanese in the later 1980s. He told his loyal
followers at the 1991 TGF meeting that he should have waited
to take out profits in Japan.

In later years he retained an affection for the Japanese,
but this was never to colour his judgement of share value. He

said in 1988 that he had nothing in Japan now, but would like to go back because its people remained thrifty, honest, hard working, organised and ambitious. But he would only do so when he could find shares there which are a better bargain than elsewhere. The Japanese market has never recovered its highs of 1989. Following a 50 per cent Japanese market fall in 1990 he looked again to see if there were better bargains there than anywhere else. He found two, Hitachi (again) and Matsushita Electric Industrial. Even with the purchase of these, from then on less than one half of 1 per cent of the fund was in Japan. He just kept on finding better bargains elsewhere.

Going Against the Crowd

As Templeton gradually withdrew from the over-hyped Japanese market of the 1980s, he scoured the globe for neglected, under-rated stocks; and these were not all in the emerging economies. He had already made a 15-fold return by buying General Public Utilities after the Three Mile Island nuclear disaster in the late 1970s, and was becoming increasingly intrigued by the low valuations of US stocks. In the midst of the demoralised market of June 1982, when the Dow Jones was at 788, he astonished commentators by his statement that he thought there was a good chance it would hit 3,000 by 1988 (it did not reach quite such heights, but it did almost treble).

He bought into a depressed Mexican market in the early 1980s and snapped up Union Carbide shares the day after the Indian plant had caused the deaths of almost 2,500 people in Bhopal. Investors dumped the shares on fears that legal suits could put the company out of business. The shares nosedived from $50 to $33. Seven months later (July 1985) the one million shares bought rose to $52. He told the 750 people gathered for the 1985 annual meeting of the Templeton funds that he buys shares when they are cheap. This sometimes means making mistakes, but, in most cases, you can sell for a profit when the bad news is over. He also said that you should avoid buying when the analysts issue buy recommendations because, by then, the shares are no longer a bargain. At this point Templeton had identified so many bargains in the North American markets that he had 40 per cent of the fund invested in the US, with another 14 per cent in Canadian stocks: Australian securities accounted for almost 12 per cent.

Another wave of pessimism drove markets down in 1990, which led to a characteristic response from Templeton. He said that he had never seen so many shares, particularly emerging market growth companies, so undervalued by the market. He found plenty of bargains in industries where there was great pessimism. So he spent the early 1990s finding bargains in far flung places such as New Zealand, Indonesia, Pakistan, Brazil and Peru. The breadth of his country knowledge was astonishing; for example in 1996 the TGF held securities in over 30 countries. However, by then there was an indication that he was already starting to become nervous of the exuberance of the late nineties because he had allocated 25 per cent of the fund to cash.

In March 2000 he went further, again demonstrating his independence from the crowd deluded by talk of the 'new era', by expressing his conviction that the equity markets were overvalued relative to earnings and growth prospects. After warning of the risks of the internet bubble he advised the editor of the *Equities* magazine to tell his readers to go into bonds. Just because for much of the twentieth century equities had been priced so low that they had been good purchases does not mean that in 2000 they were now better buys than bonds.

For his funds he bought US zero coupon government bonds, thinking that when the internet bubble burst the value of the bonds would rise as the Federal Reserve, fearful of a recession, lowered interest rates. He also purchased zeros in Canada, Australia and New Zealand on similar logic. In March 2000, Canadian 30-year zero coupon bonds yielded 5.3 per cent. Three years later they yielded 4.9 per cent. The return over three years was 31.9 per cent, or 9.7 per cent per year. Because the value of the US dollar dropped in that period the dollar return was 43.4 per cent (12.8 per cent per year). On top of this, to finance half of these investments Templeton had borrowed in Japanese yen at around 0.1 per cent. Because he had used 2x leverage the return jumps to 86.8 per cent. (To reduce the risk of the Japanese yen appreciating during the time of borrowing he placed the borrowed money in the currencies of countries with a favourable trade balance, small budget deficits or surpluses and small total government debt to GDP ratios – not in US dollars.) Bear in mind that during this three-year period many stock exchanges more than halved.

In April 2000 Templeton gave an interview to the *Miami Herald* in which he said that the time had already passed when the investor could profit from technology and internet companies. He said that the markets had reached the point of 'maximum enthusiasm' and that all such enthusiasms are temporary. By the time this interview was granted he had been shorting tech stocks for a year.

He had devised an ingenious plan to exploit the over-inflated stocks of 1999 for his personal investment portfolio. During the period following an initial public offering (IPO) of shares there is a 'lock-up' period during which the company insiders are not permitted to sell any of their shares. He figured that many of these directors/founders would be impatient to sell as soon as they could, often in the belief that the shares were caught up in a bubble; they could see the risks that their venture might not mature into a long-term viable business and wanted some wealth in cash. Also the sales by insiders would unleash an avalanche of negative momentum trades – insider selling would become a trigger for this but not the main driving force.

He only shorted those trading at more than three times their original price.

Templeton sold short 84 companies just before the end of the lock-up period (around 11 days before), and then bought them back again to close his position after they had fallen due to the pressure of insider sales. He only shorted those trading at more than three times their original price. In his disciplined fashion he set precise targets at which he took profits. If shares unexpectedly rose he ruthlessly cut his losses. He bet $2.2 million each time and was reported to have made almost 50 per cent on his overall bet of $185 million, a profit of $86 million.

Templeton had rules for short selling:

- Control your losses. State a level at which you will cut your losses by covering the stock. Remember Keynes: 'The market can stay irrational longer than you can stay solvent.'

- Take profits in a predetermined way. For the 1999 trades he used either when (a) the share is down 95 per cent or (b) the trailing PER dipped below 30.

South Korea

From the Korea story we can see the importance of patiently accruing knowledge while waiting for the right opportunity. As far back as 1983 Templeton declared that he thought South Korea would be the next 'Japan', but he did not invest his clients' money there because of the restrictions on capital removal from the country. In a talk at the Templeton funds meeting in 1991 he mentioned Korea as one of the less developed nations (alongside China, Brazil, Thailand and Turkey) with the most 'exciting investment opportunities'. The restrictions on removing money from the country were relaxed in 1992, but it was not until after the 1997 Asian financial crisis that he really started to focus money in the country.

South Korea had followed the same plan for economic development that Japan used: high savings rates, determined exporters and high education levels. This resulted in the highest average economic growth in the world between 1970 and 1997. The Korean conglomerates, known as chaebols, took on grossly inflated levels of debt to permit ever more ambitious expansion. The 1997 crisis hit hard – currency down, shares down and debt rising. When they failed to pay interest due some chaebol sought bankruptcy protection (e.g. Kia Motors, Haitai). In return for financial aid the country, now in deep recession, agreed to further open its markets.

The 2 January 1998 edition of the *Wall Street Journal* reports Templeton buying Korean-focused vehicles (e.g. mutual funds). He was quoted as saying 'I think the Korean market is somewhere near the bottom ... All my investment career, I have always tried to buy at the point of maximum pessimism ... The pessimism in Korea has been so intense in recent months.' He was betting that (a) Korea would not re-impose capital controls, and (b) the economy would return to its old growth rate. Price–earnings ratios were around 10.

Templeton chose to avoid stock picking with Korea. Instead he hired The Matthew Fund, run by people who had studied Templeton for many years and followed his approach, who had greater familiarity with specific stocks in Korea. Note that he chose the Matthew Fund even though it had a very poor recent record – it had fallen two-thirds in five months – compared with mutual funds in other markets. Many other investors had abandoned it or ignored it. Templeton could see that the poor performance was due to the Korean circumstances, not bad management. In the two years after Templeton bought in 1997 the Matthew Fund rose 267 per cent.

Templeton continued to take an interest in Korea, and began to pick shares. For example, in 2004 (when he was 92) he found Kia Motors on a PER of 4.8 while exhibiting a long-term growth rate in earnings per share of 28 per cent per year. This is compared with General Motors PER of 5.9, with a decline in earnings per share. Also Kia's net profit margin was three times as great as GM. He bought $50 million of Kia Motors in August 2004. By December 2005 the share had risen 174 per cent.

The Kia Motors example also gives us a glimpse of the character and principles of the man. Coincidental with the investment in the company he needed to buy a new car. He visited the Kia showroom and was very impressed with the car. His assistant, May Walker, asked why he had not bought one: 'Too expensive for me.' She persuaded him to buy it. 'I knew he wanted to buy it, but the man just doesn't spend money.' He never let his financial success change his thrifty behaviour.

China

In 1995 Templeton told us of the huge growth potential in China. His analysis was based on the liberating effect of economic freedoms. Even the small amount of freedom to engage in enterprise was enough to have a major effect given that the people were coming from such hopeless and poor conditions under communism. China Mobile had 68 per cent of the market. It had an estimated long-term growth rate in earnings per share of around 20 per cent, but was trading on an historical PER of only 11. It was one of the cheapest telecommunication shares in the world. Templeton looked at the PER based on earnings ten years into the future (2014). He thought this PER to be less than two, so he bought American Depository Receipts (ADRs) in 2004. To estimate ten years into the future is a good discipline. You need to think about the competitive position of the company; in particular, the potential for the entry of rivals into the industry. Between September 2004 and September 2007 China Mobile ADRs rose by 656 per cent. China Life Insurance ADRs were also purchased on the New York Stock Exchange in September 2004. They rose 1,000 per cent in three years.

Foundation

Templeton was always concerned to make sure he continued to 'work in harmony with God's purposes'. He would spend time praying and meditating. He even opened director and shareholder meetings with a prayer. The prayers were not for financial success but rather to clear the mind and focus on the really important. He saw free enterprise as a great way of enriching the poor, by reducing costs, increasing variety and improving quality. But if business was not ethical then, he said, it will eventually fail. He used his wealth to benefit others, maintaining thrifty habits for himself. He had a deep sense of stewardship. This encompassed a sense of responsibility for people's assets entrusted to him, but also stretched to cover a sense of responsibility and duty about his personal assets, such as talent, given by God, for him to use wisely. This encouraged him to work tremendously hard and to regard worldly goods as not his own, but God's, to be used according to His wishes.

In his late 30s he started giving away to charity 20 per cent of his earnings. In the 1960s he developed a respect for the Bahamians as people of deep spirituality, and so wanted to live amongst them. He also wanted to spend more time on religious and philanthropic work. So, in 1968 he, his second wife, Irene Butler (who he married in 1958) and his children moved to live in Lyford Cay, Nassau. His office became two rented rooms above a barber shop and he had a part-time secretary. He wanted to become an involved member of the community and so became a subject of the British Crown (the Bahamas was a UK colony until 1993), renouncing his US citizenship. He still controlled one mutual fund, the Templeton Growth Fund. Apart from running this he looked after family investments and gave away a fortune.

In 1972 he established the Templeton Prize for Progress in Religion – over $1 million annually – to recognise exemplary achievement in work related to life's spiritual dimension. This was Templeton's way of underscoring his belief that advances in the spiritual realm are no less important than those in other areas of human endeavour. Recipients include Mother Teresa of Calcutta, Billy Graham and Alexander Solzhenitsyn as well as numerous physicists and other scientists. Templeton was a universalist, believing that there are significant elements of truth in all religions. He wrote numerous books on spiritual matters.

He endowed the former Oxford Centre for Management Studies as a full college, Templeton College, in 1983. For his charitable work he was knighted by the Queen in 1987. The John Templeton Foundation was created in the same year to finance work on the big questions connecting science, religion and human purpose. To this day it still gives vast amounts of money (over $70 million per year) in grants funding scientific research in areas such as evolutionary biology, cosmology, theoretical physics, cognitive science and social science relating to 'love, forgiveness, creativity, purpose and the nature and origin of religious belief'. It has an endowment fund of over $1.5 billion.

What Retirement?

In 1992 the Templeton Funds were sold to the Franklin Group, when they had $25 billion under management, for $913 million. Franklin agreed to allow the 78 mutual funds to be operated separately, with Sir John becoming chairman emeritus (there were over 200 people working for the Templeton organisation by then). His wife, Irene, asked him if the sale would reduce his usual 12-hour working day. His only concession being that he would *sometimes* not work on Saturday afternoons.

He did not slow down; three years later, at 83 years old, he said that he wanted to work every day he could so that he could help as many people as possible. He declared he was working harder than he had ever worked in his life – including evenings, Saturdays and Sundays – and what is more, he found it thrilling that he could do that. Much more of a thrill than watching television or playing golf. He found so much joy in trying to help people. Even in his ninety-fifth year he worked extremely hard. The London *Guardian* reported that between 1954 and his death in 2008 an investor of $10,000 in the TGF would have experienced a rise to $7 million.

The Key Elements of His Approach

Templeton drew on a wide range of factors when selecting investments – see Figure 4.1.

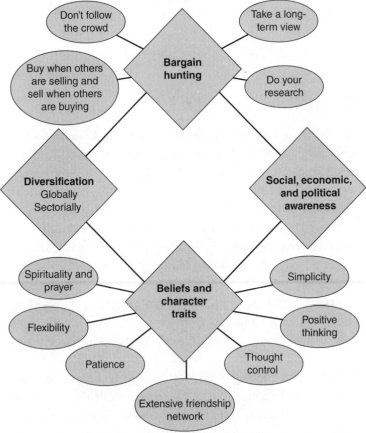

Figure 4.1   The key principles used by John Templeton

Bargain Hunting

Don't Follow the Crowd

Templeton developed a knack for looking at investments in a different way to other investors, whether in a different country, with a different time horizon, using a different valuation method, or with a different level of optimism or pessimism. He would say that share picking is the only activity where you do not follow the advice of experts. If you had a medical problem and asked the advice of ten doctors and they all agreed, you'd probably follow their advice. But if ten professional share analysts say that this share is a good buy then you should not buy it. Anything great about the company is already in the share price. It is often wiser to do the opposite of what the experts say.

Finding that others disagree with your buy and sell decisions is something that goes with the territory for a bargain hunter. If the consensus was favourable it would not be a bargain. Bargain hunters are independent-minded and have faith in their own judgement.

Humans seem to be hard-wired to overreact to a situation. They also respond to the actions of the other buyers and sellers around them rather than apply sound reasoning. Take advantage of people with less clear thinking, who are dumping stock or hyping stock on the basis of emotion. Easy to say, difficult to practise:

> Of course, you may say, buy low, that's obvious. Well it may be, but that isn't the way the market works. When prices are high, a lot of investors are buying. Prices are low when demand is low, investors have pulled back,

people are discouraged and pessimistic. When almost everyone is pessimistic at the same time, the entire market collapses ... investors are on the sidelines, sitting on their wallets. Yes, they tell you: 'Buy low, sell high', but all too many of them bought high and sold low. And when do they buy? The usual answer: 'Why, after analysts agree on a favorable outlook.' This is foolish, but it is human nature.[4]

To nurture separation from the crowd in an intellectual sense may mean choosing to be physically separate. Templeton's performance improved after the move to the Bahamas. Being in Nassau helped him think differently to Wall Street. Note that other great investors also keep away from major financial centres, e.g. Warren Buffett in Nebraska, Philip Fisher and Charlie Munger in California. By avoiding the standard company presentations and talk on the Street they were able to think freely.

When it came to initial public offerings Templeton said he found few bargains. While the crowd often became excited by initial public offering shares, he did not. He thought it best to wait until the crowd lost interest or became disillusioned, when he could pick up the same shares at a better price months or years later. There are few bargains to be had in IPOs.

He did not follow the crowd when it became enamoured of the Nobel Prize winning theory of the capital asset pricing model, with beta as its measure of risk. He thought betas were unreliable because they change. Over a five-year period

---

4. John Templeton's list of investment rules printed in *Christian Science Monitor*, February 1993. Reproduced in Ross, N. (2000) *Lessons from the Legends of Wall Street*, New York: MJF Books.

the beta for a company can look quite different at the end compared with the start. Instead of beta look for yardsticks of real value.

Buy When Others are Selling and Sell When Others are Buying

One of Templeton's most famous mottos is 'to buy when others are despondently selling and to sell when others are avidly buying'. This policy may require a great deal of fortitude but it pays the greatest ultimate reward. Another is to buy when there's blood on the streets. Crisis leads to panic as sellers are driven by fear. Fears become exaggerated. Difficulties in the economy often appear worse at the outset, but all crises subdue in time. When the panic dissipates share prices rise. For example, in August 1979 there were many reasons for pessimism: inflation, high interest rates, oil prices and fears over oil supply, Japanese competition. On the cover of *Business Week* were the words, 'The Death of Equities'. Even pension funds reduced their equity holdings and bought inflation hedges such as gold and real estate. However, Templeton thought the US equity market to be incredibly cheap by historical standards – the average Dow PER was 6.8, the lowest on record, compared with the long-term average of around 14. He invested heavily, apportioning 60 per cent of his funds to the US.

Templeton maintained a 'wish list' of well-run companies, with bright prospects and good managers, but with high share prices: thus he could not bring himself to buy them – he had to wait. Then, when a major market decline occurred he could pick a few of these as the share prices fell into the bargain range. This approach forms a bulwark against the psychological blocks that arise as the market falls and you seem to be acting alone, against the consensus. In this way you are not swayed by immediate events.

If you adopt the approach of buying when the market declines, many of your key buy signals occur when the economy is in or close to recession. Be sure that the companies on your wish-list have sufficiently low debt levels to prosper even in a downturn.

To obtain a bargain price, you have to search for where the generality of investors are most frightened and pessimistic.

On the point of maximum pessimism Templeton said that we should wait until the ninety-ninth person out of a hundred gives up. Then the market can only go up because there are no more sellers left. Bear markets are to be welcomed, because then shares become cheaper and present bargains to buy. If you can understand the paradox that you should *not* be looking where the outlook is good, but where it is most miserable, then you are well on your way to being a Templeton type investor. In other walks of life, such as being a manager of a manufacturing firm you would try to go to where the outlook is best, e.g. to build a factory where the prospects are best. But, when it comes to shares, you have to do the opposite. The reason is that your objective is to buy a share at the lowest possible price in relation to what the company is worth. A share becomes a bargain because other people are selling. There is no other reason. To obtain a bargain price, you have to search for where the generality of investors are most frightened and pessimistic.

At the point of market euphoria there is much talk about a new financial paradigm, a new age where old measures of value no longer apply. Templeton would say that the four most expensive words in the English language are 'this time it's different'. He stuck to his belief that in the long-run stock market indices fluctuate around the long-term upward trend in earnings per share. In that context bear markets are temporary and tend to start to turn a year before the business cycle turns, while rampaging bull markets will eventually end and prices crash to reflect more realistically the trend in earnings (with the possibility of an over-reaction in the short-term correction).

Templeton described himself as an 'accommodator' rather than a contrarian; when over-excited greedy investors jumped in to buy at the top of a bull market he accommodated them by selling them his shares. When frightened investors were selling at the bottom, he accommodated them by buying.

When it came to taking profits on current holdings Templeton would only do so only once he had found a much better share to replace it. By 'much better' he used the rule of thumb of around 50 per cent better, to avoid excessive portfolio churn creating wasteful activity. Thus if you hold a share that is worth $100 but its current market price is $50 and you are considering buying another share with a true value of $100 when the current market price is $40, should you do so? No, because the percentage difference $10/$40 = 25 per cent is not the 50 per cent you need. If, however, you wait a few weeks and the $40 share goes to $30 then there is a $20/$30 = 66.7 per cent gap so you should switch.

His biographer, William Procter, said in 1983 that his average holding period was around six years, but the time period was not a factor that guided him. What matters was

whether he had found something else that was an excellent
bargain. He would look over his portfolio to see which share
was the least good bargain – and sell that. But in this process
he does not ask himself whether he had owned the share for
one month or ten years: it is not relevant. Continually making
comparisons between shares in terms of the size of the gap
between their value and their price is useful because you are
forced to constantly assess the attractiveness of your investments relative to those available in the market. So, if say your
investments in Peru are currently caught in a wave of euphoria
you remain busy comparing these holdings with bargains
available elsewhere in the worldwide market, making you less
inclined to be swept up in the euphoria; you do not just sit
back and wallow in the recent rise in your portfolio. The reason
Templeton ran down his portfolio in Japan long before the final
stage of the bubble was not a conscious choice to switch out of
Japan as a country, but rather a share by share comparison of
value in Japan compared with, say, individual US companies or
New Zealand companies.

People have criticised Templeton (and other value investors)
for leaving money on the table and selling an investment too
soon. However, as an investor you have to accept that a share
may often be sold before it reaches its maximum, if there are
cheaper bargains elsewhere.

Broker recommendations are not to be trusted as guides
to bargains because if a stockbroker has recommended a share
to you then he has probably recommended it to hundreds of
others; so it is not going to be as good a bargain as one you have
found yourself. If a company or industry gets on the front pages
of the newspaper, it's too late to buy it because other people
have already pushed the price up.

Take a Long-term View

Templeton generally focused on what a company could earn two to five years down the line. The great majority of share traders look to the short term – what is going to happen to earnings next month or next year. By looking to the medium term you filter out short-term noise that is currently preoccupying the market. Taking a longer view gives the bargain hunter a psychological edge, allowing the exploitation of temporary problems in business. By asking about the company's strategic position and the quality of management in terms of their focus on long-term shareholder value you gain a superior perspective relative to traders in the market. The sorts of questions you are forced to answer include: what gives this company a competitive advantage? Will they maintain their earnings power over a long period, in bad times as well as good? Is the quality of the brand such as to provide durable pricing power?

In defining 'value' he said he tries to work out what he thought was the best estimate of earnings in five years' time. He then would pay no more than five times this figure for the shares. This has the advantage, when buying into companies reporting problems and therefore diminished share prices, of distinguishing between those with temporary, solvable, problems and those with a deep-seated strategic disadvantage or unattractive industry economics.

He told us not to speculate but to invest. The stock market should not be viewed as a casino, it has a more important purpose. That said, if you spend your time continually moving in and out of shares to gain some supposed advantage from a few percentage points moves, or you play with options and futures, then the market will start to become a casino for you, as you become a gambler rather than an investor. You may win a few times but will lose eventually. Your profits will be consumed by commissions. Keep in mind the words of Lucien O. Hooper, a Wall Street legend:

> 'What always impresses me', he wrote, 'is how much better the relaxed, long-term owners of stock are with their portfolios than the traders with their switching of inventory. The relaxed investor is usually better informed and more understanding of essential values, more patient and less emotional, pays smaller annual capital gains taxes, and does not incur unnecessary brokerage commissions.'[5]

When asked what he thought of the likely movements in the stock market over the next few months he said, he did not know of anyone who can judge this, including himself. Over a short time frame share prices are mainly influenced by emotion, by excitement or gloom.

While Templeton normally held shares for years there were one or two tempting short-term plays. For example, following the September 11 crisis eight airline companies were on low PERs. He placed an order with a broker to buy any of the eight if the share price fell by more than 50 per cent during 17 September, the day the market reopened. He had the objective of selling after six months. This was purely an exploitation of a short-term panic. In the event, three of the airlines fell more than 50 per cent and he bought. Subsequently, AMR (American) rose 61 per cent, Continental rose 72 per cent and US Airways by 24 per cent (the government came to the rescue).

---

5. Ibid.

Do Your Research

It is important that you do your own research, that you investigate before investing. Understanding what makes a company successful is vital. How does the business work? What is its performance over time and how does it compare with the performance of competitors? What stimulates sales activity? What pressures might prevent a growth in sales? In answering these types of question you can increase your accuracy in judging why the company is currently out of favour and whether a poor situation is temporary or the company will be consumed by it.

He would spend a great deal of time studying an industry, the competitive position of the firm and personal qualities and competence of the management. He would home in on the key value drivers for the industry, e.g. with mines it is reserves, with retailers it is profits and competitive strength.

When researching a company he would spend as much time researching its competitors as the company itself. Indeed, the best information comes from competitors rather than directly from the company. Competitors put a great deal of effort into competing and thus develop a deep knowledge of the weaknesses and strengths of the opposition. Ask various company executives which company in their industry they would invest in, other than their own. They are generally optimistic about the prospects for their own firm and so may give a less than frank assessment. But if you ask about a competitor within 30 seconds you'll have a fulsome analysis.

An indicator that the firms in a particular industry are under-priced is an increase in merger and acquisition activity; if they are buying each other at bid premiums of 50 per cent or more perhaps share prices are too low. Also, companies buying their own shares because they regard them as ridiculously underpriced may be taken as a positive signal.

The investor has a hundred yardsticks, similar to the doctor searching for many symptoms, to consider.

Templeton likened corporate analysis to making a medical diagnosis. The investor has a hundred yardsticks, similar to the doctor searching for many symptoms, to consider; while you cannot ignore any of them, you learn that in most situations only three or four are important to the case, and you should concentrate on them. In security analysis you deduce the basic values of a company from a particular set of measures but you do not pay a lot of attention to measures that do not apply. A different set of measures will be the main focus when it comes to another company – just as a doctor will look differently at the symptoms of each patient who comes in. A further analogy is that of reviewing a restaurant: do not expect the quality of a share to be 100 per cent perfect in every respect, but you do want the overall quality to be high enough to warrant three or four stars.

Some of the key factors (within the 100 yardsticks) he has written about are:

- **Price–earnings record**. The past year's earnings is less interesting than the earnings five to ten years into the future. Look for a share priced exceptionally low relative to its long-term earnings growth prospects.

- **Competitive advantages**. Does it have competitive advantages other companies cannot replicate? Is it the undisputed low-cost producer? Or is it the technological leader? Or does it have the strongest brand?

- **Profit margin on sales**. He looked for companies that had the widest profit margins and the most rapidly increasing profits.

- **Price to book ratio**. If this is less than one then the net assets of the company are greater than the price paid. It may be a bargain, or it may be running itself into the ground. In 1979 the P/B ratio for the average US share was under one. Furthermore, because of high inflation, the replacement value of assets was higher than the recorded book value. By adjusting the book value to replacement value, taking into account the expected rise in inflation between the time of purchase and 1982, Templeton found that the P/B ratio fell from 1.0 to 0.59: shares were priced at a 40 per cent discount to the value of the company's net assets. Whereas most people saw a P/B ratio of 1.0, Templeton saw 0.59.

- **Long-range plans of senior executives**. Interview the top executives to find out what they plan to do in the future.

- **Market share**. A strong position often produces high earnings power.

- **Is it well capitalised?** Is there sufficient equity capital? Too little equity capital can mean excess debt and more risk, or restricted growth.

- **Return on capital employed**. A high figure means that additional money used in the business, such as retained earnings, will probably generate high shareholder value.

- **Share price to sales ratio**. A low figure might indicate that the market is not sufficiently allowing for the potential of profit margins on sales to improve.

- **Share price to cash flow multiple**. A low multiple is often a sign of undervaluation.

- **Share price to liquidating value**. There are a number of ways in which value can be generated for shareholders if the assets are lowly priced, not least a takeover.

Templeton said that it is important to pay attention to both the earnings statement and what is on the balance sheet. However, as the following quote shows, most of the time he placed emphasis on earnings:

> When I was a student under the famous Benjamin Graham, he taught me about using book values and to search for companies selling for less than net working capital ... And I've used it. But it won't work in America today [1987] because you won't find any companies selling for less than net working capital. Ben was a very wise man. He had a splendid method. But if he were alive today, he would be relying on newer and more varied concepts. The yardstick of value we've used most often is price relative to probable future earnings. Others we have used include price relative to cash flow, and price relative to liquidating value, not book value ... Future earnings are more important than current or past earnings.[6]

When Templeton was asked whether he used technical analysis (charts of price or volume histories) he replied that he did,

---

6. John Templeton quoted in the *Financial Post* (Toronto), 25 May 1987, p.25. From an interview by Professor Eric Kirzner, University of Waterloo. Reprinted by permission.

but only as a supplement – and that he had not found much in technical analysis that's worth a lot of study.

Here are two valuation examples:

Case 1: Skaggs

Skaggs merged with Acme to form American Stores in 1979. Templeton said that although Acme was not profitable at the time, he was confident that Skaggs' management would raise its profit margin to the same level as Skaggs, i.e. 2 per cent. He started buying the shares at $25 when sales volume per share was $700. If 2 per cent margins are achieved throughout the merged company then $14 profit per share is to be expected. Thus Templeton was buying American Stores for under two times the potential per-share profit. The shares rose over 500 per cent.

Case 2: Ito-Yokado

Ito-Yokado, a large supermarket chain was selling on a PER of 10. Templeton estimated its earnings growth at 30 per cent per year. He compared Ito with other supermarket companies, asking what price he would have to pay for a dollar of future probable earnings.

$$\text{Price–earnings to growth ratio (PEG ratio)} = \frac{\text{price–earnings ratio}}{\text{long-term estimate of growth in earnings}}$$

Ito-Yokado   **Safeway**

PER: 10   PER: 8
Est. growth: 30% p.a.   Est. growth: 15% p.a.

PEG = 10/30 = 0.33   PEG = 8/15 = 0.53

Ito-Yokado was cheaper because the growth rate of future earnings is so much higher. However, some caution is needed: is the 30 per cent growth assumption reasonable?

Diversification

Templeton would say that the only people who should not diversify are those who are right 100 per cent of the time; few investors are right more than two-thirds of the time – he included himself in this assessment. As a guideline every investor should have at least ten shares. Those running multi-million dollar portfolios should have many more. Even if you are extremely careful in your share selection you cannot predict the future. A major oil spill, an unexpected technological advance by a competitor or a government dictat can remove half the value from the company. In addition, you may not have spotted serious internal problems when you first undertook the analysis. Thus you must diversify – by company, by industry, by risk and by country.

Templeton was a bottom-up analyst, examining shares at a company level first.

Templeton was a bottom-up analyst, examining shares at a company level first. If that led to a concentration in a particular country that year, then so be it. This concentration may appear to be a comment on the macroeconomic prospects of a country, but it was not intended as such. Regardless of this initial approach Templeton would try to avoid over-commitment to a single country.

He was shocked that so few mutual fund managers diversified by taking a worldwide viewpoint. Apart from being able to find more and better bargains risk can be reduced if your assets are in many nations. A single nation's economy fluctuates, as do single stock markets. Other countries, at the same time, might be in a completely different phase. When the UK is going through a bear market Japan may be having a boom.

Social, Economic and Political Awareness

Templeton spent a great deal of time trying to understand the social, economic and political dynamics of countries around the world. These must be taken into account by investors when estimating future earnings and the risk attached to those earnings – bargains cannot be identified without this.

He had observed first-hand the power of allowing free-enterprise to release the entrepreneurial spirit and witnessed the stifling effect of extreme socialism. This can lead to nationalisation (or even confiscation) from which the investor is unlikely to receive fair value. Controlled economies may also impose price controls and other distortions in the economy that dissuade entrepreneurs from creating wealth.

Templeton looked for governments that set their economies on a path toward capitalism and free markets. On his post-Oxford trip in 1936 he visited India and Hong Kong. Both were very poor, with people dying on the streets. When he returned years later he noticed a dramatic change in Hong Kong, but not in Calcutta; a change he attributed to the difference between enterprise and socialism. The government in India had a tendency to regulate everything so there was little progress; whereas in Hong Kong the government kept its distance, allowing businesses wide latitude. The result was that the standard of living multiplied ten-fold over 40 years in Hong Kong, while it hardly improved at all in Calcutta.

His knowledge of the workings of Hong Kong and China meant that he could see the potential of China as the economic constraints were relaxed on the mainland and the talents of Hong Kong could be put to use among over one billion people following reunification. China would not only gain a sophisti-cated financial centre to speed up progress, but also a cadre of experienced businessmen and women. With hindsight the transformation of China may seem obvious, but in the late 1980s, when Templeton was examining the issue, it was not at all obvious.

His knowledge of Japanese society and character helped him identify its potential for growth in the 1950s: hard work, thrift and social cohesion were there already. He saw all of this long before most western observers – and made a fortune by backing his judgement of the social, economic and political structure of Japan.

When there was deep pessimism in the US in 1990 due to recession, high federal debt and a prime rate at 21 per cent Templeton counted the blessings for the world economy. He predicted that the world would enter the 20 most prosperous years in history because of the collapse of communism and the Berlin Wall. In the following decade the Dow more than tripled.

Clearly, being a good market historian helps you as an investor. Patterns of events do have a tendency to repeat themselves. A new generation of traders overreacts in much the same way as a previous generation. Being able to see the start of a new playing out of an old pattern can allow the investor to jump in at the right moment. When, in 2003, the US consensus was positive, Templeton drew on his much wider perspective to point out some weaknesses. Imbalances (e.g. insufficient saving in the US) were building up in the world economy making the dollar vulnerable; there was a nascent bubble in housing. He said he saw the potential for a 50 per cent decline in stock prices.

Beliefs and Character Traits

Templeton said that the seven character traits presented in Figure 4.1 can be acquired to some degree by any reasonably able person with sufficient desire and self-discipline.

Spirituality and Prayer

He believed that high ethics and religious principles formed the basis for success and happiness in every area of life. His prayer life gave him clarity of mind and depth of insight that were decisive in his success.

Flexibility

It is important to remain flexible and open-minded about the different types of investments you might include in your portfolio. There is no one type of security that is always best. There are good times to buy bonds and good times to buy blue-chip equities, or cyclical companies or other investments. If a particular type of security is currently very popular with investors then it is usually a bad time to hold it. And always keep the flexibility of mind to think that there are times to sit on cash. Holding cash allows you to take advantage of investment opportunities.

If you have an area of investment, say oil shares, that has done well for you in recent years then it may be the time to ask whether this is a good place for you to be in the future. Look around and ask, 'What is depressed in price *today*?' Oil shares may have been bargains two or three years ago, but they may not be now and it would be foolish to stick with them. Look for those securities that performed *worst* in the recent past and assess whether they are now bargains.

Patience

Buying shares with a long-range view in mind requires patience because it frequently takes the market quite a while to catch up and revalue what you've bought. These shares can continue to be neglected for several years. Templeton's prescient purchases of Japanese shares in the 1950s and early 1960s were not rewarded until the late 1960s and 1970s, when, after a long wait, he surged ahead of other fund managers.

Buying things that others have not yet thought about means waiting until the short-term prospects become good. When the near-term earnings start to take off this attracts the attention of those less focused on the long-term, i.e. those traders who respond to things that are staring them in the face – then the prices rise.

Do not switch to current risers.

Even experienced investors find it difficult to stomach periods of underperformance. When it seems like everyone else is making money and your shares are down you can start to doubt the wisdom of your approach. Templeton taught us to expect and accept years of underperformance. Maintain faith in your method; if you have done your homework then eventually you will triumph as the market comes round to recognising the value in your chosen stocks that it previously missed. Do not switch to current risers – if your reasoning and analysis are sound your bargain purchases will pay off better in the long run.

Extensive Friendship Network

Templeton was naturally gregarious, and he built up a wide circle of friends. Many of these friends were very knowledgeable about an industry or a country and he was able to call them if he wanted to know something. He said that he had hundreds of friends with whom he had a first-name relationship in almost every industry and in a variety of nations They were very helpful to him in selecting investments. If he wanted to know something about, say, the car industry in the UK he could pick up the telephone and talk to a friend who has an intimate knowledge of that industry. While we may not have been as fortunate in building up a network of informed friends as Templeton, I think the general principle of making the effort to maintain contact is worth taking on board.

Thought Control

Templeton quoted St. Paul in saying that one of the nine fruits of the Spirit is thought control. It is important for every human being to give a great deal of attention to what is going on in his own mind. He said 'A person is what he thinks, and if you want to be a better person, you have to control what you are thinking … using it for purposes that you believe are worthwhile and admirable.'[7]

His personal techniques of thought control enabled him to concentrate, persevere and work hard. He regarded this discipline within the grasp of everyone. He recommended the crowding out method in which you fill your mind only with good and productive thoughts. That way you will not have room for the others. Try to crowd out feelings of self-centredness, criticism, envy, hatred, covetousness, revenge. Also get rid of time-wasting thoughts that do not relate to your ultimate goals in life. He rarely read novels nor watched much television, saying that he did not have enough time, given all the important things making demands on his life.

---

7. John Templeton quoted in Proctor, W. (1983) *The Templeton Touch*, New York: Doubleday, pp.90–1.

Positive Thinking

Have a can-do attitude. Direct your thoughts and actions to building up rather than tearing down.

> It's very difficult to build a corporation if you're a pessimist. You almost have to be an optimist to build any substantial organization, whether it's a business or a church or a charity. To be successful you have to *expect* success.[8]

Failure is not a defeat, but an opportunity to learn. Even the highly successful Templeton had more than a dozen failed business ventures in his lifetime. The really successful people learn from their mistakes and the mistakes of others.

He told us that as soon as we open our minds in the morning we should think of five things that we are deeply grateful for. This will help set the pattern for your day. You are less likely to suffer from self-pity or loneliness, or believe that you are discriminated against, if your mind is filled with thanksgiving.

Try not to be fearful or negative too often. For the last century those who have been optimistic about the economy and shares have been the winners. While there will be downturns, even crashes, shares will rise over time. Indeed, as the world becomes even more integrated and with greater freedom of enterprise business is likely to bloom.

I leave the last word on positive thinking to Templeton:

> Yes, I would definitely describe myself that way [positive thinker]. I'm so grateful and thankful for

---

8. Ibid., p.93.

the millions of blessings that God gives us, for having been born in this particular time, that I can't see how anybody could be anything except joyous all day long. In addition to that, I do believe that positive thinking is a great help – not only in spiritual growth and human relations, but a help in financial matters and every other activity in life.[9]

However, he never let his positive thinking cloud his rational evaluation of companies based on research and hard-headed comparison of one corporation with another.

Simplicity

Simplicity does not mean foolish or ignorant. It means focus on the essence of an industry or company *after* a thorough gathering and assimilation of information. List the strengths and weaknesses clearly and simply. Don't make it too complicated. Avoid mathematical formulae, and don't go in search of every last detail of every corporation – look for basic principles.

Simplicity extended to his private life, from using an office above a barbers shop when he was a multimillionaire to travelling economy throughout his life.

---

9. Ibid., pp.92–3.

Difficulties and Drawbacks

It is not easy being a Templeton follower. Here are some of the problems:

- It is time consuming and intellectually demanding to gain sufficient knowledge about so many markets and companies around the world.

- Not all of us have the social skills, the position in society or the length of investing career to develop a wide circle of professional friends knowledgeable about firms in other countries.

- The extraordinary discipline Templeton developed is something many of us would aspire to, but are unlikely to achieve because we have other priorities in life, e.g. working 60 hours per week may not be considered a good work-life balance if you have a working partner and children. Also, the extreme thrift habits of Templeton may not be compatible with family demands.

- It takes a lot of nerve to go against the crowd regularly – not all of us are cut out for that.

The Legacy of Templeton

Even if we cannot emulate Templeton in all regards, at least we take away some sound principles:

- When all is doom and gloom, when there is blood on the streets, this is often the best time to be buying. When all is looking bright and it seems easy to make money this is the time to be cautious. Also, be careful in assuming that because the market is down that it has entered bargain territory. For example the fact that UK, European and US shares were lower in 2007 than they were in 2000 did not make them bargains. Tip: take a look at the cyclically adjusted price earnings ratio, CAPE (the price of shares in an index divided by the average earnings per share over the past 10 years) and compare it with its long-running average to judge whether there is real blood on the streets (really low prices relative to earnings prospects) or traders are just howling because of short-term losses. In the past two decades we got used to the authorities bailing out economies and sectors, e.g. banks or car assemblers, and so gradually the fear element in the 'greed and fear' that drives markets was removed, there was always the expectation that the authorities would intervene with low interests rates, etc. and the markets would bounce back. This resulted in a failure for the equity markets to fall to bargain territory – except for short bursts such as a few days in the winter of 2008–09. It has been a very long time since we had PERs in single digits for a significant period, which is the quarry Templeton hunted. Having said that individual shares may be bargains even if the market is merely fairly or over-valued. And if real fear returns we may find ourselves over-whelmed by many bargains.

- Look at countries other than your own for bargains. You do not need to build up familiarity with a long list of countries. A handful will allow you to find a greater number of bargains than if you were purely domestically focused, and be better diversified.

- Estimate a company's value based on a projection of earnings five years into the future. This forces you to focus on the key factors giving the company value, such as strategic position and managerial quality.

- Continually examine the difference between the price of a share currently in your portfolio with its value. Then compare the extent of this difference with potential investments. Buy the best looking alternative if its gap between price and value is significantly greater than the lowest gap in the current portfolio.

- Learn about the political, social and economic developments going on in the world. You could do worse then start by reading *The Economist* and the *Financial Times* regularly.

- Develop the right character traits such as patience, thought control, simplicity, analytical rigour, ethical behaviour, clarity of thought that comes through prayer, and fortitude to withstand years of underperformance.

- Be admirable and generous: 'The only success worth having, you know, is success that reaches out and touches others.'[10]

---

10. Templeton, J.M. and Ellison, J. (1992) *The Templeton Plan*, New York: HarperPaperbacks.

CHAPTER 5

George Soros

George Soros is the most respected of the hedge fund managers investing in broad asset categories, sectors and economies, based on his view of assets being at 'far-from-equilibrium' prices. He has made a fortune for himself and the backers of the Quantum Fund. For instance, he achieved an annual rate of return of nearly 35 per cent over the first 26 years of the fund. A $1,000 investment in 1969 grew to be worth millions by the mid-1990s.

There is so much you can learn from Soros:

- A new way of looking at the behaviour of market prices: they result from a two-way feedback mechanism with participants (e.g. investors) moving prices and fundamentals in response to their (faulty) perceptions, and their perceptions, in turn, formed by market movements – this can help identify bubbles and irrational downward spirals.

- The exploitation of crowd irrationality.

- To act with independence of mind and decisiveness.

Soros sees himself first and foremost as a philosopher. Early in life he developed his philosophy of how people in social structures operate as a group occasionally to lead the economic (or political or social) fundamentals away from a near-to-equilibrium state to a far-from-equilibrium state. His observations and anticipations of financial market movements are but a sub-set of manifestations of his theory of 'reflexivity'. The same philosophical base can be used to describe and analyse, for example, the movement of a society from an open, rule-of-law, democratic form to one increasingly closed and authoritarian. It can also be used to describe and explain individual human interactions such as love and hate, amongst a host of other applications.

He has written a number of books to try to convey the essence of his idea of reflexivity – in which a two-way feedback loop, between the participant's views and the actual state of affairs exists. His amazing life experiences have taught him that individuals do not base their decisions on the actual situation that confronts them. Rather, decisions are based on people's perception or interpretation of the situation. Furthermore, their decisions can change the situation, alter the fundamentals (e.g. the price of houses in a country or the price of dot.com shares). The changes in the fundamentals thus caused are liable to change the perceptions of individuals. And so on.

Because so few people understood the concept properly from his 1980s tracts he would, for a time, describe himself as a 'failed philosopher'. He wanted to be taken seriously, as someone who has important things to say about the way society works, and so persevered with his writing, making it progressively clearer. Then, when his ideas were shown to have considerable explanatory power regarding the underlying causes of the 2008 financial crisis he finally won the recognition he deserved in intellectual, policy-making and market circles. The Nobel-prize winning economist, Joseph Stiglitz said of Soros 'By those economists interested in ideas, I think his work is taken seriously as an idea that informs their thinking'.[1] Larry Summers, former head of Harvard and President Obama's chief economist said: 'Reflexivity as an idea is right and important'.[2] Paul Volcker's view: 'I think he has a valid insight ... an imaginative and provocative thinker ... he's got some brilliant ideas

---

1. Joseph Stiglitz quoted in 'The credit crunch according to Soros', C. Freeland, *Financial Times*, 31 January 2009.
2. Larry Summers quoted in 'The credit crunch according to Soros', C. Freeland, *Financial Times*, 31 January 2009.

about how markets function and dysfunction.'[3] Soros now says
he no longer feels a failed philosopher.

Not only has Soros become famous as the man who
made $1 billion dollars in a few days by betting against the
pound maintaining its high rate against other currencies in the
European Exchange Rate Mechanism (1992), to name but one
financial triumph, but he has become the largest benefactor
promoting open society around the world (donating over $5
billion) as well as a confidant of leading figures, including
President Obama. Not bad for a penniless teenager who had
to dodge Nazi terror, endure communist totalitarian brutalism
and British indifference.

Nazis and Communists

The early experiences of his life were very important in leading
Soros away from conventional thinking about the formation
of prices, political structures or other human constructs and
towards a new theory of the world in which the act of humans
trying to understand and respond with action to the fundamentals they see can cause both the fundamentals to change,
and, when the fundamentals change, the understanding (or
misunderstandings) on the part of the human actors changes.

Soros was born into a Hungarian Jewish family in August
1930. His mother was a loving woman, but very introspective,
delving deeply, taking a highly self-critical, even self-
flagellating, posture. Soros says that he has internalised his

---

3. Paul Volcker quoted in 'The credit crunch according to Soros, C.
   Freeland, *Financial Times*, 31 January 2009.

mother's self-critical attitude. He says that one of the driving forces for him to become a big winner was the need to subdue a sense of being a big loser inside.

His father, Tivadar, was outgoing, gregarious, genuinely interested in other people's fate. While holding these virtues he was very reluctant to reveal anything of himself to others. Soros idolised him. Tivadar had been an ambitious young man, then the First World War broke out. He volunteered and was promoted to lieutenant, but was captured by the Russians and taken to a prison camp in Siberia. He remained ambitious – for a while. He edited the camp newspaper called *The Plank* (it was written by hand and nailed to a plank). He was well respected and was elected prisoners' representative. When some prisoners from a neighbouring camp escaped, the prisoners' representative there was shot dead to set an example and provide a disincentive. Tivadar decided that his best approach was to escape rather than wait to be shot in retaliation for the escape of others.

Tivadar chose 30 people because they had the right mix of skills – carpenter, cook, doctor, etc. – and they broke out of the camp, made a raft and started to float down a river to the ocean. The problem was that the rivers of Siberia flow towards the Arctic Ocean. It took weeks to realise the mistake; then started a long trek across a Siberia in turmoil due to the fight between the Red Russians and the White Russians after the First World War. He witnessed horrendous acts of violence and thereafter greatly valued simply being alive, losing all ambition; wealth and influence were no longer important – he simply wanted to enjoy life. Nevertheless his searing experiences in a chaotic society gave him both key survival skills and an insight into the potential of societies to go through periods of far-from-equilibrium states.

*Soros was chosen because it could be
pronounced in any language and in Magyar it
means 'the one who is next in line'.*

Before George was six the family name had been Schwartz, but those with Jewish names were subject to severe discrimination in Hungary. Tivadar involved the whole family in searching for a new name. Soros was chosen because it could be pronounced in any language and in Magyar it means 'the one who is next in line' – the fact that it is a palindrome also appealed.

Surviving the Holocaust

George Soros was an indifferent student, preferring to concentrate on sports and games (*Monopoly* being his favourite). He was particularly poor at mathematics, but very interested in reading classical philosophy. When he was 13 Soros was walking home from an art gallery when he saw German tanks in the streets – it was March 1944 and the Germans had invaded their Hungarian ally.

George later said that this was the most exciting time of his life. Tivadar quickly recognised that these were not normal times and normal rules did not apply. George says that this was his father's finest hour. He understood that obeying the law was a 'dangerous addiction' and that flaunting it was the only way to survive. With Tivadar as a teacher the Second World War became an advanced course in survival, providing skills for George to use in investment later in the century. The Russian Revolution had taught Tivadar what to do. He acted with decisiveness, obtaining false identity papers for his family, and finding places for them to live or to hide. It was not just his family he helped; he saved dozens of lives. Soros sees this time as the happiest years of his life. It may seem paradoxical that under Nazi rule and when the Holocaust was reaching its height he was so happy, but he was an adventurous 14-year-old who could see the father he adored in command of the situation helping others. Soros says that none of the risks he took as an adult were as great as those he took trying to evade and out-smart the Nazi invaders.

The Soviets

The Russian occupation of 1945 brought a period with some adventures, but mostly drudgery as the communist dead-hand was laid over the country. Living under both Nazi and Communist regimes provided Soros with a healthy respect for the objective aspect of reality. His experiences of living in the far-from-equilibrium conditions of first the German and then the Russian occupation of his country provided insight which played an important role in preparing him for a successful career as a hedge fund manager. Tivadar had the Russian Revolution as his teacher in how to survive and George had the Nazi occupation. Taking all these experiences together George was able to think through his conceptual framework to be able to recognise far-from-equilibrium situations when they arose.

Soros felt restricted under the controlling state of communist Hungary. He also felt that his father's sway over him was excessive. He said to Tivadar that it was not natural for a 15-year-old to think like a 50-year-old and he needed more freedom to grow. His father suggested that he strike out on his own and asked where he would like to go. George said either

England (he had listened to the BBC and was impressed by the British sense of fair-play and objective reporting) or the Soviet Union (to find out the nature of the system they had to live under). Tivadar said he had been to the Soviet Union and could tell him all about that – so he went to England.

London

Soros arrived in London shortly after his seventeenth birthday in September 1947. He had no money and no friends, and discovered a deep sense of loneliness and rejection. He found post-war London austere, aloof and emotionally cold. Distant relatives let him sleep on their couch, but did not welcome him with open arms.

He went from one menial job to another: a swimming pool attendant in Brentford; washing dishes; painting houses. A particular low point, for a young man with a high expectations, was when the headwaiter of a restaurant where he worked said that, given his bearing, one day, if he worked hard, he might rise to be an assistant headwaiter.

Despite some positive steps, such as enrolling on an English course, he felt a downward spiral of brooding despair for a year and a half, which was topped off by a failure to gain admission to the London School of Economics due to his poor English. He felt he had touched bottom. But, he did manage to find within himself some positive thoughts and decided that he could only rise from there. The pain of being penniless and friendless marked him for life. He readily admits that he has a kind of phobia about having to live through it again. And thinks that this is one of the reasons he became so determined to make serious amounts of money.

Instead of university he went to Kentish Town Polytechnic for a while, until in the spring of 1949 he passed the examinations for LSE.

When writing at 78 years old, after explaining in a clear way his reflexivity idea, he drew on his formative years to highlight the differences between near-equilibrium situations and far-from-equilibrium situations. He said that he had grown up in a stable, middle-class environment – a normal near-equilibrium. Then the Nazi terror and the Communist repression had created fear and disequilibrium. This was followed by his experiences as an outsider in England where he could only peer in through the window at a stable, self-contained society. He, more than most, became aware that stability is a commodity that comes and goes.

LSE and Karl Popper

Soros chose to study economics but quickly found it a trial for two reasons: (1) he was poor at maths, and economics was increasingly becoming a mathematical discipline, and; (2) he was more interested in addressing the foundations of economics, such as the assumptions of perfect knowledge, while his teachers preferred algebraic constructs built on such time-honoured assumptions.

The bright spots in his university experience were his encounters with Professor Karl Popper, who supplied inspiring ideas and engaged with Soros seriously.

> Karl Popper ... maintained that reason is not capable of establishing the truth of generalizations beyond doubt. Even scientific laws cannot be verified because

it is impossible to derive universally valid generalisations from individual observations, however numerous, by deductive logic. Scientific method works best by adopting an attitude of comprehensive skepticism: Scientific laws should be treated as hypotheses which are provisionally valid unless and until they are falsified ... He asserted that scientific laws cannot be verified ... One noncon-forming instance may be sufficient to destroy the validity of the generalisation, but no amount of conforming instances are sufficient to verify a generalization beyond any doubt.[4]

The economists' need to maintain the assumption of perfect knowledge on the part of economic actors directly contra-dicted Popper's contention that understanding by humans is inherently imperfect. Yet economists kept trying to create a discipline with generalisations comparable with those of Isaac Newton in physics, resulting in a discipline increasingly convo-luted and mathematical.

Tivadar's experiences of the unexpected and sudden arrival and departure of unforeseen consequences of human thought and action meshed with Popper's emphasis on fallibility.

In rejecting the standard economists' model and influenced by Popper, Soros started developing a framework of human behaviour in which misconceptions and misinterpretations play a major role in shaping the course of history. Market partici-pants do not base their decisions on knowledge alone because biased perceptions have a powerful impact not only on market prices but also the fundamentals that those prices are supposed

---

4. Soros, G. (2008) *The Crash of 2008 and What it Means*, New York: Public Affairs. pp.35–6.

to reflect. Note for now the two influences of biased perceptions – many readers of Soros' work only take on board the first
and thus glibly conclude that he is not saying anything particularly original – the original bit is the second element:

- First element: influencing market prices.

- Second element: influencing the fundamentals those prices
  are supposed to reflect.

(Reflexivity is explained later.)

---

*Soros was fascinated by ideas; he was attracted
by the 'adventure' of ideas.*

Soros was very keen on a career as an original and influential
philosopher, a yearning he carried with him throughout his
life. He wanted to establish human fallibility as an accepted
principle. However, he achieved merely a lower second class
degree, and so an academic career was unlikely. Also another
thinker, Alfred North Whitehead, who wrote *The Adventure
of Ideas*, inspired Soros to use his new perspective in the
practical world of business rather than engaging in a life of
philosophical speculation. Soros was fascinated by ideas; he
was attracted by the 'adventure' of ideas. But, he was wise
enough to realise that when it came to economic or finance
ideas he could learn a great deal more through action than
through contemplation. His thinking led to action which, in
turn, improved his thinking.

A Fancy Goods Salesman and an Arbitrage Trader

High-level thinking jobs were in short supply for lower second class degree graduates, so to make ends meet Soros became a salesman for a company selling items such as leather handbags, souvenirs and cheap jewellery. He would tour around the coastal resorts of Wales in his company car selling to tobacconists and other retail outlets. The job took him very far away from his concept of himself and what he wanted to develop into.

He obtained the *Stock Exchange Yearbook* and wrote to the managing directors of all the merchant banks in London and eventually, in 1954, secured a position at Singer & Friedlander, as a trainee doing various humdrum tasks, which he did badly. He came to settle in the arbitrage section, buying in one market and selling in another, trying to gain a profit from small price differences in the two markets. He was regarded as the fifth wheel in the team (or in any team he had been assigned to) and told that it was unlikely they would find a permanent position for him. He asked if they would have any objection to his looking for work elsewhere, to which he received the depressing reply 'No, you can go with our blessing.' Luckily, a fellow trainee at the firm, Robert Mayer, mentioned that his father's small New York brokerage, F.M. Mayer, was looking for an arbitrage trader on Wall Street.

New York

So, at 26, Soros arrived on Wall Street. He started in international arbitrage, buying securities in one country and selling them in another. There was much American interest in European securities following the formation of the European

Common Market and Soros was engaged in trading these as well as acting as security analyst and salesman.

F.M. Mayer

Soros had a five-year plan. He would work hard on Wall Street, save $500,000, and then return to the UK to pursue his philosophical studies. He was put to work trading European gold and oil shares. This business was given a terrific boost when the Suez crisis dislocated the movement of oil, causing oil stocks to become very active. He was able to use his London connections to obtain shares that could be offered to Americans.

He worked incredibly hard, unable to miss a day's trading – he didn't even take time off to meet his parents off the boat when they arrived to settle in New York. He did not build friendships and became something of a loner. But he was loving it. He developed relationships with some of the leading finance houses and he became increasingly confident, as he made deals with the likes of Morgan Stanley and Warburg. He was well ahead of his five-year plan.

Wertheim

By the end of 1959 he had married Annalise Witschak and, feeling restless at Mayer, decided to move to a much larger and richer firm, Wertheim & Co. At that time European company accounts were opaque, much more so than for US companies. Soros had to estimate true value rather like a detective piecing together scraps of information, such as tax returns. His language skills (speaking good German, French, English as well as Hungarian) permitted him to interview senior managers and gain superior knowledge relative to other European security analysts in New York. He was a path-breaker, being the first to discover a number of companies that went on to great success including Dresdner Bank, Allianz and some pharmaceutical companies.

One of the strengths he discovered in himself was a capacity for self-criticism. He admits that he has made as many mistakes as any investor, but his self-critical posture allowed him to discover them quicker than most and to correct them before too much damage was caused. Soros became a bold, even arrogant person at work, but he remained shy of telling people about his passion for philosophy – he would regularly work evenings and weekends at his philosophical ideas, trying to connect his view of fallibility with historical developments.

Losing European Trade and a Hedge Fund

Following a disagreement with a superior, Soros left Wertheim to join Arnhold & S. Bleichroeder in 1963. He was hired as a broker and asset manager, focused on global research and trading. Unfortunately, that year President Kennedy intro-duced a tax which effectively imposed a 15 per cent surcharge on the purchase of foreign securities abroad. Suddenly, Soros' main activity ground to a halt. For a while he was occupied with selling European securities back to the Europeans, but found himself with less and less to do.

Fortunately, his job was secure, so he switched his attention to philosophy, which he regarded as his main project for three years.

In 1966 Soros refocused on business. He wanted to learn about US securities so he set up a model account with $100,000 of the firm's money. He divided the money into 16 parts. Each part was invested in a company's shares he thought promising. He wrote short memos explaining his reasons for purchase and followed up with monthly reports reviewing the portfolio and discussing developments. He was trying to get a handle on growth rates, risk and return, and how to maximise portfolio returns. Not only was he developing a new business, but also teaching himself how to invest. He was forced to emerge from his philosophy-writing vacuum and come into contact with the investment community. When he tested his investment ideas on a few investors he got a good response.

From the model account emerged a small investment fund called First Eagle Fund in 1967, with Soros serving as manager. The fund, established as a mutual fund, had $3 million in capital. This was followed by the Double Eagle Fund in 1969 ($4 million of capital). Set up as a hedge fund, this allowed Soros more latitude in investment strategies and tools (e.g. selling short, use of leverage).

It was the Double Eagle Fund that allowed Soros to bridge his philosophical musings with investment practice. Here, he could elaborate his concept of boom and bust reflexivity. At last, his philosophy took on a practical application, which he found very exciting.

As the two funds grew a potential conflict of interest arose. Arnhold & S. Bleichroeder, as a broker, was a firm that recommended courses of action to its clients, such as the purchase of a particular share. At the same time it was running funds. Unscrupulous brokers who also run investment funds have been known to encourage clients to buy shares with the simple intention of hyping and artificially forcing up the value of shares they had previously bought for their funds. The Securities and Exchange Commission had safeguards to minimise the potential conflicts of interest and Soros knew that Arnhold & S. Bleichroeder could not continue to run a fund as well as its main business as a broker. He reluctantly chose to leave and set up a fund on his own. He liked the people at Arnhold & S. Bleichroeder, but the attraction of receiving all of the management fees rather than merely a fraction, on top of the SEC's concerns, encouraged him in 1973 to set up Soros Fund Management.

Soros Fund Management and the Quantum Fund

The entire staff at Soros Fund Management (SFM) consisted of Soros, Jim Rogers as a junior partner and two secretaries, located in a two-room office in Manhattan. The shareholders of Double Eagle were offered the options of staying with Arnhold & S. Bleichroeder or going with SFM. Double Eagle had grown to $20 million, and $13 million of that transferred to SFM. Some other investors joined 'The Soros Fund' so that within a year it contained just over $18 million.

He called the fund Quantum, in homage to Heisenberg and his uncertainty principle.

Soros did not want his name to be prominent and so he called the fund Quantum, in homage to Heisenberg and his uncertainty principle which had undermined the concept of causality in physics and alluded to notions of fallibility, reflexivity and incomplete determinism – it also incorporated the idea of a sudden and large increase in values.

Most of the investors were wealthy Europeans – individuals rather than institutions. Indeed, over the next few decades Soros' funds were held by a remarkably small number of people – never more than 1,000 in total – despite the value of the later funds being worth tens of billions. He never went out to seek shareholders and the fund issued few additional shares. It simply grew internally. As he says, if you compound at around 40 per cent you grow rather quickly.

The partnership with Rogers was very productive; he is one of the few people who understand his concepts of dynamic two-way interactive change in markets and investor perceptions. Rogers was highly regarded by Soros as an exceptional analyst and very hard working.

They invested in shares, bonds, currencies, commodities and anything else that seemed a good bet. They went long and short and leveraged to the hilt. When investing in shares they would borrow 50 per cent of the amount put in. When it came to bonds they would borrow a lot more. For $1,000 of the fund's capital they could buy at least $50,000 worth of long-term bonds. They also sold shares and bonds short after borrowing them from other institutions. Generally they were able to buy them back later at less than what they were sold for.

Soros Fund Management was entitled to 20 per cent of annual profits as a performance fee plus 1 per cent of all assets under management. Most of these fees went to Soros and so he became very wealthy.

He worked incredibly hard, rising at 5 a.m. and going to bed exhausted at 9 p.m. Within five years the fund had reached $100 million, but Soros was not enjoying it. He was totally absorbed in his work and found it extremely painful. The day-to-day stress, particularly with the short selling, was enormous. It got so bad that he likened the fund to a sort of parasite of his body. He said he felt that he had his nerve endings in the fund. So, even though the fund had made him very rich (around $25 million), he was so unhappy he was close to breaking point. He decided to pull back from the fund while remaining in overall charge and making the big decisions. This allowed more time for other things, including travel and book reading.

As the business grew Soros recognised the need for more staff, but Rogers was very reluctant to admit more – he liked the intimacy with Soros and did not want to admit any outsiders. When they could not agree on the need for more people (and on the need for treating those that were hired in a less critical and unforgiving way) Soros decided to break up their partnership. This was in 1980. By September 1981 Soros had farmed out most of the capital of Quantum Fund to other managers, with Soros acting as supervisor rather than active manager.

However, Soros found it difficult to find managers he could trust (or perhaps he could not let go) and so re-entered the fray as a manager in 1984. Stanley Druckenmiller was drawn to Soros after he had read his book *The Alchemy of Finance* in 1987. Druckenmiller had found the book intellectually stimulating and they discussed some of its ideas. In 1988 Druckenmiller took charge of the macro investing. Soros was still the boss, but was increasingly absent because he was involved in assisting the creation of open societies in Eastern Europe, Russia and China. Eventually Soros and Druckenmiller settled down to a coach-and-player relationship. Druckenmiller and the other managers would go to Soros for advice and to bounce ideas off him. By now half of the profit of the management company was reserved for the management team.

Breaking the Bank of England

In 1992 sterling was part of the European Exchange Rate Mechanism (ERM), which allowed currencies to fluctuate against each other, but only by a small amount. With the collapse of the Soviet Union and the reunification of Germany the ERM was thrown into what Soros describes as dynamic disequilibrium. For political reasons the East German currency was permitted to be exchanged for the deutschmark at a very high rate. This, together with a large injection of capital from West Germany to East Germany (much of it government deficit spending) created strong inflationary pressures within the German economy.

The Bundesbank, being a thoroughly independent central bank, was obliged to counteract the extra inflation by pushing up interest rates. Much of the rest of Europe, the UK in particular, was still in recession; high interest rates were totally inappropriate for them. By following a tight monetary policy the Bundesbank could no longer serve as the anchor of the ERM. That shift resulted in the ERM moving from near-equilibrium to dynamic disequilibrium.

At the same time the politicians were talking about establishing a common European currency. This threatened the existence of the Bundesbank. As Soros observed there is a strong imperative within organisations for survival. The Maastrict Treaty was seen as a threat to the very existence of the Bundesbank and its people did not like this.

There were three causes of conflict. First, monetary policy in Germany needed to be tighter than the rest of Europe. Second, the Bundesbank thought the German government were pursuing an excessively loose fiscal policy. Third, the Bundesbank was fighting for its survival. In Soros' view, the most important of the three conflicts was the third. It was also the least understood.

Soros listened to a speech given by the President of the Bundesbank in which he stated that he thought investors were making a mistake to think that the European Currency Unit (ECU) would be a basket of fixed currency rates. Soros thought he was alluding to the weakness of the Italian lira. He asked the president after the speech whether he liked the ECU as a currency: 'He said he liked it as a concept but he didn't like the name. He would have preferred it if it were called the mark. I got the message. It encouraged us to short the Italian lira, and, in fact, the Italian lira was forced out of the exchange rate mechanism shortly thereafter. That was a clear sign that sterling was also vulnerable.'[5] Soros thought that the Bundesbank was determined to break the Exchange Rate Mechanism (ERM) in order to preserve itself as the arbiter of monetary policy in Europe.

Sterling had entered the ERM at an absurdly high exchange rate. Then German interest rates rose. To stop sterling from falling below the lower boundary set by the ERM as investors sold sterling and bought marks, UK interest rates were raised to try to make holding sterling more attractive. They went to 10 per cent, then to 12 per cent, and finally, a massive 15 per cent at a time of deep recession. These high interest rates were having an oppressive effect on UK consumer demand and company investment. Furthermore the high rate of sterling against the US dollar caused great difficulties for exporters. Soros and Druckenmiller saw the interest rate increases as acts of desperation by the British government. Their position was

---

5. Soros, G. (1995) *Soros on Soros*, New York: John Wiley and Sons Ltd., p.81.

untenable: they could not avoid the devaluation of the pound and the alternative was further output deterioration.

Soros encouraged him to 'go for the jugular'
and raise the stake to around $10 billion.

Druckenmiller explained to Soros his reasons for expecting a significant sterling depreciation, and thought they should take a large position against the pound – putting money into the deutschmark and other strong currencies. The response from Soros was emphatic: if Druckenmiller really believed that sterling was going to fall why was he betting 'only' $2 or $3 billion. Soros encouraged him to 'go for the jugular' and raise the stake to around $10 billion.

Within days sterling was devalued, $1 billion of profit was taken, and Soros was dubbed 'the man who broke the Bank of England' and instantly became world famous. The secret to his success was that he was prepared for a complete shift, a regime change. Other players in the markets were still thinking about the prevailing regime; they found it difficult to contemplate revolutionary change to the same degree as Soros. He had a much greater awareness of the potential for revolutionary change due to his childhood experiences. While others were convinced by the British government's reassurance that the ERM was rock-solid, Soros and Druckenmiller did not trust that all would continue as before.

Reflexivity

To understand Soros' trading triumphs you need to develop a deep understanding of reflexivity. I attempt in this section to explain it:

- We first look at the key assumptions behind the opposing but generally accepted paradigm of classical economics.

- Then I'll discuss the theory behind reflexivity.

- Finally, I'll apply reflexivity to explain how bubbles in asset prices can develop.

Classical Economics

The Enlightenment view of the world is that reality lies there, passively waiting to be discovered. Reason acts as a searchlight to illuminate that reality. Thus, there is a separation between, on the one hand, people's thoughts and understanding of the world and, on the other, the object. The thinking agents cannot influence the underlying reality. Thus in natural science we can explain and predict the course of events with reasonable certainty.

Economic and other social areas of 'study' – Soros does not permit the use of the word 'science' with social disciplines – tried to imitate Newtonian physics and develop 'laws' to describe the fundamental processes. To make their models work in a 'scientific' manner economists would simplify reality by making assumptions, for example, that market participants base their decisions on perfect knowledge, or that supply and demand curves could be taken as independently given (with supply not influencing demand, and demand not influencing supply, except through the classical interaction on the economist's diagram).

For the physical scientists it is obvious that to gain knowledge there must be a separation between thoughts and their objective. The facts must be independent of the statements made about them. So, the Earth will move around the Sun in a fairly predictable pattern regardless of what the observer thinks about the movement. Many economists follow a sequence of logic analogous to the physics model in trying to describe economic outcomes – see Figure 5.1.

Figure 5.1   Classical economics

When we move away from the physical sciences we frequently encounter a problem. In social phenomena it is often difficult to separate fact from thoughts. The decision maker, in trying to make sense of the world, attempts to be a detached observer, but can never fully overcome the fact that they are part of the situation they seek to comprehend. For example, people and human organisations, such as lending institutions, try to understand the underlying facts about the housing market, but in doing so – and in taking action – they influence the reality of the housing supply, demand and prices. Under the classical economics paradigm demand and supply curves are supposed to determine the market price. But, it seems reasonable to suggest that in many cases these curves are themselves subject to market influences, in which case prices cease to be uniquely determined. We end up with fluctuating prices rather than equilibrium.

Another example: It is thought that the markets are on the look-out for a recession looming over the horizon, that they anticipate it. Soros takes a different viewpoint believing that it is more correct to say that markets help to precipitate recessions; that

- markets are always biased in one direction or another; and

- markets can influence the events they anticipate.

For example, it would be difficult to argue that the *reaction* of the financial markets to news coming out of the US residential mortgage market in 2008 did *not* influence events that took us into recession.

Soros' Paradigm

So, the widely held paradigm that financial markets tend toward equilibrium is both false and misleading. Soros contends that, first, financial markets never reflect underlying reality accurately, and, second, that, occasionally, these distortions affect the fundamentals that market prices are supposed to reflect, providing profound insight into both the setting of prices and the movement of underlyings. Market participants' misconceptions, misunderstandings and misjudgements affect market prices and, more importantly, market prices affect the fundamentals.

The economists' classic model does allow for deviations from the theoretical equilibrium, but only in a random manner, and the deviations will be corrected in a fairly short time frame. Soros says that market prices do not reach the theoretical equilibrium point; they are in a continual state of change relative to the theoretical equilibrium.

The role of perceptions is key to understanding reflexivity. Participants in the financial markets have expectations about events. These expectations affect the shapes of both the supply and the demand curves. Decisions to buy or to sell an asset are based on expectations about future prices and future prices are, in turn, contingent on buy or sell decisions in the present.

How can self-reinforcing trends persist if supply and demand curves are independent of market prices?

The assets that are currently rising in price often attract buyers, whereas those that are falling encourage more sales – self-reinforcing trends. Anyone who has spent time in the financial markets becomes aware that reinforcing trends exist. Soros asks rhetorically: How can self-reinforcing trends persist if supply and demand curves are independent of market prices?

The act of thinking by market participants has a dual role. On the one hand, they are trying to understand the situation; on the other, their understanding (or misunderstanding) produces actions which influence the course of events. The two roles interfere with each other. The participants' imperfect

understanding leads to actions and the course of events bears
the imprint of that imperfection.

The term reflexive comes from a feature of the French
language, where the subject and the object is the same. It also
means reflection (not reflexes).

We are all taught to think in terms of events as a sequence
of facts – one set of facts leads to another set of facts, and so on,
in a never-ending chain. However, this is not how the part of
the world affected by humans actually works. The facts are first
subject to the participants' thinking, then the participants' thinking
connects to the next set of facts. As can be seen in Figure 5.2

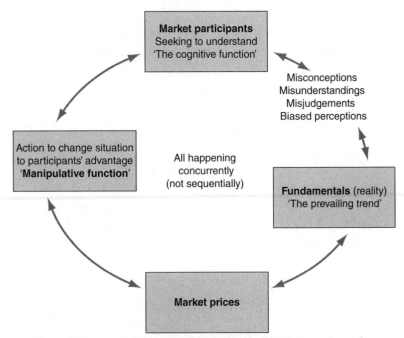

**Figure 5.2   A two-way reflexive connection between perception
and reality**

market participants look at the fundamentals through a fog of misconceptions, misunderstandings and misjudgements. They have biased perceptions. In trying to understand – 'the cognitive function' – they make mistakes. In their biased state they then take action – 'the manipulative function' – and this moves market prices.

So far, so conventional: standard economics allows for the less well-informed actors to make misinterpretations and poor decisions because markets are not perfect, and for them to do so as a herd. Soros' insight is that, rather than a return to theoretical equilibrium as the participants realise their errors (or the errors are merely part of a large set of off-setting random events), the distortions in market prices create distortions in the fundamentals – the 'prevailing trend' itself is altered – and simultaneously the perceptions of participants is altered in response to the fundamentals changing, resulting in an indeterminate outcome, as perceptions feed off the course of events and the course of events feeds off perceptions. We get indeterminacy in both the cognitive and manipulating functions because of the reflexive connection between them.

In most cases the reflexive interaction is relatively insignificant, because there are forces at play that bring thinking and reality together, such as people learning from experience or new evidence coming to light. These are termed 'near-equilibrium conditions' and the impact of reflexivity can be disregarded. In these cases classical economic theory applies, and the divergence between perceptions and reality can be ignored as mere noise.

Occasionally, however, the reflexive interaction can lead to massive market distortions, with no tendency for them to come together – 'far-from-equilibrium conditions' – leading to boom/bust sequences. In this case the theories developed around the assumption of equilibrium become irrelevant. We are presented with a one-directional process in which changes in both perceptions and reality are irreversible (at least for a period). Just as mutation has a role in biology so misconceptions and mistakes play a role in human affairs.

When thinking about Figure 5.2 try to picture the stages presented following one another so quickly that the whole thing becomes a blur of concurrently occurring (and cross-impacting) cognitive function, manipulative function, market prices and fundamentals. People taking decisions make an impact on the situation (the manipulative function), which changes the situation, which is liable to change their perceptions (the cognitive function):

> The two functions operate concurrently, not sequentially. If the feedback were sequential, it would produce a uniquely determined sequence leading from facts to perceptions to new facts and then new perceptions, and so on. It is the fact that the two processes occur simultaneously that creates an indeterminacy in both the participants' perceptions and the actual course of events.[6]

If we take the stock market, for example, we observe that people trade shares in anticipation of future prices, but those prices are contingent on the investor's expectations. We cannot assume that expectations in the market is a form of knowledge in the same way that a physical scientist can predict the motions of the stars – the movement of the stars is truly independent of the expectations of the scientist. In

---

6. Soros, G. (2008), p.10.

the absence of knowledge, participants bring in an element of judgement or bias into their decision making. Thus, outcomes diverge from expectations.

Soros uses 'equilibrium' as a figure of speech. He does not see a stable equilibrium from which deviates the occasional boom/bust process. Equilibrium should be seen as a moving target because market prices get buffeted by the fundamentals they are supposed to reflect.

- Example of a reflexive statement outside of finance: 'You are my enemy'. Whether this is true or not depends on how you react to it. It is indeterminate.

- Example of an act of the manipulative function that failed to achieve the outcome intended: 'President George W. Bush declared a War on Terror and used it to invade Iraq on false pretenses. The outcome was the exact opposite of what he intended: He wanted to demonstrate American supremacy and garner political support in the process; but he caused a precipitous decline in American power and influence and lost political support in the process.'[7]

Bubbles

Soros sees bubbles as consisting of two components:

- a trend based on reality;

- a misconception or misinterpretation of that trend.

---

7. Soros, G. (2008), p.38.

Usually financial markets correct misconceptions, but, occasionally misconceptions can lead to the inflation of a bubble. This happens when the misconception reinforces the prevailing trend. Then a two-way feedback might occur in which the prevailing trend, now puffed up by the initial misconception, reinforces the misconception. Then the gap between reality and the market's interpretation of reality can grow and grow. In maintaining the growth in the gap the participants' bias needs a short circuit so that it can continue to affect the fundamentals. This is usually provided by some form of leveraged debt or equity.

At some point the size of the gap becomes so large that it is unsustainable. The misconception is recognised for what it is, and participants become disillusioned. The trend is reversed. As asset prices fall the value of collateral that supported much of the loans for the purchases melts away, causing margin calls and distress selling. Eventually, there is an overshoot in the other direction.

The boom/bust sequence is asymmetrical. It slowly inflates and accelerates, followed by a more rapid reversal. The stages of a number of examples drawn from recent history are described later.

Soros says that there are eight stages to the boom/bust sequence. We will take the example where the underlying trend is earnings per share ('the prevailing trend') and the participants' perceptions (cognitive function) are reflected in share prices through the manipulative function, i.e. they buy or sell shares pushing the prices up or down. In turn, the change in share prices may affect both the participants' bias and the underlying trend.

Thus, share prices are determined by two factors:

- the underlying trend – EPS;
- the prevailing bias.

Both are influenced by share prices, hence a feedback loop.

In Figure 5.3 overleaf the divergence between the two curves is an indication of the underlying bias. (Soros said that the true relationship is more complex than we are representing here because the earnings curve includes, as well as the underlying trend, the influence of share prices on that trend. Thus the prevailing bias is expressed only partially by the divergence between the two curves – it is also partially already reflected in those curves.)

Stage 1 – no trend recognition

The underlying trend is gently sloping upwards, but is not yet recognised.

Stage 2 – recognising the trend and reinforcement

The trend is recognised by market participants. This changes perceptions about the underlying. The newly developing positive prevailing bias pushes shares along. At this stage the change in share prices may or may not affect the underlying trend, i.e. the level of earnings of companies. If it does not then the reflexive boom does not materialise – the correction in share prices leads to the loss of the underlying trend, i.e. EPS do not continue to rise abnormally.

If the underlying trend is affected by the rise in share prices then we have the beginning of a self-reinforcing process, and we start to move into a far-from-equilibrium state. The underlying trend becomes increasingly dependent on the prevailing bias and the bias becomes increasingly exaggerated.

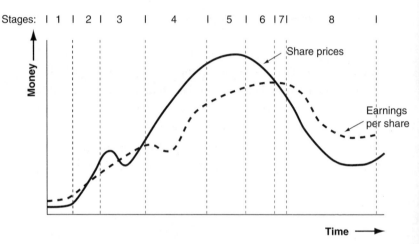

Figure 5.3   The boom/bust model

Stage 3 – testing

Both the prevailing bias and the trend are tested by external shocks – there may be several tests, but here we show only one. Prices suffer set-backs. If the test causes the bias and trend to fail to survive then the potential bubble dies.

Stage 4 – period of acceleration

Survival through the tests make both the bias and the trend stronger. The underlying trend (EPS) becomes increasingly influenced by share prices. Also the rise in share prices becomes increasingly dependent on the prevailing bias. Both the bias and the trend become seemingly unshakable. Conviction is so strong that share price rises are no longer affected by setbacks in the earning trend. Now far-from-equilibrium conditions become firmly established – the normal rules no longer apply.

Stage 5 – unsustainability

Exaggerated expectations reach such a peak that reality can no longer sustain them. This is 'the moment of truth'.

Stage 6 – twilight period

Participants realise that their prevailing bias is high and they lower their expectations. The trend may be sustained by inertia, but is no longer reinforced by belief, so it rises at a lower rate. This is the twilight period or period of stagnation – people no longer believe in the game, but continue to play.

Stage 7 – tipping point

The loss of belief eventually causes a reversal in the trend that had become ever more dependent on an ever stronger bias. When the trend reverses we have the crossover or tipping point.

Stage 8 – catastrophic downward acceleration

A downward trend reinforces the now negative prevailing bias – the gap between share price, as a reflection of expectations, and the EPS levels is now negative. A crash occurs. Eventually the pessimism goes too far and the market stabilises.

Reflexivity Does Not Follow a Predetermined Pattern

Soros emphasises that this is only one possible path resulting from the interplay of a trend and a prevailing bias. Some far-from-equilibrium reflexive situations follow this pattern of initial self-reinforcement, unsustainability of the gap between thinking and reality, followed by collapse, creating an historically significant event. But there are also reflexive interactions that correct themselves before they reach boom proportions, and thus do not become historically significant. There is nothing determinate or compulsory about the boom/bust pattern. The process may be aborted at any time. Also, there are many other processes going on at the same time, e.g. changes in other asset markets, changes in the regulatory environment, changes in the political or social environment. The various processes may interfere with one another leading to boom/bust sequences being hit by external shocks. There may be patterns that tend to repeat themselves in far-from-equilibrium situations, but the actual course of events is indeterminate and unique.

Applying Reflexivity

Stocks or sectors?

There have been times when Soros concentrated his energies and his fund's money on particular shares and other times when he selected entire markets or market segments. He has no particular rule here, all depends on the circumstances.

Trend follower or contrarian?

Despite his independence of mind Soros was very cautious about going against the herd. He says that to do so raises the real risk of getting trampled on. Indeed with initially self-reinforcing, but eventually self-defeating trends, the way to play it is to regard the trend as your friend most of the way. But at inflection points pure trend followers tend to get hurt. So most of Soros' investing is as a trend follower, but what makes him perform exceptionally well is that his theory allows the identification of inflection points before the crowd. Then he can get out of long positions and exploit the downward leg.

Cutting losses or doubling up?

If he is confident in his original thesis then despite something looking as though it is going wrong (perhaps the damage is coming from an extraneous source) he is more likely to increase his position than to sell out.

Case Studies

To reinforce our understanding of reflexivity we will look at four case studies in which Soros made a fortune:

- First, during the conglomerate boom of the sixties he exploited the trend by going with the crowd as they pushed prices to ever more irrational levels and then selling the shares short just before the peak.

- Second, during the real estate investment trust mania of the

1970s, which he predicted and bought into early, to later profitably short.

- Third, the debt crisis of the 1980s caused by over-borrowed developing country governments.

- Fourth, the housing bubble of the 2000s which is a sub-part of a much larger super-bubble that stretches back to the early 1980s.

Case Study 1: The Conglomerate Boom

The conglomerate boom of the 1960s was the first time Soros systematically put into practice his theory. Managements of high-technology defence companies feared a slowdown in sales after the Vietnam War, e.g. Textron, LTV and Teledyne. They used their highly priced shares to buy other companies. By purchasing companies on relatively low price-earnings ratios (PERs) in exchange for shares in themselves (which had high PERs) they pushed up their earnings per share, EPS.

Managers quickly learnt that there are two ways of pushing up EPS and thus the share price, allowing them to raise more capital.

Managers quickly learnt that there are two ways of pushing up EPS and thus the share price, allowing them to raise more capital. The first is to become more efficient and raise organic earnings from existing businesses. The second was to regularly buy companies on low PERs with highly priced shares. The second method became quick and easy if they could rely on their investors continuing to price their shares at a high multiple. For this they needed to convince their investors that the acquired companies would be transformed to faster growing businesses and thus the combined earnings produced should be accorded a high PER based on last year's EPS. Investors were on the lookout for growing EPS but were unable to tell whether the reported numbers were growing because of greater efficiency at acquired subsidiaries or simply because of a continuous flow of low PER-company purchases.

Imagine two firms, Crafty plc and Sloth plc. Both earned £1 million last year and had the same number of shares. Earnings per share on an historical basis are therefore identical. The difference between the two companies is the stock market's perception of earnings growth. Because Crafty is judged to be a dynamic go-ahead sort of firm with management determined to improve earnings per share by large percentages in future years it is valued at a high PER of 20.

Sloth, on the other hand, is not seen by investors as a fast-moving firm. It is considered to be rather sleepy. The market multiplies last year's earnings per share by only a factor of 10 to determine the share price

	Crafty	Sloth
Current earnings	£1m	£1m
Number of shares	10m	10m
Earnings per share	10p	10p
Price to earnings ratio	20	10
Share price	£2	£1

Because Crafty's shares sell at a price exactly double that of Sloth's it would be possible for Crafty to exchange one of its shares for two of Sloth's. (This is based on the assumption that there is no bid premium, but the argument that follows works just as well even if a reasonable bid premium is paid.)

Crafty's share capital rises by 50 per cent, from 10 million shares to 15 million shares. However EPS is one-third higher. If the stock market still puts a high PER on Crafty's earnings, perhaps because investors believe that Crafty will liven up Sloth and produce high EPS growth because of their more dynamic management, then the market capitalisation of Crafty increases and Crafty's shareholders are satisfied. Each old shareholder in Crafty has experienced an increase in EPS and a share price rise of 33 per cent. Also, previously Sloth's shareholders owned £10 milllion of shares in Sloth; now they own £13.33 million of shares.

	Crafty after the takeover
Earnings	£2m
Number of shares	15m
Earnings per share	13.33p
Price to earnings ratio	20
Share price	267p

This all seems rational and good, but shareholders are basing their valuations on the assumption that managers will deliver on their promise of higher earnings growth through operational efficiencies, etc. Managers created special accounting techniques that enhanced the impact of the acquisitions – accounting rules were lax.

Thus was created an 'underlying trend': earnings were rising. Voices initially sceptical about the potential for raised earnings per share were heard less and less. As companies showed accelerating EPS growth rates the multiples assigned to their shares expanded instead of contracting. The success of the pioneers was imitated by other companies. Investors recognised conglomerates as a group and increasingly turned away from valuation based on merit and more towards valuation based on type of company. Even quite ordinary companies could attain high PER multiples simply by going on an acquisition spree. Eventually, high multiples were awarded to companies who merely promised to put their capital to good use by making acquisitions. It became very easy for conglomerates to raise more capital.

Thus we have a 'misconception': that companies should be valued according to the growth of their reported per-share earnings no matter how the growth was achieved. Managers exploited the misconception by using their overvalued shares to purchase companies on advantageous terms, leading to the inflation of their shares even further. Soros calls this a form of equity leverage: selling shares at inflated prices to generate earnings growth (similar to using debt leverage to increase EPS).

If investors had understood reflexivity the misconception could not have arisen because they would have realised that equity leveraging creates something of an illusion. As EPS multiples became outlandishly large there came a point where reality could not sustain expectations. An increasing proportion of investors realised that there was a serious misconception lying behind the boom – but they still continued to play the game.

The managers of the illusion had to make larger and larger acquisitions to maintain the momentum of earnings growth, but beyond a certain point this is impossible. Once share prices started to fall, the decline fed on itself. In a situation of reduced overvaluation of their shares the managers could not make new acquisitions. Now the chickens had come home to roost; the managers had been sweeping all sorts of internal problems under the carpet during the period of rapid external growth – they did not have time for day-to-day management as they created 'earnings growth' a quicker way. Now these problems began to surface. Shareholders became disillusioned and were now open to all the negative news about these companies. Prepared to believe the worst they pushed the share prices down and down.

When Soros recognised the reflexive nature of the boom he took advantage. First, he rode the wave as the acquisitions grew, then he sold short when the price approached the peak.

Case Study 2: Real Estate Investment Trusts (REITs)

These companies, also called mortgage trusts, were subject to special tax provision: if they distributed more than 95 per cent of their income, they could do so free of income tax. This was largely unexploited until 1969 when they really started to take off. Recognising the boom/bust potential, in February 1970 Soros published a research report in which he said that the conventional method of security analysis should not apply to REITs:

> The true attraction of mortgage trusts lies in their ability to generate capital gains for their shareholders by selling additional shares at a premium over book value. If a trust with a book value of $10 and a 12 per cent return on equity doubles its equity by selling additional shares

at $20, the book value jumps to $13.33 and per share earnings go from $1.20 to $1.60.[8]

Say there are 10 million shares to start:

	Book value	Dollar return	Per-share earnings
Originally (10 million shares)	$100m	$12m	$12m/10m = $1.20
New shares (5 million shares sold at $20 each)	$100m	$12m	
Totals following new share issue	$200m	$24m	$24m/15m = $1.60
Book value per share	$200m/15m = $13.33		

Why would investors be willing to pay above book value for new shares? Because of the high yield and the anticipation of per-share earnings growth. The more the premium goes up the easier it gets for the trust to fulfil this expectation. The whole process is a self-reinforcing one. Once it is started, the trust can keep showing growth in EPS despite distributing 95 per cent of all its earnings as dividends. Those investors who buy into the process early enough gain the benefits of a high return on equity, a rising book value, and a rising premium over book value.

It was pointless trying to predict future earnings and (through discounting these) work out a price investors are willing to pay (the conventional approach) because the price investors are willing to pay also determines the future course of earnings. It is important to recognise the self-reinforcing nature of the process. Investors can only try to predict the

8. 'The case for mortgage trusts' research report, written by George Soros, February 1970. Reproduced in Soros, G. *The Alchemy of Finance*, New York: John Wiley and Sons Ltd., p.61.

future course of the entirely, initially self-reinforcing, but eventually self-defeating, process.

He sketched out four stages to the drama that was to unfold over the forthcoming three years or more.

Act One

In 1970 there was pent-up demand for housing and new houses found ready buyers. Because of a shortage of funds going into housing companies and REITs, those that do get funding will achieve high returns. Also, suppliers (builders, labour and materials) are reliable and available in this slack time. Investors are starting to recognise the mortgage trust concept, permitting the creation of many more and the rapid expansion of existing ones. Thus the self-reinforcing process begins.

Act Two

A housing boom begins and bank credit is available at advantageous rates. Mortgage trusts take on higher leverage. The premium of mortgage trusts' share price over book value increases as investors anticipate high returns in a booming housing market. Mortgage trusts take advantage of the high premium to increase in both size and per-share earnings. Many new mortgage trusts are established, as there are no restrictions on entry.

Act Three

Mortgage trusts take a significant proportion of the construction loan market. Competition increases and they take on more risk. Bad loans increase. Eventually, the boom slackens off and housing surpluses appear. House prices decline. Lenders to mortgage trusts panic and demand that their lines of credit be paid off.

Act Four

Investors are disappointed and downgrade the whole investment category. The premium over book value reduces which, in turn, lowers per-share earnings growth. Mortgage trusts go through a 'shake-out' period. Maturity is reached where there are few new entrants, regulations will be introduced and existing trusts will settle down to moderate growth.

Soros' report received a warm welcome from the financial community and it was widely distributed. The few mortgage trusts that did exist at the time of publication became very popular – their share prices doubled within a month or so. A self-reinforcing process got underway. In response to the increased demand many more trusts were established and events generally took the course outlined in his report.

Early in the process Soros had invested heavily in mortgage trusts and took some profits when he saw the amazing response to the report. When it became clear that there was an inexhaustible supply of trusts prices fell and Soros' remaining holdings were caught in the temporary downdraft. He hung on and even increased his positions. After a year or so he sold his holdings with good profits He lost touch with the market for the next few years as he attended to other projects.

> *Most REITs went bust and Soros reaped more*
> *than 100 per cent profits on his short positions.*

Following a re-reading of his report he sold the group short more or less indiscriminately. Then, as shares fell, he continued to sell short, following the market down. Most REITs went bust and Soros reaped more than 100 per cent profits on his short positions. He had made money on both the self-reinforcing stage and the self-defeating stage of the boom/bust sequence.

Case Study 3: The International Banking Crisis of the 1980s

The first two case studies are examples of the use of equity leverage; the international banking crisis, on the other hand, was caused by debt leverage. The story starts with the oil shock of 1973, following which the main international banks experienced large inflows of deposits from oil producing countries. They lent this money to oil-importing countries – petrodollar recycling. In judging the size of loan to grant (and interest rate to charge) lenders estimate the borrower's ability to pay. Many people view the valuation of collateral as independent of the act of lending. This may be a false assumption in many cases – it is possible that the act of lending increases the collateral value.

The sovereign borrowers did not always pledge collateral in the normal sense, e.g. a charge over property, so the international banks had to take a broader view of 'collateral'. They relied on debt ratios to judge creditworthiness. Typical ratios included:

- external debt as a percentage of exports;

- debt service as a percentage of exports;

- current deficits as a percentage of exports.

The act of lending permitted these countries to maintain these ratios at a high level because widespread low interest rates and voluminous lending stimulated the world economy and the developing countries enjoyed strong demand for the commodities they exported. Thus the collateral ratios and the lending were reflexive. This reflexive interaction led Soros to postulate that there would be a slowly accelerating credit expansion followed by credit contraction.

East European countries borrowed, expecting to repay from the products produced by the factories built with the money; South American countries expected to repay their loans from the export of commodities.

For the first few years international lending was very profitable and banks took an eager and accommodating attitude, asking few questions of borrowers. Often the banks did not know how much a borrowing country had borrowed from other banks before they lent to it. Soros noted that there are large personal incentives for bankers to participate in bubbles even if they suspected that a bubble was being blown up. If the banker refuses to lend in what seems like profitable business (at least profits are being reported on an annual basis by many banks before the bad debts start to flow in) he or she is liable to be pushed to the side. There are many other banks anxious to take the bank's place. For bankers, as for many in the financial sector, it is okay for one's career prospects to make bad long-term decisions for the institution, just so long as the rest of the industry is doing the same. As Keynes noted, it is wise to lose by being conventional rather than risk being unconventional.

Thus, even those aware that the international lending boom was getting out of control found themselves obliged to participate or lose their places. There is an important observation here: in a number of situations, even fully informed participants who are smart enough to foresee a bust are not in a position to prevent a boom from developing. Even Soros participated in the real estate investment trusts boom despite predicting an eventual crash. He suggests that we need to learn how to be a participant at the right time rather than abandon the sector.

The lending might have seemed profitable, but, given that most of it was in the Eurodollar market, which is not regulated and therefore minimum reserve requirements are not needed, we do not know if it really was all that profitable even in the early years.

The borrowing countries frequently spent the money unwisely, buying white elephants or armaments. Consumption remained at high levels, while savings withered in the face of low or negative interest rates. The booming economies created more demand for oil. Oil exporters grew even richer and provided even more money to lend.

Prices and wages rose at ever-increasing rates. To counter accelerating inflation interest rates jumped to very high levels (helped along by the Monetarist philosophy). Economies around the world plunged into recession.

The debtor countries were hit by a number of simultaneous adverse movements:

- energy costs rose;

- commodity prices fell;

- interest rates rose;

- the dollar rose;

- worldwide recession resulted.

As a result the ratios measuring their creditworthiness deterio-rated rapidly. Banks became reluctant to lend. When they did muster up the courage to do so they lent on shorter maturities.

By 1982 Mexico was in financial crisis, Brazil was clinging on by using the interbank market to finance its balance of payments deficit.

Case Study 4: The Housing Bubble and the Super-bubble

In the aftermath of the financial crisis of 2007–08 Soros provided explanations for the housing crash. But more than that, he pointed out that the housing problem was but a part of a much larger and more broadly based super-bubble that started in the early 1980s.

Housing Bubble

The US housing bubble followed the course described by Soros in his boom/bust model. Lax lending standards were supported by a prevailing misconception that the value of the collateral for the loans was not affected by the willingness to lend. Loans were packaged up into financial securities and sold on to unsuspecting investors around the world. Those securitised bonds issued in the early stages of the boom showed a low default rate on the underlying mortgages. Credit rating agencies based their estimates of future default rates on the recent benign past – another misconception. As house prices rose the rating agencies became even more relaxed as they rated collateralised debt obligation (CDOs) – instruments that repackage securitised bonds. In trying to perceive future risks and returns all participants failed to recognise the impact that they, themselves, made.

People who had no job and nothing to put down as a deposit on a house were being granted mortgages.

While Wall Street was creating all these weird and obscure financial instruments – and getting fat fees for arranging them – mortgage originators became increasingly aggressive in encouraging ordinary people to take on the responsibilities of a mortgage. The value of a loan as a proportion of the value of a house got higher and higher. Towards the end of the boom people who had no job and nothing to put down as a deposit on a house were being granted mortgages. The attraction of fee income lies at the heart of this. The mortgage arrangers received a fee for arranging the mortgage regardless of what happened to the house owner thereafter; the banks received fees for arranging securitised bonds, and yet more fees for CDOs, and yet more fees for even more complex instruments.

But, all of this was okay, if you believed that the value of homes and thus collateral for the loans, was growing and would continue to grow. This belief, for a while, created its own fulfilment: faith in the housing market led to more loans; the additional demand for housing stimulated by the availability of cheap mortgages led to house prices rising, providing more collateral; confidence in the housing market rose due to the additional collateral; more loans were forthcoming; and so on.

People became dependent on double-digit house price rises to finance their lifestyles. As they withdrew housing 'equity' through remortgages the savings rate dropped below zero. When home owners became over-extended and house prices stopped rising they had to cut back on remortgaging. There was a reduction in demand from both people moving and from people staying put and remortgaging. The moment of truth came in the spring of 2007 when New Century Financial Corp. went into bankruptcy. People started to ask questions: perhaps the value of the collateral for mortgages was not destined to rise forever and was artificially supported by the willingness of lenders to make fresh loans? If they stopped perhaps much of the 'value' in houses would prove to be an illusion?

A twilight period followed when house prices were falling but participants continued to play the game – new mortgages were signed and securitisations created. In August 2007 there was a significant acceleration in downward price movements. Over the next year contagion spread from one segment of the financial markets to another, until Lehman's collapse sparked a further downward lunge.

The Super-bubble

The super-bubble also reached its tipping point in 2007–08. This reflexive process evolved over a period of a quarter of a century. The main prevailing trend was ever-more sophisticated methods of credit expansion, supported by the trend to globalisation and the trend of the removal of regulations with increasing financial innovation.

The prevailing misconception was 'market fundamentalism', which promotes the notion that markets should be free to find their own level with very little intervention by regulators. Market fundamentalism became a guiding principle in the financial system in the early 1980s.

The long-term boom combined three major trends, each of which contained at least one defect.

Trend 1 – Ever increasing credit expansion

The long-term credit expansion was manifest in rising consumer loan-to-value of asset (i.e. house) ratios and the expansion of credit as a percentage of GDP. This trend had been helped along by the authorities' response to any sign of economic downturn or threat to the banking system. Learning lessons from the Great Depression they were quick to stimulate the economy through counter-cyclical lower interest rates or loose fiscal policy, and if anything endangered the banks there would be bail-outs.

After a few years of intervention the participants started to think there was an asymmetry to the risk of credit expansion. If they expand credit (lower lending standards) and things go right, then the lenders are the winners. If they expand and things go wrong, then they will be bailed out by the authorities. This is an example of the moral hazard problem, in which the presence of a safety net encourages adverse behaviour.

High levels of leverage became normal. Indeed, hedge funds and private equity firms thrived on it. Credit terms for auto loans, credit card debt, commercial loans as well as mortgages all reached absurdly easy levels. Japan was another source of credit expansion. During its grindingly long recession it held interest rates near to zero. This encouraged the 'carry trade': international financial institutions borrow in yen and invest the borrowed funds elsewhere in the world at higher yields.

The US was not alone. The love of leverage infected other economies from the UK to Australia.

Trend 2 – Globalisation of financial markets

The process of globalisation of financial markets accelerated with the petro-dollar recycling in the 1970s, but it got a significant boost with Thatcherism and Reaganism in the 1980s. Thatcher and Reagan saw globalisation of financial markets as a useful development because freeing up financial capital to move around the world makes it difficult for any state to intervene, to tax capital or to regulate it because it can evade such moves by transferring somewhere else. Financial capital was promoted to a privileged position. Governments often have to put the aspirations of their people in second place behind the requirements of international capital – we saw this in 2010 with the eurozone financial crisis as governments desperate to impress the financial markets with their stewardship of the economy cut budget deficits. The market fundamentalists, who dominated political and financial thinking in the quarter century until the 2007 crisis, thought that taking our lead from the markets was a good thing.

According to the market fundamentalists, globalisation was to bring about a level playing field. In reality the international financial system ended up in the hands of a consortium of financial authorities answerable to the developed countries. The whole system has favoured the US and the other developed countries at the centre of the financial system, while penalising the developing economies at the periphery. The 'Washington consensus' (IMF, World Bank, etc.) sought to impose strict market discipline on individual less-developed countries if they run into difficulties. But when the western financial system is threatened the rules are bent.

Furthermore the US has the benefit of the dollar being the main international reserve currency, accepted by central banks around the world – they would often invest current account surpluses in US government and agency bonds. This permitted the US to intervene in markets to counter its downturns and financial crises – inflating credit – while other countries were forced to live within their means. Also, it was safer to hold assets at the centre, and thus the US sucked up the savings of the world as US consumers went on a spending spree. Perversely, capital flowed from the less-developed world to the US.

Trend 3 – Progressive removal of financial regulations and the accelerating pace of financial innovation

Between the end of the Second World War and the early 1980s banks and markets were strictly regulated. President Reagan, however, would refer to the 'magic of the marketplace' especially after market fundamentalism received a significant fillip from the manifest failures of communism and other forms of state intervention. An amazing array of new financial instruments were invented, and many were widely adopted. The more complicated the financial system became the less participants and regulators could understand what was going on.

Periodic financial crises over the quarter century served as tests of the prevailing trend and the prevailing misconception.

Periodic financial crises over the quarter century (such as Long Term Capital Asset Management, the dot.com bubble crash, the 2001 terrorist attack) served as tests of the prevailing trend and the prevailing misconception. When these tests were passed, the trend and the misconception were reinforced. Progressively, in an atmosphere of *laissez-faire,* the authorities lost control of the financial system and the super-bubble developed.

The US housing bubble brought the super-bubble to a point of unsustainability – both the trends and the misconceptions became unsustainable; then a tipping point was reached for both bubbles, with the sub-prime crisis acting merely as a trigger that released the unwinding of the super-bubble.

The flaw in the market fundamentalist view is that just because state intervention is subject to error does not mean that markets are perfect.

The cardinal contention of the theory of reflexivity is that all human constructs are flawed. Financial markets do not necessarily tend towards equilibrium; left to their own devices they are liable to go to extremes of euphoria and despair. For that reason they are not left to their own devices; they have been put in the charge of financial authorities whose job it is to supervise them and regulate them ... The belief that markets tend towards equilibrium is directly responsible for the current turmoil; it encouraged the regulators to abandon their responsibility and rely on the market mechanism to correct its own excesses.[9]

Philanthropy

We cannot leave an account of George Soros' work without noting his enormous contribution to societal improvement throughout the world. Until he was middle-aged Soros openly disparaged philanthropy, but by the time he was in his 60s he really threw himself into it, giving away over $500 million.

Soros called his first foundation the Open Society Fund in honour of Karl Popper and his ideas. It focused on aiding the formation of open societies where they did not yet exist and helping currently open societies fight their enemies.

In my philosophy, open society is based on the recognition that we all act on the basis of imperfect understanding. Nobody is in possession of the ultimate truth. Therefore, we need a critical mode of thinking; we need institutions and interests to live together in peace; we need a democratic form of government that ensures the orderly

---

9. Soros, G. (2008), pp.94–104.

transfer of power; we need a market economy that provides feedback and allows mistakes to be corrected; we need to protect minorities and respect minority opinions. Above all, we need the rule of law. Ideologies like fascism or communism give rise to a closed society in which the individual is subjugated to the collective, society is dominated by the state, and the state is in the service of a dogma that claims to embody the ultimate truth. In such a society there is no freedom.[10]

Some of the projects he has supported include:

- a loan guarantee scheme for thousands of black South Africans during the apartheid era;

- scholarships to Eastern European dissidents and organisations, e.g. Solidarity in Poland;

- promoting democracy and open society in the Soviet Union before its collapse;

- school construction, building communities and civil society in Albania;

- supporting Human Rights Watch;

- printing millions of textbooks in Russian;

- sponsoring writers and youth leaders in Hungary;

- reform of early childhood education in more than 30 countries;

- retraining of thousands of communist military officers for civilian life;

---

10. Soros, G. (1995), pp.112–13.

- linking Soviet bloc universities to the internet;

- backing international peace initiatives in the Balkans;

- financing the Central European University;

- helping the Ukrainians to develop their economic reform programme;

- financial assistance to Macedonia.

Difficulties and Drawbacks of Soros' Approach

It is very difficult to identify a far-from-equilibrium situation that is likely to continue to expand and allow you to benefit from exploiting the irrational up-swing. It is equally difficult to establish, before the event, the point at which the participants become disillusioned and the process goes into reverse. Even Soros misjudged a number of asset price directions in 2008 (described in his 2009 book). Many embryonic far-from-equilibrium trends simply fizzle out before they can be properly exploited. Others, even though well-established, are hit by other large events that interfere with the idealised pattern of boom and bust, which means that the trend you thought was predictable turns out to be very unpredictable.

At various points in his career Soros found himself unhappy with the worry and the workload; there were even times when he was near to nervous breakdown. With these macro-plays you need to be close to the market watching for the moment to strike, to take your profits, to switch to shorting or simply to close positions before you lose too much. This edge-of-the-seat type investing is in contrast to the other investors in this book who, while they work hard to analyse a company before purchase, can, to a large extent, relax for a few years while the rest of the market catches up with them and re-rates the share. Of course, all shares in the portfolio need to be monitored to ensure that they still meet the investing criteria, but this does not require the same intensity and timing-dependence that a Soros-type position might need.

Soros uses a lot of financial gearing – not something the rest of us can or should attempt.

Soros uses a lot of financial gearing – borrowing as well as purchasing instruments such as futures on margin. This is not something the rest of us can or should attempt. For most of us the financing facilities are simply not available and for all of us we really need to know what we are doing if we are going to leverage up our positions. It requires so much skill to avoid losing everything in a few days of trading that most of us should stay clear.

Having said all these negative things we can still all take away a number of insights from Soros' thinking:

- Far-from-equilibrium situations exist and it makes sense to learn how to recognise them and position ourselves so that we do not suffer too badly – and can perhaps even exploit the situation. For example, the housing bubble of 2004–07 is plain for all to see with hindsight. Those people who understood Soros' message beforehand might have been able to save themselves from a blunder – or even made profits out of the folly of others. A similar disaster might have been averted/exploited in the equity markets in 1997–2000.

- Take a global perspective: there are many asset classes that you can invest in, and there are many economies in the world. Being less parochial and more in tune with opportunities worldwide could pay dividends. If an exploitable far-from-equilibrium situation is not brewing in Europe this year perhaps it is in America. If commodities are not experiencing a two-way reinforcing feedback then perhaps Chinese equities are.

- We should all be more cautious in accepting the conclusions of those economists who think in conventional equilibrium terms.

In Conclusion

The failed philosopher became one of the most successful men of his generation; not only an esteemed philosopher and economist, but a towering figure in the world of finance respected both for his wealth (many billions) and his intellectual leadership. As if this were not enough he had the heart to use his money and position to improve the lives of millions. He is so well respected and is on first name terms with so many leading figures on the world stage that he has earned the sobriquet as the only man in the United States who has his own foreign policy and can implement it.

When he was asked how he would like his work to be summarised he pointed to the three aspects of his working life: as a speculator in financial, philanthropic and philosophical matters. He succeeded brilliantly, not just as a speculator in these, but as a creative force in all three areas.

CHAPTER 6

Peter Lynch

Until his retirement in 1990, Peter Lynch was renowned as the best-performing fund manager. He achieved this status whilst acting as the portfolio manager of Fidelity's Magellan Fund. During the years from 1977 to 1990, he achieved an annual rate of return of 29.2 per cent, turning a $1,000 investment 13 years later into $28,000. His fund performed consistently, beating the US stock market in all but two of his 13 years at the helm. The asset base grew from $18 million to $14,000 million, making it the largest in the world, and attracted over 1 million shareholders by the time he decided to quit. At the age of 46, he chose to spend more time with his wife and daughters and doing charitable work. (This is the same age at which his own father, a mathematics professor then senior auditor, had died. A memory which may have motivated his decision to stop his workaholic habits.)

When looking at an investment, Lynch seeks a particular combination of characteristics. Some of these characteristics are common to some of the other investors in this book, e.g. a strong, competitive business with financial strength; others are peculiar to Lynch. He liked to favour the best-performing company in an unpopular industry. He is strongly of the opinion that small, private investors can have consid-erable advantages over professional fund managers, and can out-perform them, so long as they do their research and stick to what they know. For Lynch, investing is not complicated. If the company analysis you are undertaking starts to get too complicated, forget that company and move on to the next share.

There is so much you can learn from Lynch:

- The value of everyday experience in leading you to some great investments – if you keep your eyes open.

- To have faith in the dedicated amateur investor who can frequently out-perform the so-called professional.

- Look for niche companies – small, aggressively-run companies offering fast but not super-fast growth in earnings.

- Place money in shares with the potential to be at least 10-baggers (1,000 per cent rise)

The Beginning

Lynch grew up in an era when everyone remembered the depression and distrusted the stock market, saying, 'Never get involved in buying shares, it's too risky. You'll just lose all your money.' However, after the death of his father, Lynch did some part-time caddying at an exclusive local golf course. Listening to the golfers, he received an insight into the investment world, and began to realise that the stock market could be a place to make money. He made his first investment in 1963 at the tender age of 19 in Flying Tigers Airlines, an air freight company into which he had done some research. He bought the stock for $7 a share, and two years later, the price had risen to $32¾. This was his first multi-bagger, which enabled him to pay his way through an MBA course at Wharton, and gave him an enduring appetite for big-baggers. It had proved to him that big-baggers existed, and he wanted to go in search of more.

Education Versus Experience

Lynch first studied at Boston College, eschewing science, mathematics and accounting, studying instead history, psychology and political science. He later viewed the choosing of shares as an art rather than a science, feeling that a logical commonsense approach, rather than mathematical precision, was the key. He thought that the people who like to rigidly quantify everything suffer from a big disadvantage. Investing simply does not require complex mathematics. All the maths needed, such as that General Electric has a few billion of debt and produced profits last year of x-amount, we all got before we were 16. Rather than maths, Lynch regards logic as the subject that is most helpful when it comes to selecting shares. Logic helps you see the illogic of much of what takes place in the equity markets. 'Actually Wall Street thinks just as the Greeks did. The early Greeks used to sit around for days and debate how many teeth a horse has. They thought they could figure it out by just sitting there, instead of checking the horse. A lot of investors sit around and debate whether a [share] is going up, as if the financial muse will give them the answer, instead of checking the company.'[1]

While at college he continued part-time caddying. One golfer he caddied for was D. George Sullivan, the President of Fidelity, and this connection paid off when he asked Sullivan for a summer job at Fidelity. He was given the job, against stiff competition, and was put to work researching companies and writing reports. He learned how to examine a company's business in some depth. This experience in the real world made him question the value of his MBA course at Wharton. 'It seemed to me that most of what I learned at Wharton, which was supposed to help you succeed in the investment business, could only help you fail ... Quantitative analysis taught me that the things I saw happening at Fidelity couldn't really be

---

1. Lynch, P. with Rothchild, R. (1989) *One Up On Wall Street: How to Use What You Already Know to Make Money in the Market*, Simon & Schuster, p.32. Reprinted with permission.

happening. I also found it difficult to integrate the efficient market hypothesis … It also was obvious that the Wharton professors who believed in quantum analysis and random walk weren't doing nearly as well as my new colleagues at Fidelity, so between theory and practice, I cast my lot with the practitioners … My distrust of theorizers and prognosticators continues to the present day.'[2]

However Lynch did gain some useful knowledge from Wharton, and also met his future wife there. During his service in the army, 1967–69, he picked up so-called hot tips from friends while home on leave, only to find that they were not all so hot as promised. He then learnt the hard way that shares could go down as well as up.

Fidelity

Lynch then returned to Fidelity on a permanent basis as a research analyst. By 1974 he was director of research, and in 1977 the momentous decision was made to put him in charge of the newly enlarged Magellan Fund. Started in 1963, by 1966 this fund had been worth $20 million, but the crisis of the early 1970s and customer redemptions meant that the fund was reduced to $6 million by 1976. Merging it with another fund gave it a viable size, and this was the $18 million Magellan fund for which Lynch first took responsibility. Cannily the directors of Fidelity gave Lynch free rein in his selection of shares, and their confidence in him was amply rewarded, with the Magellan Fund becoming the best performing fund in the world.

---

2. Ibid., pp.34–5. Reprinted with permission.

Problems for the Professionals

For a fund manager, Lynch is astonishingly scathing about his profession. His number one rule is to stop listening to the professionals! He is convinced that ordinary people 'using the customary 3 per cent of the brain' can perform just as well, if not better, than the average 'expert'. He really believes that there are a lot of dumb investing decisions made by those who are paid large salaries and bonuses to look after other people's money. On the other hand, the amateur has many built-in advantages that could lend to market out-performance – and out-performance of the professionals.

---

*The professionals face a number of constraints
that the amateur can avoid.*

The professionals face a number of constraints that the amateur can avoid. There are social and political obstacles stopping fund managers being different from the crowd. If they take a chance and it turns out badly then they will be blamed – it is better for them to go along with the crowd. Then, there are all the institutional rules and regulations that prevent rational investing:

- They are restricted to investing in only certain types of share. Committees may create lists of companies for the manager to choose from. If the list contains dynamic and exciting companies then that is fine, but too often only those that satisfy all 30 committee members are included. Thus they usually exclude the exciting young small company that has found a very profitable niche. Just as no great symphony was ever written by committee, no great portfolio has ever been created by one. The committee members hardly know the firms they are excluding or including. They certainly have not visited the companies or investigated their future potential.

- They cannot invest a significant fraction of the fund in a handful of outstanding bargains but have to spread the fund very thinly across the market investing only a small percentage in any single share.

- They are limited to buying only highly capitalised companies. Because of the amount they are investing they have to purchase shares in sizeable companies. They like to buy only those shares with high liquidity.

Whilst admitting that there are some exceptional fund managers, the majority are 'run-of-the-mill fund managers, dull fund managers, comatose fund managers, sycophantic fund managers, timid fund managers, plus other assorted camp followers, fuddy-duddies and copycats hemmed in by the rules'.[3]

The Oxymorons

Lynch and Warren Buffett use this term to describe professional fund managers, who they think fail to qualify as investors as they understand the word. What is it that these people do wrong? Why do they perform badly compared to the stock market or capable and industrious amateur investors? Lynch observes that the profession has an unwritten law that states that it is okay to fail in a commonly accepted conventional way, but that you will lose your job if you try to be unconventional

---

3. Ibid., p.40. Reprinted with permission.

in order to out-perform and then fail. Those caring about job security gravitate towards 'acceptable', safe holdings, not daring to buy any out-of-the-ordinary shares. If they stick to the conventional way of doing things, e.g. just invest in the blue-chips solid shares that have advanced well in the recent past then if they suffer a reversal they will not be blamed because (a) other conventional thinkers (e.g. a boss) will not condemn the purchase of such solid 'good' companies as say IBM or Procter & Gamble, and (b) because they are just one of hundreds of managers to suffer in the downward movement. Their bad decision is lost amongst the herd's bad decision.

Thus, for most fund managers it is important not to look bad if you fail. So, when faced with a choice of buying into an unknown company with a chance of making an unusually large profit and the virtual guarantee of slightly underperforming a benchmark index by buying an established company, the incentives within the fund management industry are such that most managers would select the latter: 'they don't buy Wal-Mart when the stock sells for $4, and it's a dinky store in a dinky little town in Arkansas, but soon to expand. They buy Wal-Mart when there's an outlet in every large population center in America, fifty analysts follow the company, and the chairman of Wal-Mart in featured in *People* Magazine ... By then the stock sells for $40.'[4] Unconventional action is possible for private investors, but does not come naturally to fund managers who know that a poor result can ruin a career – mediocrity is the order of the day.

Lynch himself was fortunate enough to be in a position closer to that of an amateur investor than a professional fund manager, in that he was given freedom to buy any and all

4. Ibid., p.44. Reprinted with permission.

kinds of shares, and not forced to adhere to any particular investment approach or a restricted list of companies. Even as the Magellan fund expanded, Lynch continued to invest in his 'niche' companies, with them forming a large proportion of the 1,400 shares in the fund.

Advantages for the Amateurs

The amateur investor is free from any list of rules that make life so difficult for the professionals and he is able to buy into small and medium-sized firms offering the greatest percentage gains, rather than diversify into poorly understood shares. He need only own a few shares; he can take time to understand an industry and look for exciting new developments; he doesn't have to explain to a committee why or what he is buying or selling; he doesn't have to compete with other investors or publish his results on a quarterly basis. In Lynch's judgement the amateur that concentrates on the study of the companies in an industry he or she understands can out-perform 95 per cent of professional fund managers.

The private investors' edge comes from the knowledge they are able to accumulate about specific companies and industries. They are able to observe great growth prospects long before the professionals get to hear about them. Investors can first encounter 10-baggers quite close to home. The average person comes across a good investing prospect two or three times a year just by being out and about. Lynch is a great believer in getting investment ideas directly from experience, and one of his favourite sources is the Burlington Mall, a huge shopping centre near his home town. This is where Lynch – and any amateur investor could easily do the same in their own patch – browses through the 160 plus retail enterprises. He thinks going through the Mall is a great form of fundamental analysis where the investor can see a long line of potential investments all neatly arranged side by side for the convenience of shares shoppers. This is a far more valuable way of spending time than attending investment conferences.

The core information that is really useful to know about a company is available to the private investor, especially so in the age of the internet. Company reports are usually available online together with a mass of other information on the company. There are brokers' reports, online chat rooms as well as the opportunity to meet the directors and managers at company general meetings.

Lynch says his best investments did not come from office conversations with CEOs, financial analysts or colleagues but are stumbled upon in everyday life. One of his big winners was Taco Bell when it was a small company – he was impressed with their burritos. Another was La Quinta Motor Inns, which he was alerted to by somebody working for the rival Holiday Inn. Apple computers was another triumph – his children had one at home. And at Dunkin' Donuts what started him thinking was their great coffee. These initial encounters are obviously not sufficient to buy the shares but they do provide a lead to be developed.

Share Categories

Lynch recognises six categories of companies, slow growers, stalwarts, cyclical, asset plays (plenty of unrecognised value in the balance sheet), turnarounds and fast growers (or niche shares). While his portfolio encompassed all categories, his favourite category is niche companies.

Slow Growers

These are companies which, while they might once have started out as fast growers, ran out of steam, lost their momentum, reached market saturation, or just get complacent and tired. Most, if not all, industries slow down in time, but these slow growers do have one advantage; they pay dividends. This can be attractive to the amateur investor, as he or she receives some income, but is not taking too much risk. Dividend payments often attract investors, and cash piles up in the company, enabling it to finance expansion when needed, or pay extra dividends out if the company runs out of ideas for future growth.

Stalwarts

These are usually well-established, multi-billion dollar companies, household names whose days of fast growth are behind them, but are still performing and advancing well. They offer the investor a buffer in times of recession, because they sell the type of goods that continue to sell in recessions, e.g. cornflakes (Kellogg's), dog food (Ralston Purina), and drinks (Coca-Cola). According to Lynch these stalwarts should provide you with a growth of 10–12 per cent, but you are unlikely to double or treble your money unless you hold onto the shares for a fair amount of time – ten years at the least.

Lynch kept some of these slow growers and stalwarts in his portfolio for protection in hard times, but his main focus was on shares which could offer good, and sometimes even spectacular returns.

Cyclicals

These are companies whose sales and profits fluctuate regularly, but not entirely predictably. In growth industries, business keeps expanding, but in cyclical industries, business expands and contracts repeatedly. Industries supplying governments can be cyclicals, as their success is dependent on the whim of transient politicians. Car manufacturers, airlines, tyre, steel and chemical companies are all cyclicals. In times of recession, the cyclicals suffer, and consequently so do their shareholders. As the recession ends, and the economy flourishes, the cyclicals prosper: when the economy is thriving, people have the money and incentive to buy new cars, or go on holidays. However Lynch thinks the cyclicals are the most misunderstood shares. Timing is everything, and if you get the timing wrong and hold the shares for too long, or buy the shares too late, you will lose money.

Turnarounds

These are companies which have performed disastrously, but somehow, against all expectations, try to make a comeback. Lynch made major financial gains on some of these, but also lost money on many others that he wishes he hadn't bought. Turnarounds, if they work, make up lost ground really quickly. Also their performances are not correlated with the general market as much as most other types; thus you can make money even in a sideways or downward market. Turnarounds come in different varieties: General Motors and Royal Bank of Scotland are examples where the turnaround is dependent on government assistance; BP is victim of the accidental oil spill in the Gulf of Mexico; Toys 'R' Us was a good company trapped inside another far less successful company, that prospered when it struck out on its own. Turnarounds then are companies which have great potential, but for reasons not necessarily of their own making are brought low.

The Niche Companies

These were Lynch's preferred investments, small aggressively-run companies offering growth of at least 20 per cent per year. This is where you find the 10- to 40-baggers, and even the 200-baggers. If you get things right in this area one or two of these can make a career. Lynch looks for companies which are strong in their balance sheets and profits while they are growing. The difficult thing to figure out when valuing them is when the growth will fall to more pedestrian levels. This is where the amateur can have a distinct advantage over the professional, who dares not take the initiative and make the first move – they wait for someone else to take the plunge. Wall Street analysts and managers all watch each other, thereby losing out by jumping on the bandwagon too late. Dunkin' Donuts was a 25-bagger between 1977 and 1986, but not until 1984 did any professional analyst turn their attention to it. When Stop and Shop was about to grow its share price from $5 to $50, there was only one analyst taking any interest in it, yet IBM had 56 analysts following its progress.

One of Lynch's favourite places to look for multi-baggers is in boring or unpleasant industries; these types of industries attracted little attention, and could be severely underpriced as a result. If everything about the company seems boring – it name, its activities and its management – then it may be overlooked. The oxymorons will simply not see it until finally the flood of good news compels them to start taking an interest. As the crowd starts to do this it becomes trendy and overpriced. Then you can sell your shares to the trend-followers.

One of Lynch's favourite places to look for multi-baggers is in boring or unpleasant industries.

Lynch focuses on certain elements which are essential to the make-up of his ideal niche company. These are shown in Figure 6.1. They are typically fast growing small to medium-size companies operating a niche business with high potential and favourable prospects. The simpler the company is, the better he likes it. An ideal company is one that 'any idiot could run', because then it has sufficient strength in its market place to withstand the possibility that one day some idiot might be running it.

Niche company			
Low price	**Financial strength**	**Owner-oriented management**	**A strong economic franchise**
• Low price-to-earnings ratio • Little interest from analysts and institutional fund managers	• Strong balance sheet • Sales and earnings per share growth, with consistency • High free cash flow • Low inventory growth	• Penny pinching in executive suite • Good labour relations • Surplus cash flow returned to shareholders • Managers owning and buying shares	• Low growth industry, high growth company • Limited competition • High barriers to entry • Plenty of room to grow • Simple business

Figure 6.1   Lynch's niche company

Strong Economic Franchise

Lynch is firmly of the belief that a company is better able to exploit its superior competitive position sustainably in a slow growing industry, ideally a no growth industry, such as funeral services. High-growth industries have a tendency of letting you down. For example, over the past ten years personal computer and mobile phone demand has rocketed, but shares in these sectors have struggled. Every time a company comes out with an innovation rival manufacturers, whether in China, the US or Finland, put thousands of engineers on the task of figuring out how to make it cheaper and better, and a new product will be on the market in six months. This doesn't happen in industries with more mundane growth, say bottle caps, coupon-clipping services, oil-drum retrieval or motel chains. If the industry is not growing at all (especially if it is one that is boring and upsets people) you generally find less of a problem with new competition allowing the best firm in that industry to gain market share.

Niche companies are generally successful in one geographic area, and are then able to duplicate their winning strategy over and over again, and take it further afield. This can lead to extremely rapid expansion and profits, largely ignored by professional analysts and newspapers, who are too busy following the struggle for superiority between the well-known 'industries of tomorrow' (e.g. bio-technology, telecoms, internet). Meanwhile the highly competent niche companies continue on their way and get to dominate their particular area. The imaginary pot of gold at the end of the exciting fast-growing sector's rainbow is a magnet to many 'wannabe' rivals, but in the unexciting humdrum sector competitors drop out, leaving the competent companies to dominate their market. Lynch thinks it preferable to hold shares in companies that are able to capture an increasingly large part of a stagnant market than to have shares in companies that are fighting to protect a dwindling portion of a seemingly exciting market. Total domination in business is always more healthy for shareholders than competition.

It is apparent that some investors confuse two concepts of growth. The first is growth in sales for the industry. This will lead to growth in the more important form – growth of earnings and shareholder value for a particular firm in that industry – only if certain conditions are present, the most important of which is that high profits are not competed away. Indeed, in most high growth industries there is great uncertainty as to the potential for translating the growth of sales into earnings growth. This uncertainty alone should put off investors, especially when they consider that there are simpler, more predictable industries where the competitive threats are easier to assess.

There are a number of clues to the strength of the economic franchise, e.g. if the company is able to raise prices year after year without losing customers; earnings per share have risen steadily; the company has duplicated its success in city after city; it is not selling a high proportion of its output to one customer; the firm has a clear local monopoly.

It is difficult to overstate the importance to companies of an exclusive product or franchise. Possession of this exclusivity puts them in a strong economic position, enabling them to raise prices year on year yet retaining their customers. Often the cost to would-be rivals of entering this exclusive market is prohibitive, as in the case of quarries. Lynch is a fan of quarries: he says that he would far rather own a quarry than a jewellery business. The jewellery business is vulnerable to competitors, both those that have already set up and potential new entrants. These days high street jewellers even have to compete with internet operators. The result of all this competition is that the customer is free to shop at dozens of alternative places. A quarry near a big city, on the other hand, can find itself the only one for a hundred miles giving it a virtual monopoly. On top of that you are unlikely to find new entrants setting up in the near future because quarries are so unpopular with local residents that gaining planning permission is fraught. Local newspapers, drug companies and chemical companies are also good examples of straightforward niche businesses that are protected from rivals by high cost of entry and cost of competing, but have plenty of room for expansion.

The ideal niche company would be engaged in a simple business. It is much easier to understand the 'story' of the simple business and draw conclusions on the strengths of the firms. Also, the management are less likely to make mistakes.

Owner-oriented Management

For investors it is vitally important that the management is interested in the progression of the company for the benefit of shareholders and not their own personal aggrandisement. Lynch favours companies that do not squander company resources on plush offices finding an inverse relation between rewards to shareholders and the extravagance displayed at head office. He was suitably impressed when he visited company headquarters that were shabby and unimposing, such as those of Taco Bell or Crown, Cork & Seal (a 280-bagger over 30 years). Taco Bell's headquarters was a 'grim little bunker' stuck behind a bowling alley. At Crown, Cork and Seal the president's office had faded linoleum and shabby furniture. The office did not overlook areas of green lawn, but instead the production lines.

As an investor, look for the combination of rich earnings and cheap headquarters. Far more important than an imposing executive suite is the capability of the management to run their business efficiently and engage in good labour relations, thereby increasing profitability. Staff should be treated with respect and fairness; no corporate class system with white-collar Brahmins and blue-collar untouchables. Workers should be well paid and have a stake in the future prosperity of the company.

Lynch disapproves of companies that use surplus cash flow to diversify unnecessarily (and often disastrously). He calls this process 'diworseification', and gives the example of Gillette, a company which had a spectacularly profitable razor business but diworseified into cosmetics, toiletries, ballpoint pens, cigarette lighters, curlers, blenders, office products, toothbrushes and digital watches – to name but a few! – before realising the error of its ways and emphasising its niche business, shaving. 'It's the only time in my memory that a major company explained how it got out of a losing business before anybody realized it had gotten into the business in the first place.'[5] When he visited Apple he asked the managers all sorts of questions but he kept coming back to the issue that seemed to be most on his mind: given that the company has so much cash will it, like so many other companies, fail to stick to its knitting and go off and spend it on something the management does not understand?

A sure sign of a healthy company is when those on the inside are buying their own company's shares. If employees are putting their own money into it then you should regard that as a useful tip-off to the probable success of the share. This insider buying is reassuring, especially when lower-ranking managers use their salaries to increase their holding in the company. If

---

5. Ibid., p.147. Reprinted with permission.

people earning a normal executive salary are spending a fair chunk of that on the company's shares then you can take it as a meaningful vote of confidence. So factory managers and vice presidents buying 1,000 shares is to be read as being highly significant – more so than when the CEO buys. Owning shares encourages managers to reward shareholders (themselves) rather than pay increases in salaries or use the spare cash on pointless or ineffective expansion. However, insiders selling shares should not necessarily be seen as a negative sign; there could be many reasons for selling – purchasing a house, school fees etc. – which are totally unrelated to the performance of the company.

Owning shares encourages managers to reward shareholders (themselves).

Low Price

Lynch is wary of companies with high price to earnings ratios, PERs, advocating rejection of these companies unless you are very sure that future earnings growth will be very high. A high PER ratio acts as a handicap to shares, just as extra weight in the saddle of a racehorse acts as a handicap: the company has to work that much harder just to match expectations. His rule of thumb on the subject was that the PER should not exceed the company's expected growth rate in earnings. If the PER is less than the growth rate, you may have found yourself a bargain and if it is half the growth rate that is very positive. These rules are perhaps less applicable in the modern era of low inflation. In an environment in which inflation is in the region of 2–3 per cent we cannot expect nominal earnings growth for the average share in the long run to be more than nominal GDP growth, i.e. 2–3 per cent of real growth plus 2–3 per cent of inflation. If earnings growth of the average share is around 4–6 per cent then you might have a problem finding shares with much greater (realistic) projections of growth than this which are also on single digit PERs. What we can accept is the general principle of aiming for relatively low PERs.

High PER ratios can be based on an unrealistic and unreasonable expectation of future earnings, and have in the past resulted in a dramatic fall in the share prices of companies such as Avon and Polaroid. In 1972 Avon's unwarranted PER ratio of 64 led to its shares plummeting from $140 per share to $18⅝ just two years later. In 1973, Polaroid shares were $143 and its PER 50. Needless to say, this situation could not last, and its shares fluctuated wildly before falling to $19 in 1981. Polaroid had been in the throes of producing a new camera, and investors were expecting incredible results from it, but in the end the camera was overpriced and suffered operating problems, and so did not bring about the anticipated earnings. These anticipated earnings, however, were totally off the wall, needing Polaroid to have sold several cameras to every household in the US to achieve them. For it to be meaningful, the PER must be based on solid fact and genuine prospect of growth.

Financial Strength

An important component of financial health is a strong balance sheet, i.e. low borrowing relative to the equity capital in the business and a suitable mix of borrowing. Poor balance sheets are often at the root of the biggest losses in shares. As well as ensuring that the assets are significantly more than the debts Lynch thinks about the type of debt. Short-term loans and debts, where the repayment dates were grouped together were a bad sign, as was the increase of debt relative to cash. On the other hand, static or diminishing debts, or cash exceeding debt, were signs of financial strength.

What also matters is the amount of investment needed for future development. Companies which need vast capital investment in order to proceed with their next project, such as paper companies, are less likely to make cash for their shareholders than companies which don't rely on capital spending. A careful eye should also be kept on the amount of inventory held by companies, which could increase to an unacceptable level or could be worth far less than its book value. When inventories grow faster than sales, it's a bad sign.

The Discipline of the Two-minute Monologue

Lynch expected his staff to be able to be as disciplined as he was, and be able to expound the merits of a company in a 'two-minute monologue'. The salient facts about any company should be extracted from the morass of information, then the decision could be taken. It was vitally important that the essence of a company could be understood and explained concisely. Thus the details of the strength of the economic franchise, management quality, financial structure and low price need to be boiled down to the key deciding factors. If more than two minutes is needed then this is an indication that the investment is too complicated and carries too much uncertainty to be considered further.

Advice for the Investor

So, what advice does Lynch give to investors for the continued profitability of their investment strategy?

Know the Facts

Among the criteria Lynch sets out for investing, first and foremost is understanding the chosen companies, and continued monitoring of them. A buy-and-forget policy is asking for trouble; constant attention is required for pursuing a profitable strategy. By learning enough about shares held, the mistake of selling too early can be avoided. It can be very tempting to sell when the value of shares has doubled or trebled, but if the company is in a strong competitive position, and the management is of high quality, there is every possibility that it could be a 10- or even a 20-bagger.

To retain a portfolio's effectiveness and profitability take sufficient time, at least every few weeks, to maintain a high standard of knowledge about each company and check on its progress. There are two basic questions to ask about a share you own: (1) is it still attractively priced relative to its proven earnings, and (2) are developments at the company going to result in a sufficient rise in earnings? The answers to these questions depend on the evolving competitive position of the firm and the quality of its management – continue to monitor these to ensure that the story is intact and the firm is still robust.

He likened owning shares to having children – don't get involved with more than you can handle. Companies progress through three stages in their life. They start up, develop their business and try to find their path to success. This is a precarious phase for the investor – it could all go wrong. Next comes the expansion phase as the company's successful strategy is able to be moved into new territory. This is where the investor can make the most profit – the company has found its niche and is capitalising on its success. Finally there is the established phase, where the market may have reached saturation point, and the company needs to find a new way forward. The investor is at risk here, as there is no guarantee that the company will be able to progress. Each of the phases can last years, and it is imperative that the investor knows what stage his chosen companies have reached, and be prepared to take the requisite action. The crucial point is acquiring and maintaining knowledge of the companies, and analysing their performance, so that the investor is investing and not speculating.

Always remember that the best stock to purchase now may be the one you already own.

Continuing to develop your understanding of the company and its industry allows you, over time, to learn more about the key influences on earnings; what can lead to permanent impairment and what is merely a hiccup. Recessions will come and go; investing fashions will come and go. If you really understand the companies in your portfolio you will begin to recognise when the market has over-blown some temporary factor. Perhaps a general decline has indiscriminately dragged down even the best shares. Perhaps an event specific to your share has led to abandonment by the fickle mass of investors. Whatever the cause of the temporary price fall it is a wonderful opportunity for the informed investor to add more shares to the portfolio at bargain prices. And always remember that the best stock to purchase now may be the one you already own.

Diversify With Care

When Lynch took over Magellan, there were only 40 stocks in the portfolio. Disregarding the head of Fidelity's advice, Lynch, unable to resist a bargain, increased this to 150 shares, and continued with this approach throughout his time in charge of Magellan, ending up with a portfolio of more than 1,400 shares. Much of this extreme diversification was forced on him because the fund became large and the regulator insists that a fund of this nature hold no more than 10 per cent of a given company and no more than 5 per cent of the fund's assets could be in one company. Also, he was able to deal with so many different shares because he and his many staff worked full time to source the necessary information: 'I've always believed that searching for companies is like looking for grubs under rocks: if you turn over 10 rocks you'll likely find one grub; if you turn over 20 rocks you'll find two … I had to turn over thousands of rocks a year to find enough new grubs to add to Magellan's outsized collection.'[6] In other words, only take on shares where enough time is available, and has been taken, to have a complete grasp of the company's situation.

Most investors are in no position to follow the sheer volume of companies that Lynch and his staff were able to track. Ordinary investors should limit themselves to researching as many companies where they have got an edge and they have the time and knowledge to ensure each company passes all the tests of prudent value investing: and in Lynch's opinion this could be

---

6. Lynch, P. (1994) *Beating The Street*, New York: Simon & Schuster, p.141.

as few as five companies. He said that if you only choose shares in five different growth companies, then three will perform as expected, one will encounter unforeseen trouble and disappoint you, while the fifth will do better than you could have imagined. Lynch does not recommend putting all the eggs into one basket but says that for small investors 8–12 companies is probably the most that a part-time stock-picker could follow.

The crucial consideration is allowing enough time to be able to develop and maintain a high level of knowledge about each of the companies. All shares in the portfolio have to pass some stiff tests and you will not know if they pass the tests unless you spend time analysing them. The private investor will not have the analytical edge over the professionals if he or she spreads intellectual resources thinly.

Accept Fluctuation

The investor must accept that the stock market fluctuates and admits that, despite 'learning in graduate school that the market goes up 9 per cent a year' he found it impossible to predict, nor could he find a reliable source to tell him, which way the market was going: 'There are 60,000 economists in the U.S., many of them employed full-time trying to forecast recessions and interest rates, and if they could do it successfully twice in a row, they'd all be millionaires by now ... As some perceptive person once said, if all the economists of the world were laid end to end, it wouldn't be a bad thing.'[7] So if the experts can't get it right, what chance is there for the amateur investor?

7. Lynch, P. with Rothchild, R. (1989) *One Up On Wall Street: How to Use What You Already Know to Make Money in the Market*, Simon & Schuster, pp.74–5. Reprinted with permission.

Recessions come and go, and fashions in investing come and go, but if the amateur investor has done his work properly, and has concentrated on understanding the essential business of a company, he will appreciate that perhaps an unpredictable negative factor, such as freak weather conditions, a trade embargo or recession, can cause a sudden but temporary downturn in a share price. He must have confidence is his research, recognise that shares fluctuate for a huge variety of reasons, and not be panicked into premature action. He must not let emotion overcome knowledge. If the market is on a downturn, he should not blindly follow the current flavour of the month with professional investors, but trust in his own choice of shares, which are the result of time well spent on proper investigations. If a share goes up or down following your purchase this only tells you that there was somebody who was willing to pay more or less for identical merchandise; it does not tell you the share's value.

Avoid the Latest Fads

The investor should not be drawn into investing in the latest hottest shares, the so-called whisper shares, on the market. These frequently turn out to be no more than hope and thin air. These shares rise in value astonishingly quickly, but there is nothing astonishing about their subsequent spectacular drop in price. There are constant whispers circulating about the latest craze, whether it be jungle remedies to cure all ills, high-tech start-ups, or bio-technological miracles, and it can be very tempting to join in. On the face of it, these new companies are on the brink of solving the world's major problems. Often, there is no substance behind all these rumours and the stock-picker can leave his brain outside because he does not have to spend time checking earnings and so forth because usually there are no earnings. Figuring whether the PER is acceptable is no problem because there is no PER ratio. But there will no shortage of microscopes and high hopes.

Lynch's favourite example of this is a company called KMS Industries, which between 1980 and 1986 engaged upon various technological 'miracles', such as 'amorphous silicon photovoltaics', 'video multiplexer', 'optical pins', 'material processing using chemically driven spherical implosions', 'inertial confinement fusion program', 'laser-initiated shock compression' and 'visual immunodiagnostic assays'. Needless to say that over this time its shares fell from $40 to $2½. Lynch's solution to this is simple: he says that if the current hot stock has such wonderful prospects, then this will be a good investment next year and the year after that. You can always put off buying into the company until later. If 10-baggers are available in companies that have already proven themselves, why take the chance with one that has not? In sum: when in doubt, tune in later.

Consistency

The amateur investor should develop their own particular method of investing, a tried and proven investment strategy that suits them, and should stick with it, ignoring transitory but probably insubstantial trends in the stock market. There will be occasions when the temptation to act rashly is overwhelming, but strength of character is needed here. Losses within the chosen strategy have to be tolerated; they are bound to occur and must be accepted, and should not cause the investor to be panicked into buying or selling unnecessarily. Remaining consistent and faithful to a strategy will minimise losses and maximise long-term profitability. As Lynch says in some years you will make a 30 per cent return, but there will be other years when you'll only make 2 per cent, or even lose 20 per cent. That is the way things are in the stock market, and you have to learn to accept it. If you raise your expectations such that you are looking to make 30 per cent year after year, the end result will be frustration at shares for defying you. Impatience will follow, which may cause you to abandon your investments at precisely the wrong moment. You may also start to take high risks in the pursuit of illusory pay-offs. If you want to maximise your long-term return then stick to a strategy through good and bad years.

Investing in the stock market is not scientific. Successful investors accept periodic losses and unexpected occurrences. The wise investor takes it on the chin and goes on searching for the next great share. If only six out of ten of your shares perform well then you should be thankful; you are doing better than the average and a 40 per cent error rate will allow you to out-perform.

Bucking the Trend

The obvious answer to the question 'When should I buy?' is when all the painstaking research stacks up, and the company looks a good bet. However there are investors who buck the trend and act contrary to the general consensus. These contrarians zig when everyone else is zagging, but true contrarians do not simply take the opposing view just to be different. They are actually acting intelligently by choosing to zig when they understand that the stock market has got it wrong and zagged. They can succeed by waiting for the excitement to die down, and then investing in companies that nobody is interested in any more, especially those companies that have begun to bore the analysts.

For him investing without research is like playing stud poker and never looking at the cards.

Lynch does not think that investors should rely on their gut feelings; they should learn to ignore them, and continue with trying to understand the fundamentals of the company under investigation. For him investing without research is like playing stud poker and never looking at the cards.

Lynch warns that shares should not be bought because they are the next of something, such as the next Microsoft or the next Disney: they almost never are what they promise. Nor should investors be influenced by companies with exciting names: dull names for a good company help to keep early buyers away, whereas a flashy name in a mediocre company seems to attract investors and gives them a false sense of security.

Pay No Attention to the Science of Wiggles

He rejected technical analysis (chartism). He said, 'I don't pay much attention to that science of wiggles.'

Do Not Try to Predict Short-term Ups and Downs in the Market

Lynch agrees with Benjamin Graham that the short-term movements (over a few months) are irrelevant to good investing except that they might offer the opportunity to buy at a bargain price if other investors are being foolish. The investor must concentrate on the underlying business of the company in question and not waste time trying to achieve the impossible. Buying and selling on the prediction of market movements is likely to result in very poor performance, as the investor is likely to be optimistic and pessimistic at precisely the wrong times. On top of which there are the additional costs of frequent trading – transaction costs and taxes:

> Every year I talk to the executives of a thousand companies, and I can't avoid hearing from the various gold bugs, interest-rate disciples, Federal Reserve watchers, and fiscal mystics quoted in the newspapers. Thousands of experts study overbought indicators, oversold indicators, head-and-shoulder patterns, put-call ratios, the Fed's policy on money supply, foreign investment, the movement of the constellations through the heavens, and the moss on oak trees, and they can't predict markets with any useful consistency, any more than the gizzard squeezers could tell the Roman emperors when the Huns would attack ... All the major advances and declines have been surprises to me.[8]

---

8. Ibid., p.74. Reprinted with permission.

Pulling the Flowers and Watering the Weeds

Do not automatically sell the shares that have risen in price, while holding on to those that have fallen hoping to come out even. Equally silly is the *automatic* selling of losers and holding onto winners. These two strategies don't make sense because they use the current movement of the share price as an indicator of the company's fundamental value. Of course, we know that recent share price movements often have little to do with the future prospects of a company. A falling price is only a tragedy if you sell at the lower price. If the prospects for the firm remain good then a fall presents a wonderful opportunity to buy at bargain prices. To make decent profits as an investor you need to train your mind to accept that when a good share has fallen 30 per cent after purchase you buy more because it is even more of a bargain than you originally thought. Just because everyone else is abandoning the company it does not mean you should do the same. If your analysis is sound, buy more. It follows that stop-loss orders are illogical – so, to have a rule that any share down by 10 per cent will be sold will mean losing some excellent niche companies and wasting a lot of analytical effort

No Derivatives

In his entire career Lynch never bought futures or options. He thinks that stock futures and options should be banned. They can be expensive and risky. The premiums on options are too costly for the protection they might afford and futures can lead you to gear up returns and losses – you can lose multiples of your initial stake if the market moves the wrong way for you over a short period.

Selling

Advice that any investor would love to follow would be 'sell before interest rates rise' and 'sell before the next recession'. If only it was as uncomplicated as that! Lynch's view on selling can be simply stated; the investor does his research, buys his investment and keeps it so long the story remains sound. If the evidence you have gathered tells you the share is going higher and everything is working in your direction, then it's a shame if you sell. This however is much easier said than done.

Two difficulties occur, both psychological: first, the share price rises; second the share price is static or falls! If the share price rises, then it can be very tempting to cash in on the shares before it is too late. It can be harder to stick with a winning share after the price has risen than it is to believe in it after the price goes down. But, if you sell at the first decent rise you will never have a 10-bagger. Just because a share has risen it does not mean it is due for a fall.

One good piece of advice is to avoid following what Lynch calls the drumbeat effect when undue influence is given to opinions in the financial world and media. Thus an investor might be panicked in to selling: 'If you flip around the radio dial and happen to hear the offhand remark that an overheated Japanese economy will destroy the world, you'll remember that snippet the next time the market drops 10 percent, and maybe it will scare you into selling your Sony and your Honda, and even your Colgate-Palmolive, which isn't cyclical or Japanese.'[9] Incomprehensible (to the man on the street) rumours about money supply, or about the Fed (Federal Reserve) led William Miller, once Fed chairman, to say 'that 23 percent of the U.S.

---

9. Ibid., p.254.

population thought that the Federal Reserve was an Indian reservation, 26 percent thought it was a wildlife preserve, and 51 percent thought it was a brand of whiskey'.[10]

In other words, don't be swayed by events and matters you don't understand. Patience is the key, and even Lynch had frequently to grit his teeth and wait for the rest of the world to appreciate a company. He got used to holding onto a share when the price is going nowhere. He said that he made most of his returns in the third or fourth year of owning something. You need a lot of patience to hold on to a company that you think is very exciting, but which everybody else seems to ignore. There will be moments when you begin to think everybody else is right and you are wrong. But if the fundamentals are promising hold on, your patience will be rewarded – at least it will be in enough cases to make it worthwhile. There are lots of advice and reasons for selling, but in the end it all boils down to one thing; the investor's determination to keep *au fait* with the evolution of his chosen companies – only then can he make sensible decisions.

However if the fundamentals of a company worsen and the price has increased, then it could be time to consider moving allegiance to another better prospect, so long as the appropriate research has been carried out on the new prospect, of course. Another hint that it could be time to sell is when prices rise dramatically but the fundamentals are wavering, and Wall Street has got excited about the stock too late. 'If forty Wall Street analysts are giving the stock their highest recommendation, 60 percent of the shares are held by institutions, and three national magazines have fawned over the CEO, then it's definitely time to think about selling.'[11]

---

10. Ibid., p.255.
11. Ibid., p.259. Reprinted with permission.

Difficulties and Drawbacks of Lynch's Approach

On the surface, Lynch's approach to investing sounds simple, and he sees no reason why the private investor cannot be as successful as any professional. However, his approach is not quite so easy to implement as it might seem. It is difficult enough to develop the skills needed to understand the management and strategic position of a company. Added to that is the fact that the amateur investor does not have access to all the snippets of information that Lynch and his staff were able to accumulate, nor is it as easy for the amateur investor to call up the CEO of a company and ask questions about the company's progress.

Lynch is very encouraging to the private investor.

Lynch and his staff had the built-in advantage of working for a world-renowned financial institution; telephone calls from them would be answered and treated with respect, and people would willingly give them information. Where the amateur investor has the advantage though is in knowledge of companies that are familiar to them, either through employment or observation. Perhaps you used to work in the medical profession and so have superior insight into medical supply companies, or perhaps you know about engineering and so can analyse some engineering firms. Lynch is very encouraging to the private investor and while you might not achieve the amazing return he did you can nevertheless do better than placing your savings in a managed mutual fund or a stock market tracker.

Writing about the personal qualities it takes for an investor to succeed, Lynch gives a comprehensive but quite daunting list of these qualities:

> It seems to me the list of qualities ought to include patience, self-reliance, common sense, a tolerance for pain, open-mindedness, detachment, persistence, humility, flexibility, a willingness to do independent research, an equal willingness to admit to mistakes, and the ability to ignore general panic. In terms of IQ, probably the best investors fall somewhere above the bottom ten percent, but also below the top three percent. The true geniuses, it seems to me, get too enamored of theoretical cogitations and are forever betrayed by the actual behavior of stocks, which is more simple-minded than they can imagine. It's also important to be able to make decisions without complete or perfect information. Things are almost never clear on Wall Street, or when they are, then it's too late to profit from them. The scientific mind that needs to know all the data will be thwarted here. And finally, it's crucial to be able to resist your human nature and your 'gut feelings.' It's the rare investor who doesn't secretly harbor the conviction that he or she has a knack for divining stock prices or gold prices or interest rates, in spite of the fact that most of us have been proven wrong again and again.[12]

So, if you can fulfil all these qualities, you would be a very successful investor: if you can fulfil some of them, you might have reasonable success with your investment portfolio. Even Lynch recognised that he frequently failed to live up to the ideal he has placed before us. His message to himself and to

---

12. Ibid., p.69. Reprinted with permission.

us is that even though we fail – regularly – we need to pick ourselves up, learn from mistakes and try to do better next time.

And Finally

Peter Lynch says that investment is simply a gamble in which you've managed to tilt the odds in your favour. Well he has given us some useful tools to tilt those odds:

- The private investor should play to his strengths:
  - be unconventional (compared with the crowd-hugging professionals) in choosing shares;
  - avoid following institutional rules and regulations;
  - avoid responding to short-term market excitements;
  - buy small and medium-sized firms, where the multi-baggers come from;
  - take time to understand every share in the portfolio;
  - find companies with great growth prospects before the professionals hear about them, e.g. in the shopping mall;
  - be prepared to buy into companies that are boring and doing unpleasant tasks at bargain prices.

- Look for companies that have an excellent economic franchise, owner-orientated management, financial strength and a low share price.

- Do not diversify beyond the point where you fail to maintain a high level of knowledge about every company in the portfolio.

- Do not think of trying to time short-term market movements or use macro-economic forecasts to time investing.

- The following are a waste of time: hot stocks, technical analysis/chart following, stop-loss orders, derivatives.

- Pulling the flowers and watering the weeds is a poor approach, as is selling losers and watering the winners automatically and being an automatic contrarian.

- Keep abreast of the story (the fundamentals) for every share in your portfolio and only sell if the story changes from strong to weak.

CHAPTER 7

John Neff

John Neff, a value investor, has developed an investment philosophy which emphasises the importance of a low share price relative to earnings. But he has not stopped there; he requires the share to pass a number of tests in addition to the price-earnings criterion, and it is through his use of these further screening tools that he successfully evolved his approach from simple low price-earnings investing to a sophisticated one.

Neff employed his investment approach in managing the Windsor Fund for 31 years between 1964 and 1995. It returned $56 for each dollar invested in 1964, compared with $22 for the S&P 500. The total return for the Windsor Fund, at 5,546.5 per cent, outpaced the S&P 500 by more than two to one. Considering that the average fund return after expenses is less than on the S&P 500 this is a very good return.

There is so much you can learn from Neff:

- How to use to your advantage knowledge of stock market behaviour.

- To go beyond simple low price–earnings ratio (PER) investing in sophisticated low PER investing.

- To look for the key fundamental factors when examining a company.

- To develop the personal traits of independence of thought, courage and perseverance needed for long-term investing success.

Standing Against the Tide of Conventional Opinion

Neff's ability to stand against the tide of conventional market opinion and make up his own mind about a company stems from his early experiences as well as his capacity for hard work. Even at a young age Neff was regarded as someone with a mind of his own (this is to put it charitably – his first grade teacher used the word pugnacious): 'I was never inclined to back down from an argument, even when confronted by the mantle of authority. My mother, in fact, used to claim that I ought to be a lawyer because I would argue with a signpost.'[1] He has managed to use to his advantage his early experiences to allow him to follow the route less travelled by more conventional investors, favouring the opportunity to make up his own mind about shares.

When he was young the family's very small food retail business went bankrupt as his uncle started to drink heavily. From this he picked up three valuable lessons: (1) do not develop an emotional attachment to a particular business, because this can fool you; (2) just because a company is down it is not always a wise investment; and (3) drinking to excess was neither a business nor a personal virtue. The first two, in particular, became key elements in his later investment success.

Neff began to learn how to separate himself from the herd when trading baseball cards during his fifth grade, observing how bidding for those cards that the enthusiasts thought most desirable could go sky high as bidders become over-excited. He observed the emotional momentum or mania and thought

---

1. Neff, J. and Mintz, S.L. (1999) p.14.

it bizarre. He thought it peculiar that the children's main focus was to sell the cards on at a higher price than the purchase price, rather than valuing the cards for any intrinsic value. He also noticed how the cards with the largest price rises eventually fell the farthest – sooner or later.

In 1950, when 18 years old, Neff joined his father's small company selling mechanical equipment to automobile dealers, service stations and farmers. From this experience he learned a lesson which has been applied throughout his investing career, that you can make good money without a glamour product. Indeed, he developed a keen interest in dull businesses – they make money because they are less likely to attract competition.

During his spell in the Navy (1951–53) he learned through poker games that the consistent winners were the ones with the better knowledge of the odds and that they were strong willed enough not to be tempted into trying to win the big money unless the probabilities were firmly on their side.

At college (1953–55) Neff took two courses taught by Dr Sidney Robbins, a follower of Benjamin Graham. He extended his education achieving a degree in banking and finance from Western Reserve University in the late 1950s while working for National City Bank, Cleveland, as a securities analyst. He was a quick learner, even though, through his own admission, his knowledge of investment was slight at the beginning. Yet he managed to be promoted rapidly within the bank. However, his desire to be more independent eventually led to a securities analyst position at the Windsor Fund in 1963, where he felt less restricted and was allowed to follow his more creative approach to share picking.

The Windsor Fund

Neff took control of the Windsor Fund in 1964 (when aged 33) and for 25 of the following 31 years managed to outperform the market. Prior to Neff's arrival the Fund had fallen far off pace and was lagging behind the S&P 500 by more than 10 percentage points due to an infatuation with small supposed growth shares in the early 1960s and a lack of attention to the durability of the growth in company earnings. The fund then continued to hold on for too long before cutting its losses, compounding its problems by then putting the remainder of the money into so called 'safe' shares only to watch the market turn, leaving them behind.

After looking through the Windsor Fund's portfolio on his arrival he quickly discovered the past errors. He said the fund was holding onto all sorts of shabby stuff as a result of the managers following recent fads and fashions. Out of 41 industrial stocks held by the Fund only eight could be called successful, and their successes were lacklustre at best.

Out of 41 industrial stocks held by the Fund only eight could be called successful.

He began to make changes. He took larger positions within some of the companies already held by the Fund, determined not to commit the sin of diversifying into mediocrity. These underrated shares were those he judged to be predictable businesses, with the prospect of steady earnings, growth potential and a low share price.

Character Traits of Good Investors

This is where we start to look at the essential differences between the beliefs of most market players and the principles followed by Neff.

Courage, Judgement and Fortitude

Success in sophisticated low PER investing requires courage. You need to be brave to buy the down-and-out shares, those rejected by your peers. You may get blank expressions as they try to understand your unusual behaviour, and you must be prepared to accept the risk of embarrassment that follows from being different.

Neff was always on the look-out for out-of-favour, over-looked or misunderstood shares that had earnings growth potential that the rest of the market had missed. He believed if you could buy shares where all the negatives were chiefly known, and therefore the share price is depressed, then any good news would have an overwhelmingly positive effect.

According to Neff a key mistake made by investors is to buy into shares where investors generally had high expectations of growth and where any negative news could have a devastating effect on the shares. He noticed how the market would tend to be led by the latest fashions and fads. This resulted in over-valuation of the in-vogue shares and under-valuation of the less glamorous but generally good shares. Investors became caught up in a frenzy and ignored the good solid companies. He says that for a successful investment career you can live without glamour stocks or bull markets. The key requirements to carry you through are judgement and fortitude: 'Judgment singles out opportunities, fortitude enables you to live with this while the rest of the world scramble in another direction … To us ugly stocks were often beautiful.'[2]

Of course failure whilst taking a conventional approach to investing – going with the rest of the crowd – is commonplace and usually produces little opprobrium. But to fail whilst investing unconventionally and not 'pull it off' leaves you open to criticism and accusations of stupidity. Most people would rather not risk this derision and so stay with the herd. If you went around and asked investors whether they had the courage to choose those shares which are unpopular you will find that most will say, 'well, of course'. This is only human nature – who wants to acknowledge that they are pulled along by the crowd? Unfortunately, too often, their claims to be independently minded don't often bear scrutiny. They are all very good at recognising a bargain in retrospect and then taking credit later for spotting it. So, if a share climbs to a price 30 times earnings, they point out that they thought it to be a bargain when it was trading at eight times earnings. But was there a great volume of buyers back then? Of course not – otherwise the price would not have been so low – most of them were cowering in fear of an announcement from the company or on the economy, while rushing to get onto the glamour shares bandwagon.

Consistency, Persistence and Patience

Neff would go for long periods of time against the wisdom of the masses and had to cope with the psychologically corrosive delay before benefiting from his superior analysis. He showed

---

2. Ibid., p.4.

perseverance, sometimes waiting years before other investors realised their mistake and appreciated the virtues of a good solid company with steady rising earnings.

His approach does not rely on a few shares doing dramatically well. To go home winners, investors need to be consistent and not to rely too heavily on any individual share. To explain the requirements of consistency, persistence and patience Neff used a tennis analogy. Some players are extremely talented and are able to adopt a playing style to win a match. They have brilliant stroke play or a winning serve, say. Most players are not like that. For the rest of us we should concentrate on our strengths, to win by not losing; to keep the ball in play as long as possible allowing time for our opponent to make a mistake.

Neff had a sense of the history of stock market behaviour and he believed this was essential to investors giving them the opportunity to take intelligent risks. Without this knowledge you are at the mercy of fads and fashions. Neff felt that over time you could feel the market's personality: it could be irrational and unsentimental; it can also be cantankerous and hostile; yet there are occasions when it is forgiving and congenial. As a long-term investor you will experience good days and bad days, good years and bad years simply because the market is going through a mood phase. Neff himself went through a very bad patch in the early 1970s, but he kept his nerve and persisted with the same approach.

The Main Factors Neff Looked For

Low PER

The Windsor Fund usually bought shares with PERs 40 to 60 per cent below those of the typical share. Neff believed that if these shares also had the promise of steady earnings growth then there was the potential for the appreciation to be 'turbocharged'. Low PER shares can get two boosts. One when the market recognises that the out-of-favour industrial sector (or company) is not so bad after all and that it has previously overreacted to the difficulties. The second boost is due to higher reported earnings per share.

For example, imagine two companies Famous Inc. and Ignored Inc. Both companies have earnings of $1 per share. However, Famous Inc. is a well-known company having been thoroughly analysed and consequently stands on a PER of 25. Ignored Inc., on the other hand, is overlooked and in an industrial sector that is currently out-of-favour. It has a PER of 12. Not only do both companies have the same current earnings, but careful analysis tells you that their future annual earnings growth will be the same, at 8 per cent. So after one year the earnings at both companies stand at $1.08. The market continues to value Famous Inc. at a PER ratio of 25 and consequently the share price rises to $27, an 8 per cent appreciation.

During the year the market has slowly come to realise that it has overreacted to the difficulties in Ignored Inc's industry and a re-rating has taken place. Now the market is prepared to pay a multiple of 20 on recent earnings. So, if earnings are now $1.08 the share rises to $21.6. This is an 80 per cent appreciation in one year!

If you can sell into that fresh interest, you should produce an impressive return.

Neff said that because investors have forced the price of the low PER share to absorb all the bad news, there is little positive expectation built into the price. Moderately poor financial performance is unlikely to lead to a further penalty – so there is a degree of protection on the downside. However, any indication of improvement may lead to fresh interest. If you can sell into that fresh interest, when other investors are fully recognising the underlying strengths, you should produce an impressive return.

Obviously not all investments in a low PER portfolio are going to turn out to be as successful as Ignored Inc's shares (the operating performance of the firm declines, say, or the market continues to ignore the company), but evidently, it is possible to succeed in a sufficient number of cases for this approach to be useful.

Modest Earnings Growth

It is not enough to simply invest in all shares with low PERs. Thorough analysis beyond PERs is still needed. The key to success in this type of investing lies in being able to distinguish between shares selling at a low PER ratio because they are out-of-favour, overlooked or misunderstood, and those which are past their best with poor prospects. Figure 7.1 shows the main factors Neff examined to find good companies.

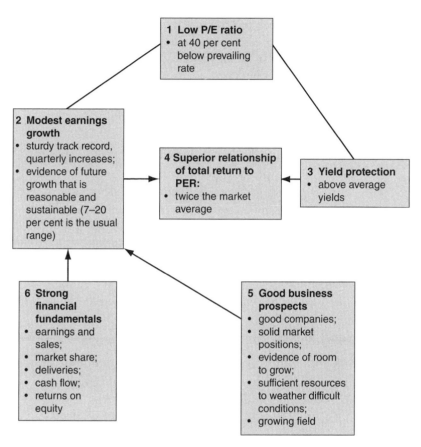

Figure 7.1   Sophisticated low price-earnings investing

Historical earnings per share figures are easily obtainable, so are analysts' projections. Although these make for a good starting point you must apply your own judgement, as even the best analysts must admit that their forward projection is nothing more than an educated guess (and many forward projections are far too optimistic – remember that the analysts often work at the brokers and investment banks that receive fees or favours from the company). You must look for evidence of sturdy earnings track records, and the assurance that there is good reason to expect sustainable growth at a reasonable pace. This growth rate needs to be fast enough to eventually catch the attention of the bulk of investors, but not too fast so that it tips the share into the risky growth stock category. (Too much hype will quickly lead to its downfall.)

As a rule Neff usually liked to find companies with earnings growth of at least 7 per cent per year but avoided companies with earnings growth greater than 20 per cent. There was too much risk if a company was growing at more than 20 per cent. He usually forecast earnings growth for five years because this constituted a timescale which forced the analyst to think about the long-term competitive position of the firm within its industry.

Dividend Yields

The dividend yield provides a near-term cash return on the investment which offers a satisfactory income while the investor is waiting for the market to recognise the earnings growth potential. It is also far safer to look for a return through dividends than waiting for the uncertain return of growth in earnings. Dividends are rarely lowered and good companies are likely to increase the payout.

The out-performance by the Windsor Fund of 3.15 per cent per year over the market average was largely attributed to its superior dividend yield. Neff believed that many investors over-emphasise higher earnings growth potential over higher dividend yields. He said that analysts tend to evaluate shares on the basis of earnings growth expectations alone, and therefore, in many instances, investors could 'collect the dividend income for free'.

He found it incomprehensible that investors would regularly pay higher prices for shares with an earnings growth of 15 per cent plus a 1 per cent yield over a share offering 11 per cent growth but a 5 per cent yield. Neff does not go into great detail about what he meant by 'superior yield' but generally it is believed he favoured a yield at least 2 percentage points over the average.

Superior Relationship of Total Return to PER

Neff's success was partly based on a formula, which he used to calculate the total return of a share as a multiple of its price earnings ratio offered in the market – a way to measure 'the bang for our investment buck'. He would calculate this by combining the growth in earnings with the dividend yield and placing this over the PER.

$$\frac{\text{Total return}}{\text{PER}} = \frac{\text{earnings growth} + \text{yield}}{\text{price} \div \text{most recently reported earnings}}$$

Investors search for high earnings growth prospects, but also need shares with the lowest price relative to current earnings and dividends. Neff, after a good deal of experience and experimentation, determined that his rule of thumb hurdle rate was to be double the market average ratio. That is, the total return for a share divided by its price earnings ratio for a particular company should exceed the *market average* ratio by two to one.

An example would be if the earnings growth for shares generally is 4 per cent and the market dividend yield is 5 per cent, taking the historical PER for the market index as 14, then the hurdle rate for a particular share under consideration would equal:

$$\frac{\text{Total return}}{\text{PER}} = \frac{4 + 5}{14} \times 2 = 1.29$$

The hurdle rate will rise to 1.8 if the market PER falls to 10.

The time period used to calculate past earnings growth is critical for estimating future growth. As a minimum Neff would use five years because this time scale allows for economic fluctuations such as extraordinarily good periods causing average earnings to rise by double-digit percentages. Common sense is required; avoid, for example, extrapolating double-digit real growth figures from bull market periods to infinite horizons. A reasonable upper limit to the estimate of future profit growth would be to follow the real Gross Domestic Product growth rate (say 2.5 per cent) plus inflation (say 2 per cent) over the long run. To assume higher growth rates is risky, leading to the abandonment of a conservative stance about future prospects.

Good Business Prospects

Unfortunately, there is no set of purely mathematical or mechanical tools out there that will allow the investor to pick and choose market-beating stocks. Neff shows us that we require both a quantitative and qualitative approach to our analysis. This includes finding out how an industry ticks. Study the firm and its rivals, the products, and the strategic positioning. He was interested in good companies with powerful competitive strengths that were under-priced and overlooked due to the market's obsession with glamour stocks.

Study the firm and its rivals, the products, and the strategic positioning.

Neff advises us to visit factories, shops and try the products sold by the specific companies you're interested in – kick the tyres. Reading trade magazines is a good way of discovering developments in an industry before the news reaches the investment community. Seek out kerbside opinion about the company, its people, its products and its competitors. A useful indication of a company's strategic position is whether it is a leader in its industry. Listen to the grapevine of opinion with regard to the company to find out its reputation as a whole, the growth outlook for the sector and its ability to dominate markets, products and services leading to premium prices (i.e. use the Scuttlebutt approach made famous by another of our great investors, Philip Fisher). It is important to consider the ease of the entry for new competitors, or the development of substitute products. Neff would look for companies with the potential for growth; the industrial sector should not be stagnant. He also required that the company has enough resources to weather difficult conditions.

Neff suggests posing a series of key questions to the CEO, or the investor relations officers. For example: will the prices charged by firms in the industry rise or fall over the foreseeable future? Are costs rising or falling? Which firms lead the industry? What are the reputations of each of the main firms in the industry? Can industry capacity meet demand? Is there a lot of capital investment taking place in the industry? Will this extra investment lead to a lowering of profitability?

Assessing the degree of sustainable competitive advantage of a company and the economics of an industry is by no means easy and perhaps due to his familiarity with the business world Neff has developed a sixth sense about the relative strengths of a firm. Although Neff only gives us a few clues into the thought processes and criteria needed to assess the degree of sustainable competitive advantage of a company the one thing he did insist on was that investors should only invest in companies where there was a full understanding of the industry and the company. Because of the difficulties of analysing industries and the competitive advantage of particular firms within those industries Neff concentrated on reasonably predictable companies in reasonably predictable industries. His motto remained 'Keep it simple' – this meant that a number of companies in fast-moving technological areas, e.g. Microsoft or Cisco, could not be analysed and included in the fund.

Neff was interested in 'good' companies, those with strong market positions. It seems odd that companies with powerful competitive strengths should be under-priced, overlooked and neglected, but the Windsor Fund seemed to find a more or less continuous stream of firms which market whims had confined to the shadows, while the spotlight was on the latest glamour share or sector.

Strong Financial Fundamentals

Neff would start the analysis by gathering a whole raft of numbers and facts. He would become familiar with the performance and financial strength of the company from a number of different angles, searching for confirmation or contradiction in the numbers. The numbers and ratios for the firm were compared with those for the industry and market benchmarks to provide a perspective on performance.

Sales should be growing, to provide a healthy rise in earnings over the long run. Improving profit margins may indicate improving pricing power as a result of an improving competitive position in the market place. He would also check that the company has been able to deliver goods demanded by customers. If it does not have a spotless recent record on this, it might be because it is inefficient in its operations or because demand is out-stripping supply. If demand is this good, then he would check to see if it is likely that the firm will soon get back on track and catch up with demand to produce profitable growth.

Cash flow (defined by Neff as retained earnings plus depreciation) should be healthy because it is important to the investor that the company's investment plans can be financed internally rather than the firm being forced to increase borrowings or raise equity capital. Investors should avoid companies that need regular injections of money from their shareholders; after all there are other firms that have such plentiful cash flow and low needs for additional fixed and working capital expenditure that they have surpluses permitting them to increase dividends or repurchase shares.

Return on equity is the best single measure of managerial performance in Neff's view.

Return on equity is the best single measure of managerial performance in Neff's view because it reveals the extent to which managers have generated good levels of profit from the equity base entrusted to them.

Where High Quality Low PER Shares Can be Found

A good starting point is to look at the list of shares posting new lows – i.e. those that have declined in price significantly in recent months. The majority of these companies will have poor prospects and should not even be considered. However one or two may be worth further investigation. It may also be worth consulting the list of the 20 worst performers of the previous day.

Significant Change

A company going through a period of change in its products, management or market may be subject to unwarranted selling pressure on its shares. The uncertainty associated with companies going through these transitional periods discourages most investors and the over-reaction that develops can push stock prices below reasonable levels. This can provide an excellent opportunity to the more analytical and patient investor. However, there must be sound reasoning and clear rationale that the company will emerge from this transformation stronger. If the share is standing on a low PER, you have every reason to assume reasonable growth and if it meets other Neffian criteria then take courage and go against the crowd.

Difficult Times

Neff would look for good companies which have fallen on hard times as investors become excessively wary, pushing the share price too low. For example, the Windsor Fund under Neff's guidance, in the late 1980s, bought into property and casualty insurers when environmental liabilities were hurting the insurance industries dragging them downwards. The Doomsday scenario did not occur and the insurance companies reserves were more than sufficient for them to cope. Then, when Home Depot's profits fell in 1985, due to pre-opening costs and expanding overheads, the forward looking PER fell to a mere 10 (the Windsor Fund made a 63 per cent return in nine months).

Small and Crack Companies

These are often companies which lack size and visibility to catch the attention of the conventional analyst and are overlooked. They may be 'crack' companies, so called because they fall between the cracks of accepted institutional coverage. These companies are often engaged in a combination of commercial and industrial activities making them hard to classify. The retail analyst may ignore a company because only 30 per cent of earnings comes from retailing, likewise an oil industry analyst is not interested due to the firm having only a small oil subsidiary and so on. Consequently, these crack companies can become incompetently valued by the market.

Changing Industry

Similar to these crack companies, are those firms making a gradual shift from an industry with poor economics to one with better strategic qualities. This is usually a gradual process and not the result of a dramatic restructure due to a merger or acquisition. It involves the slow movement of the main area of the firm's activity and profits. There is a delay in recognition as the market still thinks of the firm as belonging to the old low value sector, and this creates an opportunity for the value investor.

Use Your Specialist Knowledge

Start with what you know and build from there. Neff advises investors to play to their strengths and use their knowledge of a particular company, industry sector or product. If you work or have worked in an industry, then you may have an exceptional insight into which firm is the market leader, which is growing most rapidly and who has the strongest management team and strategy. You can keep honing this knowledge by keeping your eyes open and your ears to the ground. Again, reading trade magazines gives you an insight into developments within an industry. Discover what products the teenagers are talking about and what are the 'must carry' lines for a retailer. Use your own experiences. Which companies do you use and why? Who gave you the best service recently? Was the food good at the restaurant chain you ate in? Was the office supply company efficient and friendly and were their goods sold at competitive prices that beat all the competition you have come across so far?

Advice on the 'Don'ts'

We have discussed at length the criteria used by Neff to be a successful value investor, however, there are several important areas that he avoids.

Don't Invest in Glamour Shares

Neff avoids shares showing fast earnings growth, as they are generally well recognised and hyped expectations drives the price up to unrealistic heights as investors get carried away. There is evidence of this in the mania shown for internet stocks in the late 1990s in the combination of over-excitement and the obligation of index trackers (and closet index trackers) to buy those shares that have risen (with small free floats), pushing prices to extreme levels. The companies had untested business models and no profits. Furthermore investors were not properly considering the possibility of market entry, competition and the introduction of substitute products.

Even well established companies can be poor investments.

Even well established companies can be poor investments. Companies such as Coca-Cola, Microsoft and Procter & Gamble are good companies, with excellent financial performances and are in strong competitive positions with good management behind them. Also, their businesses are broadly-based, worldwide and sound. They are safe and will almost inevitably be around in 20 years' time. But, they will not produce good returns to the share buyer if they are purchased at a time when everyone knows that these are great companies. The share price has usually been bid up to reflect the widespread belief that the company will perform well. But, any hint of trouble will send the price plummeting downwards as the crowd become aware that it has been priced for perfection. As Neff says you cannot up the ante forever – eventually, even great stocks runs out of gas. Even good companies have a price ceiling. Believing that Apple is a buy at a P/E of 50, because it might go up to 70 times earnings is battling against the odds. As a value investor you must always keep the odds in your favour.

Don't Do Crystal Ball Reading Using Charts

Neff advises an investor to study a company inside and out, analyse the figures and look into past performance, but he would never advise predicting market movements over the next few months. He suggested that the best approach would involve 'hitting behind the ball instead of anticipating market climaxes six to eighteen months ahead of the investment crowd. Poor performance often occurred as a consequence of a technical orientation that tried to predict peaks and troughs in stock charts. It assumed that where a stock has been implies where it is going.'[3]

Don't Follow the Bull Market Hype

Over time, markets will go through cycles and the pack of investors will go through periods when they invest in quality and use a more selective and risk averse approach to their stock picking. However, as their confidence grows in a rising market, these investors can get carried away. As the market continues to grow beyond expectations so does the inexperienced investor's frenzy to follow the latest fad and fashion. These investors get so caught up with the prospect of making a quick buck, they fail to follow a rational investment strategy undertaking a funda-mental evaluation of stock. Shares are bought and sold on the

---

3. Ibid., p.44.

basis of tips and superficial knowledge, investing without clear understanding and calm reflective thought. Investors seem to have an almost infinite capacity at times to believe in something too good to be true.

It will, at some point, dawn on the crowd that some players have cut their losses and figured out that things have gone too far. Like sheep, group panic sets in as everyone runs for the exit. Unfortunately, the aftermath of these bull markets is not a pretty sight and most of the followers go home empty handed. Neff's advice would be to stay clear of the markets that have lost touch with the fundamentals. Don't try to play the greater fool game – buying even though you are not convinced of the fundamental value in the hope of selling the stock on to someone else before the market decline comes – you might end up being the biggest fool.

Don't Forget History's Lessons

Neff believes a great investor requires a knowledge of market history in order to succeed. Because only then can you truly get the perspective required to make clear and rational decisions. Neff refers to most market participants as amnesiacs, because their memories are notoriously short. Examples of lessons can be easily found throughout the mistakes made by previous generations of the stock market from the 'go-go stocks' of the 1960s, the Nifty Fifty in the 1970s, the oil companies of the 1980s and the dot.com boom of the 1990s. Long before all of these were the 'new era' stocks of the 1920s (e.g. radio companies).

Each generation believes it is observing a rewrite of the rules of economics so that a few amazing companies will have an almost infinite ability to grow. Investors then jump aboard to ride the new fad before it is too late believing that 'this time it is different':

> At least a portion of Windsor's critical edge amounted to nothing more mysterious than remembering lessons of the past and how they tend to repeat themselves.[4]

Neff illustrates the point wonderfully with the story of the two moose hunters who hired a plane to take them to moose country in Canada. The pilot agreed to return to pick them up two days later. He told them that they could only return with one moose for each hunter to keep the weight in the aircraft at a safe level. When the pilot returned the hunters had prepared two moose each for the flight home. The pilot said that he had told them to bring only one home each. 'But you said that last year,' whined one hunter 'then we paid an extra $1,000 and you managed to take home four moose.' The pilot agreed. An hour into the flight the gas tanks ran low, the engine sputtered and the pilot was forced to crash land. All three managed to emerge from the plan unhurt. 'Do you know where we are?' asked one of the hunters. 'Not sure,' said the other, 'but it sure looks like where we crash landed last year.'

Don't Invest Where You Have No Discernible Edge

Another of Neff's beliefs is to invest only in sectors where you have a superior knowledge of the business. For example, he avoided technology stocks for three main reasons: (1) they were too risky; (2) they failed to pass the total return to price earnings

---

4. Ibid., p.127.

ratio test; and (3) he admitted that he had no 'discernible edge' compared to other investors in the market place. Neff felt it was essential to have an analytical advantage as well as an in-depth knowledge of the business.

Don't Over-diversify

Some degree of diversification is necessary to lower risk and bolster performance, yet to over-diversify could lead to hobbled performance. Neff said 'By playing it safe, you can make a portfolio so pablum-like that you don't get any sizzle. You can diversify yourself into mediocrity.'[5] Whilst at the Windsor fund Neff generally ignored market weightings,[6] favouring areas of the market where there was evidence of undervaluation. There were some sectors of the market that were completely unrepresented in the portfolio, yet others that were over-represented. He reasoned that it was stupid to own, for instance, forest products companies if the market is excited about this sector and you can reap exceptional returns by selling them. It was usually the case that the vast majority of the S&P 500 was not held by the fund as only a mere four or five of these well-known companies satisfied his requirements for inclusion. At one stage when the fund was valued at $11 billion, 40 per cent of the fund was made up of only ten stocks (it generally held only 60 in total). Windsor would often buy 8 or 9 per cent of the outstanding shares in a company.

---

5. Ibid., p.49.
6. Investing portions of the fund in proportion to the size of the industry in the stock market.

Don't Incur Unnecessary Expense

The Windsor Fund under Neff had exceptionally low expenses, running at a mere 0.35 per cent per annum. He was able to maintain these low cost levels mostly by avoiding high turnover of shares held in the portfolio thus saving on transaction costs and taxes, but also by not using expensive sophisticated equipment or people to carry out the determination of share values as he felt they could be understood without them. Keep things simple.

Don't Automatically Go Against the Crowd

As discussed at the beginning of this chapter Neff is an individual who makes up his own mind about companies and their shares. His ability to go against the fads of the stock market have made him a great investor. However, he never became ego-driven or obstinate and was prepared to listen to others. He did not assume that the market was always wrong and used his tried and tested techniques to analyse companies closely before making an informed decision. He did not unthinkingly or automatically take a contrarian line; he took a sophisticated one. He advises us not to bask in the warmth of just being different:

> There is a thin line between being contrarian, and being just plain stubborn. I revel in opportunities to buy stocks, but I will also concede that at times the crowd is right. Eventually, you have to be right on fundamentals to be rewarded ... Stubborn, knee-jerk contrarians follow a recipe for catastrophe. Savvy contrarians keep their minds open, leavened by a sense of history and a sense of humor. Almost anything in the investment field can go too far, including a contrarian theme.[7]

---

7. Ibid., pp.100–1.

When to Sell

Deciding when to sell is the toughest investment decision. Unfortunately it is far too easy to fall in love with the shares in your portfolio. You must remember that your shares represent a business and if the underlying business is not performing now, and you see no upward turn on the near horizon, you must part with them.

Each share in the portfolio must have a clearly visualised potential for growth.

All the Windsor Fund's shares were for sale, yet Neff was not averse to holding some for three to five years. However, at times if a share was not living up to expectations it may only be held for a month. Thus, a share may be sold if the fundamentals of the business have changed (e.g. strategic position or management) since the purchase or a mistake in the original analysis is revealed. Each share in the portfolio must have a clearly visualised potential for growth.

There are two major hurdles an investor must clear when making the decision to sell.

1. Parting with a share and admitting you made a mistake in its purchase in so far as it has not lived up to your expectations. You must swallow your pride and exit as swiftly as possible. This requires the investor to be extremely self-critical and analyse the company on a regular basis. If you are simply holding on because of your past enthusiasm or your love for it, you must put these feelings to one side and consider only its earnings growth potential.

2. More difficult still is timing the sale of your successes. The knack is to sell at the time when the share is fairly valued and not hold on for too long and miss the boat. Neff stressed that many investors hold on to a share for too long as they are loathe to miss out on what they think will be 'the best part of the gain'. The fear of selling a share only to then watch it continue to rise in price is why many hold on for too long; to avoid this regret. Neff admitted even he was unable to time sales of shares at their peak and gain all the reward. He was prepared to sell into the rise and leave a little on the table for the buyer. He feels the risk of being caught in a sudden downshift is too great. The important thing to remember is that the profit made can be used to buy more undervalued stock and so begins the cycle again. 'An awful lot of people keep a stock too long because it gives them warm fuzzies – particularly when a contrarian stance has been vindicated. If they sell it, they lose bragging rights.'[8]

The Difficulties With this Approach

A Neffian approach requires a lot of background work as well as critical self-examination. You must have a good working knowledge of economics, finance, accounting and strategy. Your analysis must be high quality, as you delve into companies, investigating the earnings growth potential. You cannot put in a little effort and apply a little knowledge; it has to be sound analysis or you will not out-perform the market. As an investor using Neff's approach you must be able to invest not only your money, but also time and mental energy.

---

8. Ibid., p.115.

This method is psychologically demanding due to the immense amount of courage and perseverance required before you can reap the rewards. A sense of market history is required along with the development of sound judgement. Honing the skills required may take years and unfortunately many of these qualities are not attainable by all of us. Neff suggests that those unable to put in the time may be better advised to place their money in collective investment vehicles (e.g. mutual funds) rather than make a half-hearted attempt at sophisticated low PER investing.

A major problem with his focus is that the vast majority of companies would not get over the first hurdle because Neff would require them to have a PER ratio 40–60 per cent below the average, to produce a high yield and have a good total return to PER ratio. A large number of high growth stocks would be excluded based on his screening tools. Such companies under a Neffian approach would be considered too risky, given the problems of distinguishing between the genuinely valuable growth stocks and those which have been momentarily buoyed up by the market enthusiasm.

Another problem is that there might be occasional long periods of under-performance. For example, the Windsor Fund suffered in the early part of the 1970s due to the rush of investors joining the Nifty Fifty bandwagon and abandoning value stocks. You must be in it for the long haul and be prepared to take at least a five-year view. If you are prepared to make the effort and have the ability to withstand the pressures then this approach can be rewarding. You must roll with the punches. You do not need a vast intellect but some capacity for informed rational independent thought will certainly be required.

Concluding Remarks

Neff's approach is accessible to most investors if they can find the time and can develop the character traits needed. It does not require genius or blinding insights, but it does require imagination, hard work and the ability to learn from the mistakes made by yourself and others.

When Neff retired in 1995 he took time to reflect on his mother's comment that he would argue with a signpost. He went on to say that he had argued with the stock market his whole career – but happily had won more arguments with the market than he lost.

Key points to take away from Neff's approach:

- Search for out-of-favour, overlooked and misunderstood shares selling on low PERs, with good dividend yields and modest earnings growth. In this, play to your strengths, e.g. in the industry in which you work, where you shop, eat, etc.

- Total return to PER ratio for a share should be double that for the market as a whole.

- Analyse the quality of the strategic position of the firm, the quality of its management and the soundness of its finances – use Scuttlebutt to do it.

- Develop character traits such as perseverance, fortitude, patience and sober reflection.

- Have a sense of history and develop judgement about market moods and underlying value over time.

- Do not turn over your portfolio regularly, over-diversify, try short-term investing to catch market movements or invest in fast-moving industries that you cannot understand.

- Be strong in the face of bull market hype and when you need to take the opposite actions to the generality of investors.

- Sell when the fundamentals have deteriorated or the shares are fully valued.

CHAPTER 8

Anthony Bolton

Anthony Bolton is widely acknowledged to be the greatest British investor of his generation. Peter Lynch describes him as one of the best investors on earth. He is a contrarian-value investor, who searches for out-of-favour, under-researched shares with potential that others have missed. He finds most of these in the small and medium capitalisation company sectors. These undervalued and unloved shares are often found where things have gone wrong (but where redemption is likely) or where the company is going through a period of change. He looks for situations where he believes that investor sentiment about a company is likely to improve in the medium term.

Bolton manages his funds with an above average risk profile. His investors are asked to live with a greater degree of volatility than the average fund. The kind of medium-sized companies he invests in will often, in a recession, fall further than the large companies. So while his approach does very well in the medium and longer term a follower of his philosophy has to accept that there will be uncomfortable periods.

Bolton has a remarkable record. The fund that he ran at Fidelity, Special Situations, for 28 years between 1980 and 2007 produced a return that averaged 19.5 per cent. This beat the benchmark FTSE All-Share Index by 6 per cent per annum. A £10,000 investment at launch was be worth £1,480,200 by the end of 2007.

It is difficult, if not impossible, to find someone who has a bad word to say about Anthony Bolton as a person. Unfailingly courteous, he is described variously as modest, genial, collegial and a great listener. He has an air of quiet efficiency, of delib-erateness in his actions, a manifestation of a very orderly mind; he reminds many people of a quintessential professor with a deep intellectual well and agile mind. Lynch says that he is 'cool' in the very best, most British sense of the word – passionately unflappable, intensely calm. He accepts that he is a fairly unemotional sort of person, but counts this as a virtue because emotional people generally make poor fund managers.

There is so much you can learn from Bolton:

- How to look for good value among the unloved, overlooked reaches of the stock market, by taking a contrarian stance.

- What makes an excellent company.

- What valuation metrics to use.

- The concept of the investment thesis.

- How to manage a portfolio.

- The personal attributes that a good investor needs.

After first looking at Bolton's early experiences we quickly get onto the key elements he examines when evaluating a company. We then explore the range of valuation measures he uses and the central importance of having an investment thesis to justify every investment you make. Some tips on how to manage a portfolio are followed by guidance on when to sell your shares. Finally, I discuss the character traits that make a good investor and some don'ts to stop you wasting time and money.

The Making of a Great British Investor

Bolton ended up in investment by chance. He had a fairly conventional middle-class upbringing: his father was a barrister, he did well at school and achieved an engineering degree from

Cambridge in 1971. After graduating he had no idea of what to do next. A friend suggested the City of London, and another friend gave him an introduction to the stockbrokers Keyser Ullmann, where he started as an investment manager trainee. At that time investment management was a backwater, only just becoming recognised as an industry; corporate finance was the area that had the glamour and attracted the best talent.

Keyser Ullmann managed money in a particular way that was to later influence Bolton's investment philosophy. First, it concentrated on smaller companies. Second, analysts and managers got out of the office and visited companies – a rarity among City folk. Third, one of Bolton's mentors, a director of the firm, used technical analysis (charts, etc.) to supplement fundamental analysis. In order to advance to investment manager rather than remain a junior, in 1976 he moved to Schlesingers.

Fidelity

He did not stay at Schlesingers for long because in December 1979 Fidelity recruited him as one of their first London-based investment managers. The family-held firm had an established reputation for in-depth fundamental analysis and consistently good performance, and had already grown to be the biggest independent investment manager in the US, but the international side of Fidelity was only just getting going. In the early 1970s Fidelity's operations in the UK were tiny, consisting of only 12 people. It has grown somewhat – there are over 3,000 today.

Bolton, aged 29, was immediately put in charge of the Fidelity Special Situations Trust, that was launched, along with three other funds, as soon as Bolton arrived at the company. It was a difficult fund to sell, and struggled along with only £2–£3 million invested for some time. (It became much easier as the fund topped the performance tables in the late 1980s.)

'Searching for capital growth opportunities in an aggressive and contrarian way.'

Bolton described a special situation as 'a company attractively valued in relation to net assets, dividend yield or future earnings per share, but additionally having some other specific attraction that could have a positive short term influence on the share price … Special Situations tend to fall into the following categories: small growth stocks, recovery shares, asset situations, new issues, companies involved in bids, energy and resource stocks, companies reorganizing or changing their business and new technology situations.' (Bolton, writing in the first Fidelity Special Situations Trust Manager's Report). He later encapsulated the idea in a single sentence: 'searching for capital growth opportunities in an aggressive and contrarian way'.

He adopted a 'bottom-up' approach, examining the facts about specific companies rather than giving more weight to macro-economic considerations. He left himself plenty of room to extend his search territory beyond the categories in which he initially thought most special situations would be found, believing that in the pursuit of high returns you should not exclude potential moneymaking opportunities simply by being too restrictive about what kind of shares you can buy.

One of the most endearing characteristics of the Fidelity approach is that fund managers are allowed to get on with running their funds, with few other responsibilities imposed on top, such as marketing and administration. Bolton has a fierce loyalty to the company, borne of the decent and respectful way in which he has been treated by the senior team. Over the years he has been approached by a number of companies to join them but never came close to leaving. The following quote gives some hint of how much store he puts on the character of the people he works with, and his sense of values:

> I remember one approach in the 1980s from what was then one of the most successful global hedge fund businesses of the time ... I met the head of international investment and I must say that I thought he was a particularly unpleasant person. He ended our meeting by saying something along the lines that he couldn't understand why British people didn't think getting rich was the most important aim in life and were motivated by other things besides money.[1]

Another indicator of integrity: when Bolton started running a fund he felt it only natural that he should stop buying shares personally and instead put all his money into the investment fund, saying that this should be standard policy for all fund managers. Why is it that so few fund managers invest significant amounts of their own money in the funds they run I wonder?

---

1. Written by Anthony Bolton in Davies, J. (2004) *Investing with Anthony Bolton*, Harriman House, p.52.

Why Out-of-favour Stocks?

Bolton believes that recovery stocks and others that are currently out-of-favour will produce the best returns because it is the opposite of going along with the herd. The stock market takes things to extremes. Your job, as an investor, is to take advantage these excesses. By spending time looking at out-of-favour shares you are forced to go against the herd. This is an uncomfortable thing to do for most people who feel much more confident doing what the herd's doing. If the press, brokers and everyone else is telling them that GlaxoSmithKline is a good company, then they want to believe that GSK is a good company.

An indicator that the herd has gone in a particular direction is when a number of brokers call him and recommend buying a certain share. The contrarian spirit in him, and common sense, says that this would be a bad move because if the market in general is optimistic the share is probably already fairly or over-priced. On the other hand there are occasions when the market gets too pessimistic on things, focusing on the short term and missing the longer-term dynamics of a business.

His ideal is a company where things have gone wrong, but where there is reason to believe that they might be changing – there is something which will recapture investors' attention before too long.

In the mid-1980s Bolton was so well respected that he was asked to take on the management of a Fidelity European equities-focused fund in addition to Special Situations – at one point he was responsible for the management of £10 billion of other people's money. He liked investing in European shares in the 1980s because they were so under-researched and because their stock markets tended to lack sophistication in their reaction to news, providing plenty of opportunity to discover hidden gems.

At the end of 2007, at the age of 57, Bolton (temporarily) retired from full-time investment management, as the pace required to look after such a large fund became too much, and he wanted to create more time for his other interests. However, he did agree to continue to mentor Fidelity analysts and younger fund managers. He also wrote a number of articles for the *Financial Times* and devoted more time to his passion for composing classical music.

The Key Elements Bolton Investigates

The key elements that Bolton investigates are shown in Figure 8.1 and explored in depth below.

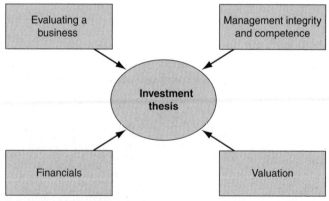

Figure 8.1   The key elements

Evaluating a Business

Bolton is in agreement with Warren Buffett and Benjamin Graham: think of shares as small pieces of a business. It is essential to understand the key factors that drive the company's performance. A useful approach is to imagine that you are buying the entire firm when evaluating shares, and ask questions such as: how good is the business? Does it have significant and sustainable competitive advantages? How is it positioned for changes in the economy or society?

Bolton firmly believes that businesses are not created equal. Only a few of them have strong franchises which can sustain the firm over a long period. A franchise (economic franchise) is the degree of pricing power flowing from its competitive advantages, especially its barriers to the entry of competitors. The strength and durability of the franchise is determined by the structure of the industry (e.g. the degree of rivalry between players in the industry) and the ability of the firm to rise above its rivals in the industry and generate exceptional long-run rates of return on capital employed. Bolton likes Buffett's 'moat' metaphor for franchise strength: a barrier that protects the firm from the incursion of rivals.

A simple way to test your conviction about the strength of franchise is to ask if it is likely that the business will still be here in ten years – and will that franchise (and therefore the business) then be more valuable than it is today? He says that it is surprising how many companies fail this test. Many firms are set up under business models that work in current economic/social/political conditions, but you cannot be confident that they will still work in changed circumstances. Some firms seem fine when, say, macro-economic factors, such as exchange rates or interest, are favourable, but when these move against them you quickly discover that the firm is unable to stand on its own two feet – it was being propped up by factors over which it has no control. The best shares to own are those in companies with control over their own destiny because of their degree of market power and which are not very sensitive to macro-economic factors.

The best shares to own are those in companies with control over their own destiny.

Given the difficulties of analysing the long-term durability of a franchise, it is advisable to avoid complex businesses, with many variables changing from day to day. In other words, favour simple businesses. Bolton refuses to look further at any business where the business model is very difficult to comprehend. After all, there are many others that are easier to understand.

In the next section we look at another important factor in the evaluation of shares – management integrity and competence. While this is important, and it would be a big mistake to invest in a company if you have any doubts about either, Bolton says that the quality of the economic franchise is the number one priority. He agrees with Warren Buffett that he would rather have a good business run by average management, rather than an average business run by good managers.

Management Integrity and Competence

If you have any questions on trustworthiness or competence then avoid the company. The people running the firm must have the highest integrity and openness. They must be candid and not prone to hyperbole. Bolton must feel that the managers are giving him a truthful and balanced view of the business. They must tell him about all the minuses as well as the pluses – because all businesses have both. They must be managers who under-promise and habitually deliver a bit more than they indicated. Be very wary of those who promise great advances because they are unlikely to deliver.

If there are blemishes on their character then be wary because people rarely change. If managers are unethical and dishonest no amount of corporate governance checks (e.g. outside directors) or accounting probes will reveal the truth; there are simply too many ways for managers to pull the wool over the eyes of investors. They can get away with spin and falsehoods for many years. He noticed that unreliable types often tend to be more extrovert. He feels that their flashiness may be used to cover up other failings. A test: does the person admit to making mistakes? Those that do not should be regarded as dangerous.

Look for management teams that display a detailed knowledge of the business strategically, operationally and financially. These people tend to be fanatical about the business, expecting high performance from themselves and from members of their team; and they work long hours.

Management objectives and incentives need to be aligned with those of the shareholders. One indicator of this is that they hold a significant number of the company's shares. Managers with very little 'skin in the game' can be more focused on prestige, status and perks rather than shareholder returns.

Meeting the Managers

Bolton is very keen on meeting managers of investee or potential investee companies. His habit was to hold three or four company meetings per day. They were usually with the chief executive and/or the finance director, but could be with the investor relations officer. If Fidelity's holding is substantial he preferred to see them once per quarter; and the meetings normally lasted one to one and a half hours. Regular meetings over an extended period of time allow him to assess management competence because he can check whether what they say will happen in the future actually turns out that way; you develop a sixth sense about who has the right qualities and who does not. He likes to set the agenda, which usually focuses on strategy, recent performance and new developments. Reading body language as the managers react to questions is an important part of the mix for Bolton, so regular contact is essential.

Key Data Prepared for a Meeting

In the initial meeting with a company, he focuses his questioning on the strengths and weaknesses of the business franchise. He goes into meetings armed with the following:

- A share price chart going back three, five or ten years to see how the share has been performing.

- Some valuation measures, e.g. price-earnings ratio, price

to book ratio, price to enterprise ratio, price to sales ratio. These will go back 20 years. If 20 years are not available then he likes to see data for at least a complete business cycle. He regards less than ten years of data as inadequate and misleading because this will not cover enough variety of business conditions. He wants to see if the current valuation is high or low relative to its history.

- Director dealings in the company's shares, going back a few years. He regards such deals as a possible lead indicator of an improving or deteriorating business. Trades by chief executives or finance directors are given more weight than those by divisional directors.

- The list of the top 20 shareholders. He wants to know if the shareholder list is diverse or concentrated, with perhaps a few investors controlling the firm. (He is also on the lookout for the names of institutional shareholders whom he respects cropping up on the share register – if they do this is a positive signal.)

- The proportion of the shares held by insiders. He likes to see manager interests aligned with those of shareholders.

- Financial strength report – see later for the criteria.

- A chart showing the net short position and how it has moved – how many are betting against this company?

- Credit default spread rates for the company (if available), showing the financial markets' judgement of the likelihood of a failure to pay interest and capital on issued debt.

- A chart of brokers/analysts' earnings upgrades or downgrades so he can quickly see whether average expectations are deteriorating or improving.

- The latest company results, other official releases and press reports.

- Recent broker notes – both positive and negative ones if possible.

- Fidelity's analyst's notes and financial models.

- A review of his handwritten notes from previous meetings. This is the element he considers the most important. He always writes notes about the meetings in A4 ruled notebooks. He started doing this in 1987 and now has over 50 notebooks recording over 5,000 UK company meetings (for European companies he has 37 books). These notes became useful supplemental material when later evaluating the company and meeting its management again.

With this background data Bolton is able to lead the discussion into division by division detail on volume of output, prices charged, gross margins, costs, operating margins, capital expenditure, debt levels, etc.

With the first meeting he is trying to get to the bottom of the business model and the main influences on the success of the firm. He probes the managers to understand strategic positioning, quality of management and their incentives and recent business trends. He wants to know what areas of the business are doing well but also those areas that doing less well. What is the senior management's view on the outlook for their various divisions and the market generally? All this questioning and thought is designed to allow Bolton to build a more sophisticated and accurate model of the company than his competitors.

Ongoing Relationship

Bolton maintains an ongoing relationship with companies and expects to be consulted about big strategic moves, such as mergers or company disposals. He also expects his views to be sought on major board changes, incentives and remuneration schemes. As a responsible shareholder he has a policy of using his votes if the company is going to make a major change. Directors often ask for feedback, and if he has a view he will give it.

Bolton is also a great believer in having a quiet word behind the scenes with directors to ensure that his views are taken into account. If a quiet word is ignored he is not averse to raising his voice and explaining his views in public. When it was proposed that ITV (the UK's independent television station) should be formed through the merger of Carlton, led by Michael Green, and Granada, led by Charles Allen, Bolton thought it wrong that these two strong characters, who were somewhat cool about each other, should share the top two posts in the merged entity – one of them had to go.

Bolton was dubbed 'the City's quiet assassin' by the press.

Bolton was dubbed 'the City's quiet assassin' by the press, because the outcome was the removal of Michael Green from the company.

He has intervened to change the way a badly underperforming firm is run. He usually does this in conjunction with other major shareholders. Bolton feels he is obliged to correct errant companies rather than sell the shares in the market and walk away. Given that he usually invests in small and medium-sized firms and he has a great volume of money to invest, Fidelity frequently ends up amongst the two or three largest shareholders. Selling can take time and result in poor prices so it makes sense to try and change an underperforming company.

Case study: the power of meetings – Nokia

In 1987 Bolton visited a Finnish conglomerate that engaged in paper production, TVs, tyres and a host of other things. One division, Mobira, was growing at 50 per cent per year but the company was not profitable. Indeed, the whole company went through a very bad time over the next few years – losing money and a series of chief executives. In 1992 the finance director, Jorma Ollilla was appointed chief executive and he visited Bolton in London in 1993. He said that all the divisions, except Mobira (later renamed Nokia), which was now profitable, were likely to be sold. Sales of Mobira mobiles in the US had taken off and Ollila was very optimistic. Until that time divisional profits had not been reported, which only served to hide the extraordinary profits of Mobira behind the losses of the other divisions. The potential of this company, once the other divisions had gone, was something that most analysts had missed. Bolton's habit of meeting managers gave him an information edge.

Financials

When Bolton first joined the City he knew very little about accounts. No formal training was forthcoming, so he taught himself how to read and analyse a firm's numbers. Here are the main elements he looks at.

Borrowings

Bolton says that balance sheet risk has been the most common factor behind his worst investments. A painful lesson Bolton learned early in his career is that companies with weak balance sheets – high borrowings – are the ones that tend to depress portfolio returns when the economy or an industry goes through a rough patch. Even if they do not go bust they may find that their bankers force them to make disposals of divisions to bring down their debt levels. Unfortunately, prospective buyers will often spot they are a forced seller and the price received is reduced to levels below what the company and investor thought they were worth.

Given that an investor has to pay as much attention to avoiding disasters as to picking winners then sidestepping highly geared firms is one way to hold fewer losers. As well as straightforward debt the analyst should take into account pension fund deficits and the value of redeemable convertible preference shares where the likelihood of conversion is slim. Also consider the debt maturity profile: what has to be repaid this year, next year, and so on. Debt covenants may be onerous for shareholders so check them out.

Some companies select year-end dates when their seasonal cash flows are at a high point. In these cases the analyst should look beyond the absolute debt levels at the year-end and consider the debt through the year. The amount paid in interest for the year may be of some help here – if it seems high relative to the year-end debt and prevailing interest rates then, perhaps the debt levels for much of the year were far higher than those reported at the year-end.

Bolton produced a poor performance for his investors in 1990–91 because the type of companies he invests in are more vulnerable than the average to recessions. He did a lot of soul searching to figure out if it was possible to retain the main features of his approach while reducing the downside risk. As a result he subsequently put a lot more effort into tracking the 'Altman Z-scores'[2] and other methods used by credit analysts to identify vulnerable companies with weak balance sheets.

He is not saying that he will never own a company with a weakened balance sheet, but that he will do so with his eyes open and then pay special attention to its progress. The holdings are also likely to be relatively small, and will be sold if there is a hint of something going wrong with the company or the economy.

Cash Generation

Will the business generate cash over the medium term? Because of Bolton's preference for firms that generate cash rather than consume it, he runs portfolios that have a bias towards service businesses rather than manufacturing. Businesses that can grow using only small amounts of extra capital are particularly attractive because the ultimate measure of attractiveness in terms of valuation has to be cash-on-cash return. He would much rather a company was a high cash generator than one that

---

2. An Altman Z-score is based on a number of financial ratios, which when combined act as proxy for default risk/bankruptcy risk.

has impressive growth of sales and profits but little in the way of cash available for shareholders.

Read the Notes

He says that vital information about a company is presented in the notes to the accounts; the analyst must discipline him or herself to read them very carefully. Often, companies hope that key negative information will be overlooked if it is buried deep in the notes.

Announcements

Read the company announcements and other information flowing from the company in the original form. Directors and their advisers often spend a great deal of time choosing the right words and so the original contains more nuance than that produced in a broker's summary. Much of this information is available free on financial websites.

Valuation

Bolton does not have a favourite valuation measure because he likes to look at a range, believing it dangerous to focus on only one. Note that for all the measures listed below he looks at them both on an absolute basis and on a relative basis. Absolute values are particularly useful at market extremes to avoid being sucked into a share at times of great exuberance.

The measures are:

- Price–earnings ratio. He normally looks at the ratio of price to predicted earnings for the current year, and for the next two years. He is particularly looking for companies that are priced at less than ten times the earnings in two years from now.

- Cash flow yield well above prevailing interest rates.

- Enterprise value[3] (EV) to gross cash flow or EV/EBITDA.[4] EV is adjusted down to the extent that there are minority interests and pension fund deficits. This is a measure examined by companies when valuing a prospective acquisition, it is therefore useful if you are interested in anticipating potential takeover bids, as Bolton is.

- Prospective free cash flow per share.

- Price of shares to sales and EV to sales (particularly useful for loss-makers or those with low profits).

- Cash flow return on investment (CFROI). This metric is a based on internal rate of return. If CFROI is above 'the risk free rate' then Bolton expects the business to trade at a premium to invested capital.

When employing these metrics Bolton likes to go back 20 years (if possible) and see how a company's valuation has changed over time to get a feel for the range of valuations that is normal for the type of company or industry. This practice is especially useful when the current valuations are abnormally high or low.

---

3. EV is the market value of the company's shares plus its net debt.
4. EBITDA – Earnings Before deduction of Interest, Tax, Depreciation and Amortisation.

You increase tremendously your chances of having a successful investment if you buy when valuations are low against history; buying when they are high increases your risk of loss. He also looks at how the company is valued relative to its industry peer group on a country, regional and global basis.

Other measures he uses in specific circumstances include break-up value. Caution is needed with this because as bull markets progress brokers tend to become less and less conservative in calculating break-up value.

It is important to use the correct measures for a particular industry.

It is important to use the correct measures for a particular industry. For example, for house building shares adjusted book value is appropriate, whereas price-earnings ratio is not, because earnings jump about all over the place due to one-off land sales and the like.

The Measures he does not Recommend

Bolton is not an admirer of the PEG ratio (the price–earnings ratio (PER) divided by the expected growth rate) because he sees little logic in the argument that the following three businesses are equally attractive:

- Company A: PER = 5, Growth rate = 5 per cent per year.

- Company B: PER = 10, Growth rate = 10 per cent per year.

- Company C: PER = 20, Growth rate = 20 per cent per year.

They have the same PEG ratio, but Bolton's sees Company A as far more attractive because it is so much cheaper relative to its proven earnings flow. A lot of hope value is placed on the future growth rate of Company C.

Dividend yield provides some downside protection, but it is not much use for valuation because it is merely derived from the more fundamental measure of earnings.

Bolton has some, but not a lot of time for dividend discount or discounted cash flow models because these require the prediction of dividends or cash flows for at least ten consecutive years as well as an estimate of terminal value; these are then all discounted using a suitable discount rate. He says that it is difficult to predict the dividends for the next two or three years, let alone those for years four or five into the future. With these models, if you make small changes in the assumptions they can have a substantial effect on the valuation. While he uses the techniques as a cross-check, he does so in the full knowledge of their shortcomings.

Investment Thesis

Bolton believes that every share you own should have an investment thesis. That is, you should be able to summarise why you own, or want to own, a share in a few sentences that your teenage son or daughter could understand.

The investment thesis should be retested at regular intervals. When testing it you should think about what might lead to the share becoming 'bad'; what might the 'bear' in the market place latch onto? Can you provide convincing counter-arguments to those who are much more negative about the share? Bolton is one of those rare individuals who goes in search of disconfirming evidence – people are naturally inclined to search for evidence that confirms their currently held views, so it takes a lot of self-discipline to hunt out disconfirming facts and opposite views. For example, he likes to read broker research that disagrees with his view and then discuss this with colleagues to firmly establish in their minds why they think the broker is wrong. It is very important to build conviction about a stock, but conviction must not develop into pig-headedness in the face of new (negative) information – keep an open mind.

Even after a collecting a lot of facts and testing your views against those of others do not think that you will be hugely sure about what you are doing at all times; business is inherently uncertain and your conviction is bound to wax and wane, and a lot of the time you are going to be uncertain about everything. However, when you do get a strong conviction then it is important to back it strongly.

The Categories of Shares he Favours

Recovery shares

These are businesses that have been performing poorly for quite some time, but there is good reason to believe that matters are about to improve. Investors, generally, like to be associated with companies that are doing well, which can lead to those in trouble receiving little attention. When a change for the better occurs most investors miss their chance to invest at a low valuation.

Change can come about because of new management, a restructuring or a refinancing. One area where Bolton has done well is in purchasing shares coming out of bankruptcy, because these companies tend to be completely ignored by most equity institutional investors.

Recovery shares must be split into two groups: those that have a strong economic franchise and those that do not. Only go for the good ones – poor franchise businesses will never recover. With recovery shares Bolton usually takes a small stake to start with – it is easy to be too early – then as his conviction grows that the worst is over he adds to the holding.

Unrecognised growth

This could be in areas unfamiliar to most investors, such as an obscure industry. Another possibility is the firm has a terrific division hidden within the company and obscured by the less attractive divisions (e.g. Nokia).

Valuation anomalies

For example, a share is the cheapest in its sector when it does not deserve to be. Another possibility is that those shares with few trades become underpriced because the market tends to overprice the highly liquid shares and underprice illiquidity. Bolton agrees with Lynch that firms that sound dull, ridiculous, depressing or are doing something disagreeable are disregarded and not owned by institutions:

> I have always started my search amongst the stocks that investors don't think are the prettiest, so that if they

change – and I'm really using my skills to find ones that
have the factors that might lead to a change – there will
be lots of new buyers for the shares as they become more
attractive.[5]

Corporate potential

Holding shares in a takeover target can result in prices rising
by 50 or 100 per cent in a matter of hours. Bolton tries to
identify those shares that are most likely to be the subject of
a takeover bid. Being biased towards small and medium-sized
firms helps because they are more likely to be targeted than
large companies. He looks in industries where future consoli-
dation into a few players makes economic sense.

Companies with only one or two large (but not controlling)
shareholders are more likely to be sold, as are those controlled by
a small group of institutions because a bidder will be able to talk to
these key players and move towards agreement. Companies with
lots of cash and no controlling shareholder are also vulnerable.

Be careful about buying shares because you have been
tipped that the company will shortly be subject to a bid.
Predicting M&A targets in the short term is very difficult (if
not impossible) without inside information and likely to lead
merely to large fees for brokers and losses for the gambler.

Asset plays

He likes companies selling at a large discount to their assets. An
example here is the Mersey Docks and Harbour Board in the

---

5. Ibid., p.56.

1980s, which was widely regarded as a very bad share because strong union power and the high cost of meeting redundancy pay greatly inhibited profit making. Bolton saw that the company was sitting on a very valuable property portfolio, with its ownership of miles of waterfront land close to a city centre. When the Thatcher government eventually relieved the company of the redundancy costs and weakened the unions the shares rose ten fold

---

One of the investment themes he avoids is growth stocks.

One of the investment themes he avoids is growth stocks. He likes to quote Jeremy Grantham (chairman of GMO) on the subject:

> Growth companies seem impressive as well as exciting. They seem so reasonable to own that they carry little career risk [to professional fund managers]. Accordingly, they have underperformed for the last fifty years by about 1½ per cent a year. Value stocks, in contrast, belong to boring, struggling, or sub-average firms. Their continued poor performance seems, with hindsight, to have been predictable, and, therefore, when it happens, it carries serious career risk. To compensate for this career risk and lower fundamental quality, value stocks have outperformed by 1½ per cent a year.[6]

---

6. Grantham, G. (2006) GMO Special Topic Letter to the Investment Committee VIII, July.

Charts/technical Analysis

When Bolton is considering a share he examines the share price chart showing the price movements going back three or five years. He likes to put the current price in the context of its recent history. A company that has caught his eye because of its fundamental value might already have a number of investors chasing after it. A glance at the chart will tell him whether other people have got there before him – is he arriving as a late comer? If the share has done very well, say tripling or quadrupling, then a lot of the potential could already be in the price and so may become a poor investment looking forward. Knowing that a share has risen considerably in recent years does not always mean exclusion from further consideration; it may still be a great opportunity, but he will treat it as more risky, especially if the market is at a high point and may be about to turn nasty.

Bolton uses technical analysis as an additional screen following fundamental analysis. If the technical analysis confirms his fundamental views he might take a bigger bet than he would do otherwise. On the other hand, if the technical analysis doesn't confirm his fundamental positive view he might review his investment thesis on a company. Thus he re-checks to see if there are some negative factors he has overlooked. He will ignore the technical view when it conflicts with the fundamental view if his conviction is very strong. In other cases if the fundamental and technical views conflict he will take a smaller bet or reduce his position.

He also uses charts to provide an early warning signal that there are problems brewing at a company he is already invested in. He sees the chart as a summation of all the fundamental views on a share at that particular moment which can sometimes give an advanced warning of problems ahead.

When it comes to potential recovery shares the share price chart can provide an indication of a change in trend, from decline to rising from the ashes.

Managing a Portfolio

Bottom Up, But Some Balancing Needed

Bolton is an investor who looks at individual stocks and invests where he sees unrecognised value (a bottom-up investor), rather than first allocating funds to sectors or countries before selecting stocks for the portfolio. He certainly does not agree with the logic of allocating money to a sector simply because other investors are enthusiastic about it and have bid up the prices, resulting in it becoming a high proportion of the overall market. For example, he refused to allocate much money to the dot.com, telecom and media sectors in 1999 when other fund managers felt obliged to take part.

Despite this he acknowledges the need to keep an overall balance within the portfolio so that it does not become too heavily weighted on a theme, sector or a market. His rules for this are that: (a) an individual holding should not exceed 4 per cent of the total fund, except in very rare circumstances; (b) he should not be more than 30 per cent overweight in any one sector; and (c) he should not hold more than 15 per cent of a company's equity.

Within these rules the size of his bet on an individual share depends on his 'conviction level' for the stock, how risky it is and how marketable it is. For the Special Situations Fund he normally started by allocating 0.25 per cent of the fund to a company, and then increased the percentage as his conviction grew (say after a meeting with the managers). Note that he ran a very large fund, so it had to be split up into 200 or more pieces to allocate to companies, otherwise it would have an excessive proportion of a small company's shares. In the early days, when running a smaller fund, he would allocate to only 30–40 companies, so individual holdings were a larger proportion of the fund.

Bolton does not make large adjustments to the size of his holdings in one step, he takes an incremental approach.

A Start from Scratch Portfolio

Each month Bolton takes a piece of paper and writes five columns across the top: 'strong buy', 'buy', 'hold', 'reduce' and '?'. Then he lists every company in the fund under one of the headings. This technique is a way of getting to 'a start from scratch' portfolio – if you were starting with cash now, how would you allocate it to shares? It helps him question his conviction levels. In some cases it will highlight the need to do some more investigation to make sure he really understands the positives and negatives, and where more information must be sought (from analysts or from the company's management).

Mistakes are Inevitable

In running a portfolio Bolton says you need to be aware that a substantial proportion of your investment decisions will turn out to be bad however skilled you are – you must not expect to be right every time. To be involved in managing a portfolio is to make mistakes regularly. If you can keep the mistakes down to only 40–45 per cent of your investment decisions then you will have a good hit rate; one that is superior to most investors. You only need a few winners to outperform – try to win by not losing too often. Even with all his experience Bolton reckoned that at least two out of five of his investment decisions are wrong.

Watch List

Bolton keeps a watch list of companies that he thinks might be candidates for purchase one day, but for which he has not yet developed enough conviction on to take action. He has piles of company information (annual reports, analysts' reports, notes from meetings, etc.) arranged alphabetically on his shelves. Then, once a quarter he reviews them to see if he wants to keep the company on his watch list.

Balance Offensive and Defensive Investing

Offensive investing is looking for new potential investments, whereas defensive investing is monitoring and managing your existing holdings. You need to maintain a balance between the two – it can be too easy to slip into the habit of dealing with the day-to-day management of existing shares and squeeze the time available for scanning the horizon for new ones: set aside time for the offensive.

When to Sell

Spotting an anomalous price is one thing; knowing when the market will correct it is something else. Thus Bolton allows himself plenty of time: he expects to hold for between one and two years, with 18 months as a rough average, but is quite prepared to wait many years for a thesis to be proved correct.

Other analysts and fund managers are looking for a signal of a near term 'catalyst' that will correct the anomalous price, but Bolton warns that it is very unusual to both observe a significant anomaly and at the same time the catalyst that will correct it. He says that if the catalyst were also obvious then the anomaly would not be there in the first place.

If the share is no longer a buy and is probably a sell, then swift action to cut losses is required.

The first two rules of selling are (1) avoid having an emotional attachment to a stock inhibiting a sale, and (2) forget the price you paid for a share. To help fight these two psychological tendencies regularly check the investment thesis. If the share is no longer a buy and is probably a sell, then swift action to cut losses is required.

The reasons for selling:

- If the investment thesis is no longer valid due to some change in circumstance. He does not set price targets for each share, but regularly checks the investment thesis to assess his level of conviction. Price targets are simply too precise in a process – changing values of investments – that cannot be exact. He does concede that price bands may make some sense.

- If he finds something better. He is constantly looking at similar companies to those in the fund and comparing the ones in the fund to the ones outside it.

Personal Attributes

Bolton believes that there are certain key attributes required if you are to be a good investor.

Common Sense

Being able to think logically and objectively is vital. Being able to go back to first principles and boil down a complex story so that its essential elements become upper-most in your mind is required; see the wood for the trees.

A common sense approach is required when something seems too good to be true. If the supposed 'good' comes out of complex structures that you cannot comprehend then stay clear. For example when everyone else was jumping in, Bolton looked at 'constant proportion debt obligations' (CPDOs) and could not figure out how they worked, so he avoided them.

Be smart about a gaining a measured sense of your own abilities – do not get over-confident. For example do not get an over-inflated opinion of your genius when you have been through a good period – some of your best performing shares could have been picked just as easily with a pin! On the other hand, do not underestimate your abilities by focusing on a poor short-run performance. Over short periods of time it is very difficult to differentiate between luck and judgement. By short Bolton means three-in-a-row years. This viewpoint helps puts into perspective the common practice of judging fund managers over a three-month period, which is absurdly short. Even highly skilled investors need time for the probabilities to work in their favour. They also need to get used to having underperforming years. Bolton himself had three in a row: 1989, 1990 and 1991.

Temperament

Similar to Warren Buffett and Peter Lynch, Bolton sees temperament as more important than IQ when managing a portfolio. A reasonably high level of IQ is required, of course, but a very high IQ without the right temperament is dangerous.

A temperament of humility is a key quality, so that mistakes can be made and accepted as an integral part of being a stock picker; be prepared to humbly learn from mistakes and not get upset by them. A temperament of humble open-mindedness and questioning will present opportunities.

You have to be able to accept setbacks from time to time. You cannot afford to become emotional about difficulties. Investment is a game of probabilities. The investor who gets it right all the time just does not exist; the best that we can hope for is to make fewer mistakes than our competitors. If you are afraid to make mistakes there is a danger of adopting an approach that is so defensive that you badly underperform.

Commitment and Organisation

Investing can (and should) become so absorbing that you become almost fanatical about it:

> investing is continuous and intangible. There's no beginning or end to it, and there is always something new that needs delving into. I think you have to be completely taken by it to do well. If you look at the investment managers I admire, none of them do it part time.[7]

Information will come to the investor in an unstructured way and it is important that discipline is displayed in the process of organising it to produce uncluttered insight. Do not let events drive your agenda. Allocate different parts of the day to different tasks – only a small part will be for responding to events. Do not spend hours looking at Reuters or Bloomberg screens; it is usually unnecessary to know the latest moves in the market and a great deal of time can be wasted.

Independence of Mind

Good investment managers think independently, being willing to challenge conventional wisdom. It is a natural human desire to want to be part of the crowd and so it takes a significant amount of effort of thought to sift through the evidence and come to one's own conclusion; sometimes (most times) you will agree with the crowd, but sometimes you will take a different view. Bolton has found that his contrarian stance has been particularly useful at market turning points when the natural

---

7. Anthony Bolton quoted in Davies (2004), p.6.

tendency to go with the crowd in their extreme pessimism or extreme optimism is strong but is completely the wrong thing to do. Independence of mind can be developed with greater experience; you will start to recognise patterns similar to those that have occurred in the past – patterns of crowd behaviour, fads and fashions. As Mark Twain said, "History never repeats itself but it sometimes rhymes."

Flexibility

Bolton calls for 'flexible conviction', i.e. the ability to change views as the facts change. To be too certain about prior conclusions is to lose the open-mindedness needed by a good investor. The world of real business is subject to constant change and so there is a constant challenge to keep up. For example, Apple may be having great success with its latest gadget this year but will competitors bring out a better product next year? You must keep up with the changing climate, and not fall in love with what worked last year or the year before.

The Seeing Eye

Investment is likened to chess by Bolton in that it is necessary to see a couple of moves ahead of competitors. Think through the secondary effects of a current change. For example, everyone can immediately see that a rising dollar against the pound is good news for UK-based manufacturers exporting to the US. What is not so obvious is the impact on the oil refinery industry given the fact that oil is priced in US dollars. And then there is the impact on inflation a few months down the line, which in turn has an impact on interest rates, which can affect company profits. Lateral thinking is often required to see things differently leading to the development of perceptive vision that is not in the grasp of linear thinkers.

Hunger for Analysis

You need to have a curious, enquiring mind wanting to know how things work. What is the process underlying the end result for a business. So, good fund managers tend to be those who will not just switch on a light and accept the result. They will want to know what is behind the process: how does the electricity flow? How does the bulb work? They don't want to be presented with the conclusions only, but they like to know the process used to get there. They are inquisitive, always questioning and always thinking.

The Detailed Generalist

It is necessary to maintain a reasonably good knowledge of a wide range of industries and businesses. This helps to get up to speed on a firm or sector within a few hours, permitting a rapid build-up of expert knowledge as the need arises. It also helps provide perspective on companies and industries to which you are already committed.

Know Yourself

Know your strengths and weaknesses, and compensate for them. Given your limitations and talents you should choose an investment style that suits:

There are many approaches to making money in the stock market and the portfolio manager needs to be able to establish what works for them personally and then stick to it. I don't believe a manager can be a jack of all trades, switching between different approaches over time.[8]

Integrity

Be honest with investors, companies and colleagues – and be honest with yourself.

What Not to Do

Don't Get Fixated on the Price You Paid for Shares

What you originally paid for shares is totally irrelevant to your decision on what to do now. This is especially true if you have to take the decision to cut losses, which may be psychologically difficult.

Do Not Try to Guess Where the Market is Heading in the Short Run

Timing the market – getting in just before a rise and getting out just before a fall – is incredibly difficult. There are a handful

---

8. Written by Anthony Bolton in Bolton, A. (2009) *Investing Against the Tide*, FT Prentice Hall, p.156.

of occasions during an entire investing career when Bolton felt strongly about the market's likely direction. And even then he would not put large bets on that view.

After decades of experience Bolton concluded that the direction of the market over the next few months cannot be forecasted with any consistency. He advises us to not even try to time the market with regard to buying or selling shares. To try and do so means that you are likely to fall into the trap of becoming more optimistic as the market rises and more pessimistic as the market falls. When the market is at the top you will hear all kinds of persuasive arguments about a rosy future, when it is at the bottom there will be no end of gloom and doom stories. Better by far to concentrate on analysing individual companies and buying them when they represent good value.

He advises us to not even try to time the market with regard to buying or selling shares.

Don't Narrow Down Your Sources of Investment Ideas

Ideas can originate from many places, so don't become too attached to the same old routines and reading matter. Bolton particularly likes sources of information not widely used by the investing institutions, thus permitting him an edge over the others.

Don't Go Along With the Crowd

If you are comfortably doing what the crowd is doing then you are probably too late:

> When nearly everyone else is cautious about the outlook, they are probably wrong and things are going to get better. Equally, when very few are worried that is the time to be most wary … the stock market is an excellent discounting mechanism. By the time everyone is worried about something it is normally largely in the price.[9]

While it is important to do your own analysis and stand your ground, it is equally important to listen to the market – it is often right.

Don't Put Too Much Weight on the Macroeconomic Outlook

Look beyond the economic projections for the next year or two. Quite often the short-term can look terrible just as the bottom in the stock market is reached; and it can look great just as the stock market reaches its peak and is about to fall. Bolton feels uncomfortable in taking a view on macroeconomic variables because he does not regard himself as having an information edge here; there are hundreds of other people looking at this data, why should he do any better? On the other hand when it comes to individual (particularly small) companies he gains an information edge. He can come out of a meeting with the senior managers feeling that he knows more about this company than anyone else. He only put bets on things where he has some

---

9. Written by Anthony Bolton in Davies (2004), p.80.

advantage over others, and betting on macroeconomic changes is not one of those things.

Having said that, there are occasions when he will adjust his portfolio to the stock market cycle which is usually linked to the economic cycle. For example, when he judges that we are in the advanced stages of a bull market he takes the prudent course and prunes back some of the more risky holdings as well as those that have done particularly well in the bull run-up. This attitude continues until he believes the trend has changed and then he starts to accept more risk.

Do Not Buy on Impulses or Tips

Invest where you have a competitive advantage based on your ability to analyse a company, not on a whim or tip from a friend, newspaper or broker.

Avoid 'Pass-the-Parcel' Shares

Shares that have a great deal of upward momentum, which is sustained by people thinking that they can sell out at a higher price because current excitement will keep pushing the share forward (rather than based on fundamental qualities) are to be given a wide berth.

Don't Close Your Mind to Disconfirming Evidence

Once a share is bought there is a natural human tendency to avoid looking at or ignoring evidence that does not confirm our original investment thesis; we have a psychological aversion to the idea that we made a wrong decision. Keep an open mind to be receptive to disconfirming evidence:

> Don't be too stubborn about your views but don't lose all your conviction. Ideally, your conviction level should be around the 50 per cent level (where 0 per cent equals no conviction and 100 per cent means you are so convinced you would never change your view).[10]

Be Prepared to Accept Criticism

You must remain open-minded when listening to advice from others about why you are not doing well. Colleagues may be able to see more clearly than you what you are doing wrong; seek their advice and be prepared to take criticism.

Be Wary of Initial Public Offering (IPO) Shares

IPO shares are usually 'priced for the seller, not the buyer' and so most of them should be avoided.

Drawbacks and Difficulties with His Approach

As with all the approaches used by great investors to out-perform, Anthony Bolton's method requires a great deal of effort. This

---

10. Written by Anthony Bolton in Bolton (2009), p.145.

means a lot of ground work before you even meet the managers and then regular meetings with the executives before and after purchase. This raises another issue for many investors: unless we are running multi-billion dollar funds we will not be able to have the one-to-one meetings that Bolton can request. Furthermore, the depth of knowledge of industry economics, corporate strategy and accounting required excludes many people from being able to emulate him.

Key Points to Take Away

- Look at special situations: unloved, out-of-favour or going through a period of change companies.

- Take a bottom-up approach: evaluate the business, look for a strong economic franchise.

- Have conviction levels about companies: buy or sell based on relative conviction levels.

- All investee companies should have managers of high integrity and competence, low borrowings and good cash generation.

- Develop an investment thesis (a quick, easy to under-stand justification) for every company you are considering purchasing.

- Devise a start from scratch portfolio that is reviewed every month.

- Keep a watch list of potential investment candidates.

- Keep an independent mind, be accepting of your mistakes and maintain a curiousity about how things work.

- Do not try to guess where the market or the economy is heading in the next few months.

- Keep an open mind to disconfirming evidence and criticism.

A Return to Investing

With the Special Situations Fund Bolton was permitted to invest up to 20 per cent of the money in non-UK stocks. In the later days of the fund about one-quarter of this 20 per cent found its way to China and Hong Kong. He wrote in 2004 that:

> China interests me for three reasons. One is that it is one of the most exciting places that I have come across in recent times to find new stocks. The second is that China has become such an important factor in determining what happens to the rest of the world from an investment perspective. Going there and finding out what is happening on the ground gives me a good chance of establishing an advantage over other investors. Finally, having given up my European responsibilities, learning about a new area is itself a new mental challenge, something to keep me interested and on my toes.[11]

In 2009 he could resist the pull of the Chinese market no longer and announced that he would return to professional investing. He had spent a couple of years indulging his passion for music, and even released a CD of his work (*My Beloved*). He had generously advised the readers of the FT, and had become an acknowledged elder statesman of the investing world. But now he wanted to go back into the fray. With his title of 'Fidelity

---

11. Anthony Bolton quoted in Davies (2004), p.30.

President of Investments' he started a new life in Hong Kong, to run a new China-focused fund. His restless intellect and the need for mental challenge will not allow him to slip into quiet retirement. He sees the centre of gravity is clearly shifting to the East and he wants to play a part in the process. He sees the development trajectory of China as similar to that of Taiwan or South Korea in the 1980s and 1990s or Japan in the 1960s.

> Many areas of the economy are in the steepest part of their development curve as consumer incomes reach a level where increasing numbers of people can aspire to own homes, cars and household goods. Because of the scale of what is happening, and the effectiveness of a centrally-run economy that other emerging markets do not enjoy, the world may never see anything like this again. All of this is why I am deferring my retirement and returning to running money. I have become convinced by the opportunities available in China today.[12]

---

12 Written by Anthony Bolton in 'Why I'm returning to running money – in China', *Financial Times*, 28 November 2009, p.8.

Bibliography

Chapter 1: Benjamin Graham

Bianco, A., 'Why Warren Buffett is Breaking His Own Rules', *Business Week*, 15 April 1985.

Warren Buffett speech, New York Society of Security Analysis, 6 December 1994.

Buffett, W.E. (1989) Letter to shareholders. www.berkshirehathaway.com

Graham, B., *Forbes*, 1 June 1932.

Graham, B. (1973) *The Intelligent Investor*, revised 4th edition, New York: Harper Business (reprinted 1997).

Graham, B. (1996) *The Memoirs of the Dean of Wall Street*, New York: McGraw-Hill.

Graham, B. and Dodd, D. (1934) *Security Analysis*, New York: McGraw-Hill.

Graham, B. (2003) *The Intelligent Investor*, revised edition updated with new commentary by Jason Zweig, New York: Harper Business Essentials.

Lenzner, R., 'Warren Buffett's Idea of Heaven: I Don't Have to Work With People I Don't Like', *Forbes 400*, 18 October 1993.

Lowe, J. (1994) *Lessons from the Dean of Wall Street*, Dearborn Financial Publishing, Inc.

Lowe, J. (1999) *The Rediscovered Benjamin Graham*, New York: John Wiley and Sons Inc.

Chapter 2: Philip Fisher

Fisher, P. (1960) *Common Stocks and Uncommon Profits,* PSR Publications (originally published by Harper & Brothers in 1958). References are for 1996 reprinted Wiley Investment Classics book: *Common Stocks and Uncommon Profits*, New York: John Wiley and Sons Inc.

Fisher, P. (1975) *Conservative Investors Sleep Well.* Previously published by Business Classics. References are for 1996 reprinted Wiley Investment Classics book: *Common Stocks and Uncommon Profits*, New York: John Wiley and Sons Inc.

Fisher, P. (1980) *Developing an Investment Philosophy,* Financial Analysts Society and Business Classics. References are for 1996 reprinted Wiley Investment Classics book: *Common Stocks and Uncommon Profits,* New York: John Wiley and Sons Inc.

Chapter 3: Warren Buffett and Charles Munger

Baer, J., 'Man on the money with Buffett', *Financial Times,* 13 July 2008.

Buffett, W.E. (1967) Letter to Buffett Partnership partners.

Buffett, W.E. (1985) 'Investing in Equity Markets', quoted in Columbia University Business School, transcript of a Seminar held 13 March 1985.

Buffett, W.E., Letters to shareholders included 1977–1999 www. berkshirehathaway.com

Buffett. W.E., 'The Superinvestors of Graham-and-Doddsille', transcript in *Hermes,* Magazine of Columbia Business School, Autumn 1984. Reproduced in the reprinted version of Graham, B. (1973) *The Intelligent Investor,* revised 4th edition, New York: Harper Business (reprinted 1997).

Buffett, W.E. (1995) *Warren Buffett Talks Business,* The University of North Carolina, Center for Public Television, Chapel Hill.

Davis, L.J., 'Buffett Takes Stock', *New York Times Magazine,* 1 April 1990.

Dickson, M., 'Lessons from History: On Berkshire Hathaway's Plan to Buy the Rest of Geico', *Financial Times,* 28 August 1995.

Dorr, R., 'Ex-Omahan Traded Law for Board Room', *Omaha World-Herald,* 3 August 1977.

Grant, L., 'The $4-Billion Regular Guy', *Los Angeles Times,* 7 April 1991.

Lenzner, R., 'Warren Buffett's Idea of Heaven: I Don't Have to Work With People I Don't Like', *Forbes 400,* 18 October 1993.

Lewis, W., 'The Dream Team's Realist', *Financial Times,* 13 May 1998.

Loomis, C.J., 'The Inside Story of Warren Buffett', *Fortune,* 11 April 1988.

Lowe, J. (1997) *Warren Buffett Speaks,* New York: John Wiley and Sons Ltd.

Lowenstein, R. (1995) *The Making of an American Capitalist,* New York: Random House.

Munger, C. (1989) Wesco Financial Corporation Annual Report (1989).

Munger, C.T. and Koeppel, D.A. (1982) 1982 Annual Report of Blue Chip Stamps.

New York Post, 'Warren Buffett Triples Profits', 14 May 1994.

Rasmussen, J., 'Billionaire Talks Strategy With Students', *Omaha World-Herald*, 2 January 1994.

Schroeder, A. (2008) *The Snowball: Warren Buffett and the Business of Life*, London: Bloomsbury.

Smith, A. (1972) *Super Money*, New York: Random House.

Train, J. (1987) *The Midas Touch*, New York: Harper and Row.

Urry, M., 'The $45bn Man Makes His Pitch', *Financial Times*, Weekend Money, 11/12 May 1996.

Chapter 4: John Templeton

Alexander, D., 'The Marco Polo of the class of 1934: Sir John Templeton', *The American Oxonian Journal*, 2004.

Barclays Capital (2009), Equity Gilt Study 2009.

Bartiromo, M., CNBC show *Market Week with Maria*, 20 May 2002.

Bloomfield, P., 'Depressed markets draw Templeton's eye', *The Financial Post* (Toronto, Canada), 28 May 1993.

Brackey, H.J., "Merger creates fund giant/Templeton, Franklin in deal', *USA Today*, 3 August 1992.

Cawfield, D., 'Don't put all your eggs in the wrong basket', *The Toronto Star*, 20 July 2003.

De Lollis, B., 'Sir John Templeton, titan of investing, declared craze for Internet stocks history', *The Miami Herald*, 18 April 2000.

Goold, D., 'Market Watch Value investing the Templeton way', *The Globe and Mail* (Canada), 19 July 1996.

Hemeon, J., 'Sir John favors Canadian stocks "They represent the best bargains" Templeton says', *The Toronto Star*, 27 July 1995.

Herrman, R. (1998) *Sir John Templeton*, Philadelphia & London: Templeton Foundation Press.

John Templeton Foundation website www.templeton.org

Kirzner, E., 'Gospel according to Templeton', *The Financial Post* (Toronto, Canada), 25 May 1987.

Marcial, G.G., 'I have never seen so many stocks … so undervalued', *Business Week*, 5 November 1990.

McIntosh, A., 'Templeton turns mishap into gains', *The Globe and Mail* (Canada), 25 July 1985.

Proctor, W. (1983) *The Templeton Touch*, New York: Doubleday & Company Inc.

Ross, N. (2000) *Lessons from the Legends of Wall Street*, New York: MJF Books.

Rubin, S., 'Sir John's outlook: For a career pessimist, fund titan is unabashedly optimistic', *The Record* (Kitchener-Waterloo Ontario), 6 August 1996.

'Sir John's game plan. Templeton is still backing stocks with fundamental value', *Equity International*, 1 June 1988.

'Taking advantage of a temporary insanity', *The Business Times*, Singapore, 23 May 2001.

Templeton, J.M. and Ellison, J. (1992) *The Templeton Plan*, New York: HarperPaperbacks.

Templeton, L.C. and Phillips, S. (2008) *Investing The Templeton Way*, New York: McGraw-Hill.

'Templeton's Creed', *Business Magazine*, 2 November 1989.

Chapter 5: George Soros

Freeland, C., 'The credit crunch according to Soros', *Financial Times*, 31 January 2009.

Kaufman, M.T. (2002) *Soros*, New York: Vintage Books.

Slater, R. (2009) *Soros The World's Most Influential Investor*, New York: McGraw-Hill.

Soros, G. (1994) *The Alchemy of Finance*, New York: John Wiley & Sons, Inc.

Soros, G. (1995) *Soros on Soros*, New York: John Wiley & Sons, Inc.

Soros, G. (2008) *The Crash of 2008 and What it Means*, New York: PublicAffairs.

Chapter 6: Peter Lynch

Lynch, P. with Rothchild, R. (1989) *One Up On Wall Street: How To Use What You Already Know To Make Money In The Market*, New York: Simon & Schuster.

Lynch, P. with Rothchild, R. (1990) *One Up On Wall Street: How To Use What You Already Know To Make Money In The Market*, Philadelphia: Penguin Books.

Lynch, P. (1994) *Beating The Street*, New York: Simon & Schuster.

Chapter 7: John Neff

Neff, J. and Mintz, S.L. (1999) *John Neff on Investing*, New York: John Wiley & Sons, Inc.

Chapter 8: Anthony Bolton

Bolton, A., 'Heed the alarms', *Financial Times*, 2 May 2009.

Bolton, A. (2009) *Investing Against the Tide*, Harlow: FT Prentice Hall.

Bolton, A., 'Why I'm returning to running money – in China', *Financial Times*, 28 November 2009.

Davis, J. (2004) *Investing With Anthony Bolton*, Harriman House.

Tucker, S., 'Fidelity's Bolton turns back on retirement to set up China fund', *Financial Times*, 27 November 2009.

Index